Justice in Japan

Justice in Japan

THE NOTORIOUS TEIJIN SCANDAL

Richard H. Mitchell

University of Hawai'i Press
Honolulu

© 2002 University of Hawai'i Press
All rights reserved
Printed in the United States of America
07 06 05 04 03 02   6 5 4 3 2 1

Library of Congress Cataloging-in-Publication Data
Mitchell, Richard H.
    Justice in Japan : the notorious Teijin scandal / Richard
H. Mitchell.
        p. cm.
    Includes bibliographical references and index.
    ISBN 0-8248-2523-3 (alk. paper)
    1. Teijin case, 1934. 2. Trials (Bribery)—Japan—
Tokyo—History—20th century. 3. Political corruption—
Japan—History—20th century. I. Title.

KNX42.T45 M58 2002
345.52'02323—dc21   2001052820

University of Hawai'i Press books are printed on
acid-free paper and meet the guidelines for permanence
and durability of the Council on Library Resources.

Designed by Jacqueline Thaw

Printed by The Maple-Vail Book Manufacturing Group

To Yoshiko

Contents

Acknowledgments

I WISH TO EXPRESS MY GRATITUDE to those who aided in the publication this book. I am indebted to Suzuki Yoshio and Imai Nakaba for providing valuable material and to Ohno Masao for correcting an error. I would like to thank Amanda Crowell for typing the manuscript. A special debt of gratitude is owed to Yoshiko for her double duty as research assistant and wife.

Teijin Trial Defendants

Saitō Cabinet

MITSUCHI CHŪZŌ: Seiyūkai member
of the House of Representatives and
finance minister
NAKAJIMA KUMAKICHI: baron and
House of Peers member; minister of
commerce and industry

Finance Ministry

AIDA IWAO: bank inspector, Special
Banks Section
KURODA HIDEO: vice-minister and
member of the House of Peers
ŌKUBO TEIJI: head, Banking Bureau
ŌNO RYŪTA: head, Special Banks
Section
SHIDOMOTO JIRŌ: retired bank
inspector

Bank of Taiwan

KOSHIFUJI TSUNEKICHI: head, First
Section, Tokyo branch
OKAZAKI AKIRA: director and secre-
tary to the president; director, Teijin
Company
SHIMADA SHIGERU: president and
director
TAKAGI NAOMICHI: director; presi-
dent of Teijin Company
YANAGIDA NAOKICHI: director

Businessmen

KAWAI YOSHINARI: director of Teijin
and other companies
KOBAYASHI ATARU: manager of the
Fukoku Chōhei Insurance Company
and director of other companies
NAGANO MAMORU: director of Teijin
and other companies
NAGASAKI EIZŌ: president of the
Asahi Oil Company and director of
other companies

A Note on the Transliteration of Japanese Words

In the transliteration of Japanese names, the standard form is used, with family name first. The names of Japanese Americans, however, are cited with personal names first. Macrons are used to mark long vowels except in the case of common words found in collegiate dictionaries (e.g., Tokyo, Kyoto, Osaka, Taisho, Showa, and Shinto).

Introduction

THE SENSATIONAL TEIJIN SCANDAL of the 1930s was Japan's most notable interwar political bribery case. Compared to numerous Japanese corruption cases of the past century, the Teijin affair not only stands out as the most sensational of the pre-1945 era, but is also a leading candidate for the most important corruption case, because it left an indelible mark on the public mind. When people think about the financial world of the 1930s, the Banchōkai and the Teijin scandal come immediately to mind.[1] And the Teijin case lives on in the postwar era.[2] For example, the political critic Yayama Tarō, writing on a political bribery case of the late 1980s, begins his article with "The Lesson of the Teijin Affair."[3] In fact, it is unusual to read a book on Japanese interwar politics or economics that does not include at least a brief mention of the Teijin affair. Nevertheless, Japanese and foreign scholars have neglected this scandal, which not only destroyed the Saitō Makoto Cabinet but also produced a record-setting trial of sixteen defendants: Finance Ministry bureaucrats, cabinet ministers, and businessmen.[4]

During the long district court trial (June 1935–December 1937), popular Tokyo procurators found themselves attacked for gross illegal abuses as the media exposed sordid tales of forced confessions and harsh jail conditions. Indeed, some critics pinned the label of "fascists" to procurators' court robes. A sensational trial verdict, by a three-judge bench, finding all defendants innocent, not only tarnished the procuratorial public image but reenforced a tradition of judicial independence just as the nation slipped into the quagmire of the China war (from July 1937). The December verdict, however, did not silence criticism of the Justice Ministry, as politicians in both major parties attacked prosecutors for violations of Teijin defendants' legal rights in this and other criminal cases. Finally, under political pressure, Justice Ministry officials began to discuss needed reforms in the criminal justice system.

Despite the importance of the Teijin scandal, basic facts about this legal case remain obscure, and too often scholars commenting on this incident repeat factual misinformation or produce farfetched conspiracy theories to explain the origins of the Teijin Incident. The need for a close study of this incident is illustrated by the fact that both a legal scholar such as Hasegawa Masayasu and the distinguished historian Itō Takashi, the outstanding authority on this period, view the Teijin Incident as a puzzling affair.[5] While the primary purpose of this book is to clarify the Teijin Incident, it will also illustrate that the flaws in the Japanese criminal justice system of the 1930s, which were reflected in the Teijin case investigation and trial, remain embedded in the postwar system.

Because distinguished and influential defendants were involved in the Teijin trial, justice authorities found it impossible to ignore demands for reform of criminal justice system abuses. Thus, the Teijin trial revitalized an ongoing legal reform movement. Unfortunately, this reform movement was stymied by an expanding war in China and the Pacific Ocean. The Allied Occupation in 1945, however, reinvigorated this reform movement, which produced significant legal changes in the constitution and other parts of the criminal justice system. Nevertheless, as the handling of criminal cases in the "new" Japan illustrates, postwar reforms have not changed the criminological attitude and the inquisitorial nature of the criminal justice system. Moreover, the structure of the current justice system encourages abuses of suspects' procedural rights. Some scholars accept a cultural explanation for the criminal justice system's sterling performance in controlling crime and producing confessions; criminal suspects are programmed internally to cooperate with authorities. From early childhood people are taught to work in groups and to obey authority, and this lifelong socialization process does influence the outcome when individuals face police, procurators, and judges. Nevertheless, the key determinant in the handling of criminal cases is not found in this "cultural explanation" but is located in the institutional structure of the criminal justice system, which the Occupation reformers sought to change. Although their reform efforts did modify the Penal Code and the Code of Criminal Procedure, they failed to dislodge basic assumptions and practices rooted in the criminal justice system. In sum, institutional conditions of the criminal justice system and the behavior of police and procurators during the postreform era bear more than a little similarity to those of the imperial era.

The book begins with a survey of the criminal justice system from its Tokugawa roots through the new legal structure introduced during the Meiji Era (1868–1912). I pay special attention to the development of notions about equitable justice and the contributions of judges who offered objective judgments; the origins of judicial independence; the expansion of the concept of "personal rights" (*jinken*); the expanding power of procurators, especially those in the important Tokyo bureau who played a key role in the Teijin case; and the role of trial judges who rendered a final verdict on the "truth" discovered by procurators.

The doomed relationship of the Bank of Taiwan and the Suzuki Trading Company provides the background to the scandal. Out of their mutual bankruptcies came the Teijin Company stocks held by the government and desired by stockbrokers, if the price was right. The purchase of a large block of these company shares in 1933, brokered by Banchōkai members, an informal group of businessmen, opened the door to charges of favoritism and bribery. The businessman, reformist politician, and newspaper editor Mutō Sanji, who exposed this stock transaction as a corrupt deal, supplied the spark that set off the political explosion. Scholars who are uncertain whether Mutō's actions were motivated by a genuine desire to expose a corrupt stock deal or whether he was merely a pawn in a political plot may be persuaded, in reading this book, that the first view is correct.

The chapter on the Saitō Cabinet explores the political setting in which the Teijin stock deal was exposed and the procurators began an investigation. Numerous groups were trying to bring down the cabinet of this moderate admiral. In fact, the anti-Saitō political activities are strikingly similar to those of earlier years: the "outs" were using a corruption scandal and dirty tricks in hopes of destroying the cabinet. Indeed, money scandals, particularly bribery cases, were a traditional weapon in the endless battle for political power. Members of the Banchōkai, some of whom were involved in the Teijin stock sale, were also involved in politics. Therefore, it is not surprising that the Banchōkai became a political target.

Key to understanding the motivation of Tokyo procurators, who indicted Banchōkai members and other Teijin defendants, is the anticorruption drive of Tokyo District Court Chief Procurator Shiono Suehiko. More specifically, however, the indictment of Teijin suspects demands a close look at the Finance Ministry's handling of the Meiji Sugar Refining Company case, which became a topic of newspaper headlines in 1932–1933, on the eve of the Teijin stock deal. One important result of this tax scandal was a public clash between Tokyo procurators and Finance Ministry officials. Procurator Kuroda Etsurō, whose name was spotlighted by journalists in this bureaucratic dispute, which Tokyo procurators lost, must have been angry at finance officials and at some Justice Ministry officials. At any rate, Mutō Sanji's newspaper exposure of the Banchōkai's Teijin stock deal provided Kuroda with an opportunity to renew his battle with the finance bureaucrats; he arrested five of them as suspects in the Teijin case investigation.

This book also covers Diet debates on the Teijin affair and analyzes the destruction of the Saitō Cabinet, which resigned after cabinet officers were targeted by the procurators' investigation. I conclude that the Teijin Incident is best understood by focusing on the motivation and actions of Kuroda and his fellow procurators who needed no push from outsiders, because they had been waiting for an opportunity to punish Finance Ministry officials. As attorney Imamura Rikisaburō put it: ever since their humiliation at the hands of finance officials, during the Meiji Sugar Refining Company investigation, "Tokyo procurators had an arrow in their bowstring aimed at the Finance Ministry."[6]

Too many scholars, puzzled by Teijin affair complexities, have a propensity to accept conspiracy theories. A favorite one centers on the "evil" former justice minister Hiranuma Kiichirō, who is accused of using Tokyo procurators to mastermind the destruction of the Saitō Cabinet. I hope this book will reveal this dark plot theory as a feverish fantasy. Many of these same scholars also identify Hiranuma as a "fascist"; sometimes they apply this label to the government as well. In a 1976 book I argued that "fascism" is not a proper political label for 1930s and 1940s Japan.[7] Fortunately, by the end of the past century, there was growing agreement that this term is nearly useless for analytical purposes if applied to Japan. As Stanley G. Payne concludes: "Japan had evolved a somewhat pluralistic authoritarian system which exhibited some of the characteristics of fascism, but it did not develop fascism's most distinctive and revolutionary aspects." Indeed, Japan on the eve of the Pacific War "in many ways approximated the development of Germany's Second Reich more than Hitler's nation."[8] Ben-Ami Shillony and Elise K. Tipton reach the same conclusion: "Japan was not an ideological disciple of the Axis. . . . The Japanese regime was restrictive, narrow-minded, and stifling, but it was not a dictatorship."[9] It "bore a closer resemblance to the eighteenth- and nineteenth-century police states of Germany, Austria and France than to its twentieth-century contemporaries in Nazi Germany, Mussolini's Italy and Stalinist Russia."[10]

Procedures for the arrest, interrogation, and preliminary trial of criminal suspects are described below. The main indictments of the Teijin suspects were for bribery, misfeasance, and perjury. As the defendants were under investigation, the Sixty-Sixth Diet debated the case, paying special attention to the defendants' personal rights (i.e., procedural rights under the law). I draw on newspaper accounts to analyze public reaction to the acrimonious exchanges in the Diet.

A three-judge bench presided over this sensational trial, which lasted for a record-setting 266 sessions, including the verdict day. There were longer trials, but they involved appeals to higher courts. The reader is taken step-by-step through the opening statements, examination of defendants, testimony of witnesses, prosecution summary, defense summary, and verdict.

In the aftermath of the Teijin affair, parliamentarians in the Seventy-Third Diet urged reforms in the criminal justice system. My analysis of contemporary publications and issues such as the Criminal Compensation Law, "fascism by the prosecution" (*kensatsu fassho*), and responsibility for the prosecution debacle indicates that the trial verdict sparked reform discussion but little systemic change.

The criminal justice reforms put in place by the Allied Occupation stressed the expansion of human rights. Some of these reforms, however, were modified even before the Occupation ended. Not surprisingly, critics of the current criminal justice system complain about abuses that were characteristic of the prereform system: forced self-confessions, suspects held for long periods in holding cells in police stations (so-called substitute prisons), and severe limitations on meetings between suspects and lawyers. In sum, critics claim that confession, and not a thorough investigation of all aspects of a criminal case, is the objective pursued by police and procurators. Thus, Teijin case procurators, if transported from the mid-1930s to today's prosecution scene, would recognize quickly that, despite extensive legal reforms, the essence of the old system remains intact. They would also discover that, while the prestige of procurators has fluctuated over the years, that of judges has remained high. The courage of the Teijin trial judges, no doubt, not only inspired other judges, but convinced the public that courts dispensed equitable justice.

CHAPTER 1
Criminal Justice System

THE TOKUGAWA REGIME (1603–1867) was a transcendental administrative state in which superiors issued orders or delegated power to inferiors; the outstanding trait of this political system was a lack of legal redress against authority.[1] A long peace and commercial development, however, stimulated the emergence of two essentials of positive law: decrees (authority) and precedents (regularity).[2] A primary concern of the growing body of positive law was to reenforce the regime's status regulations by a harsh criminal code. In 1742 the Kujikata osadamegaki assembled important precedents and statutes in a two-volume code; book 1 was mainly administrative orders, and book 2 was mainly criminal regulations.[3] Concomitant with the expansion of positive law was the expansion of judicial machinery for dispute settlement. "Judges" began as administrative officials, but by the time of the two-volume code, "the outlines of a purely judicial organization had begun to appear."[4] Moreover, during the Tokugawa era, the ideal of a transcendental judge who offers objective judgment took root among the people. This ideal judge is personified by Ōoka Echizen-no-kami (Ōoka Tadasuke), whose official life stimulated many trial legends that circulate until today. Dan Henderson notes that "the strong popular admiration in Japan for this basic equitable type of justice called Ōoka sai-ban . . . is an important part of the jural tradition."[5] Ōoka Tadasuke was appointed to the position of Edo city magistrate in 1717 by Shogun Yoshimune, who launched an ambitious reform program to reverse a decline in government finances. Together with other officials Ōoka attempted to create an impartial legal system: restrictions were imposed on the official use of torture; judicial procedures were circulated to officials; punishments were reduced.[6] These legal reforms and others had a profound impact on society. Stories involving the law and above all Yoshimune's chief legal adviser, Ōoka Tadasuke, were still circulating among the common people long after the Tokugawa government itself had disappeared.[7] In stories from the volume *Cases Handled by Magistrate Ōoka* (*Ōoka seidan*), written for the common people in the eighteenth century by unknown authors, readers see an illustration of a fair and incorruptible official who never fails to distinguish between evil and good and who dispenses equitable justice.[8]

There is evidence that peasants, who were conscious of a stable system of political and social norms, had a strong sense of justice. According to Irwin Scheiner, "This system guaranteed them . . . justice from the political overlord; it determined the structure and pattern of social relationships within and without the village." Thus, "by general law and specific statute their individuality was dissolved into their functions as peasants and then further subsumed by their role as members of the corporate village."[9] Some peasants who demonstrated against harsh regulations used terms like "justice," "injustice," and "reason" as they demanded respect for their status rights.[10] Overlords understood this message, because from early Tokugawa they "recognized that a viable government must heed the needs of the peasant for a just and benevolent government, since the economic basis of the state rested on the productivity of the peasant."[11] Moreover, many overlords were influenced by Neo-Confucianism, which spoke of benevolent rule and moral duties.[12] One scholar suggests that the notion of justice among peasants was due to more than interaction with overlords. A notion of justice, she writes, developed through their participation in market exchanges. "According to their expectations, their ruler, like any merchant, should give them fair value."[13]

Stories circulated about peasant leaders who sacrificed their lives for their villages. These martyrs were praised, because they championed the cause of justice. Most famous among them, Sakura Sōgorō (or Sōgo of Sakura), was crucified in the seventeenth century for petitioning the government for famine relief. According to the legend, village headman Sakura challenged the evil deeds of the local overlord by appealing directly to the shogun. This audacious act brought relief to the peasants but death for Sakura and his family. It is impossible to know how widely Sakura's story circulated, but by the 1750s a published version appeared, and in 1776 Yuasa Gensen, a Confucian scholar, wrote *A Tale of Sōgo and His Enemy*. Moreover, after the Meiji Restoration of 1868, thirty Tokugawa era manuscript versions of this story were found in farm storehouses from northern to central Japan.[14]

The most spectacular protest against official injustice was led by Ōshio Heihachirō, a former government police inspector who headed a

Confucian private academy. Angered by official inaction to help the poor
during a famine and certain that it was his moral duty to save the people,
he incited residents of Osaka and surrounding villages to join him in rebellion on February 17, 1837. Word of Ōshio's revolt quickly spread, spark-
ing other protests, the best known of which was led by another samurai,
Ikuta Yorozu, in Tatebayashi Fief. This May revolt, like Ōshio's, failed.[15] A
failure in life, Ōshio became a cultural hero in death. City people and farmers "idolized Ōshio for many years after his death, referring to him rever-
ently as 'Heihachirō sama,' usually in the context of casting opprobrium
on Bakufu officials in Osaka." Leaders of later uprisings in Bingo, Echigo,
and Settsu regarded themselves as disciples and supporters of Ōshio—
"thus prolonging the myth that Ōshio had not died."[16] Indeed, Ōshio's
fame as a champion of justice left such an indelible mark that during the
mass protests over the high price of rice in 1918 (the so-called Rice Riots),
urban crowds called out for someone like Ōshio to lead them![17]

In sum, on the eve of the introduction of Western legal ideas, the
Tokugawa era had already produced the beginning of a system of positive
law, and ideas about specific "rights" were circulating in society. For example, the shogunate "pledged itself implicitly to offer redress when merited
to all the people of the nation, including those under the immediate jurisdiction of the daimyo . . . and regardless of what the state acknowledged,
the people perceived a traditional right of appeal on a variety of grounds."[18]
Furthermore, subjects presumed that they had a "right" to petition or sue,
perhaps as an unintended result of the fact that everyone was now recorded in the population registers and thus identified as a subject with public
duties.[19] Notions about equitable justice circulated among peasants and
townspeople, and even the concept of a fair judge who offered objective
judgment was well established by late Tokugawa.

Confession played a central role in the Teijin trial, and it was central to
the Tokugawa criminal justice process. Authorities not only attached great
importance to a confession but usually considered a case incomplete without one. Torture, carefully regulated, was used to obtain a "truthful" confession, but from the mid-eighteenth century torture was officially
permitted only in specified felonies.[20] Hiramatsu Yoshirō, an authority on
Tokugawa criminal justice, notes: "First, the acknowledgment of the suspect was indispensable for conviction. Presumably, this is because of a
desire to bring about recognition of the bakufu trials, and accordingly of
public authority; to bring about trust therein, and to bring about compli-
ance therewith. . . . So long as the suspect continued to deny the crime, the
crime went unpunished."[21] Moreover, Hiramatsu writes that a person

could be convicted solely on the basis of a confession, without any confirming evidence. Since a confession was nothing more than a formal written account of the suspect's testimony, and since torture could be used, "it was by no means difficult for either the suspect or the official, or both, to create a false confession. Furthermore, it was entirely possible that punishment—including the death penalty—might be determined based solely upon such a fabricated statement."[22]

A New Legal Structure

The opening of Japan in the mid-nineteenth century, followed by the Meiji Restoration (1868), prompted wholesale changes in the nation's legal structure: new codes, new courts, and a constitution. This era of conflict and change also introduced the disturbing issue of "personal rights" as defined by law.

On January 1, 1882, the Penal Code (*Keihō*) was promulgated by the Great Council of State; the Code of Criminal Instruction (*Chizai hō*) became effective on the same date. The Penal Code, which totally repudiated traditional law, classified crimes into three types: felonies, misdemeanors, and police offenses. Under the new code arbitrary sentences by judges were limited. Moreover, the old idea of collective criminal responsibility was removed, and the individual was solely responsible for a crime. Furthermore, the old rule-by-status system was swept away by establishing the principle of equality before the law. Finally, the code protected criminal suspects from official violence: Article 278 provided punishment for officials who violated rules for arrest or who illegally imprisoned an individual; Article 282 listed punishment for police officials, procurators, or judges who injured criminal suspects in forcing confessions.[23]

During the early years of the Meiji period (1868–1912), the administration of justice remained mixed with executive branch duties, but in August 1871 a new Department of Justice was organized. Efforts to define the duties and status of the new department more clearly moved forward rapidly after the appointment of Etō Shinpei as the new head in June 1872. Etō, who is considered Japan's first justice minister, tried, with some success, to carry out far-reaching reforms (e.g., placing all courts under the control of his department and issuing the first comprehensive regulations for the new department). Under Etō's direction the department divided judicial business among the courts, the procurators' offices, and the Meihoryō (a law school). Unfortunately, for reformers who hoped to create a judiciary independent of the executive branch, the status of the department remained low, and reforms made after Etō departed in 1873 were inadequate to create a completely independent judiciary. The position of the Supreme Court, for example, remained inferior to that of the executive center. Indeed, an early attempt to raise the status of the court, and other courts as well, failed when Minister of the Right Iwakura Tomomi refused the concurrent position of chief justice.[24] "By default the next choice for Chief Justice had to be a judge of the first grade. Yet no one in the judiciary was qualified . . . and Tamano Seiri, a judge of the second grade, was appointed Assistant Chief Justice instead. Failing to fill the Chief Justice position with a person of high status and hence elevate the Supreme Court to an equal position with the Genrō-In, where it would be situated just beneath the Central Chamber, the Supreme Court at length fell to rest in a place next in line to the departments of state."[25] This lack of status for the highest court spilled over into the status of the new Department of Justice (and this lower status among the various departments—later called ministries—continued as a problem for justice officials throughout the era of the imperial state). Nevertheless, throughout the Meiji era judges gradually replaced local officials in the administration of justice, and judges developed a degree of independence from the executive, including the administrative headquarters in the Justice Ministry.[26]

On February 11, 1889, Emperor Meiji promulgated the Constitution of the Great Empire of Japan. The preamble rejects Western ideas about limitations on the government imposed by natural rights or social contracts. Although a number of articles in the constitution guarantee rights for people, none are unconditional; all can be removed by government legislation.[27] Thus, the constitution plus the various legal codes reenforced Tokugawa ideas about avoiding limits on law-making power and means of redress against authority.[28] Despite these limitations on the rights of subjects and limitations on courts (for example, administrative matters were outside their jurisdiction), the constitution did provide for an independent court system (Article 57).[29] As one noted scholar puts it: "No organ or branch of government was supreme. None had the power to direct or check the others. Only the judiciary could claim full autonomy from all direct outside interference—hence judicial independence—as it alone had both the authority and power to act 'in the name of the Emperor.' "[30]

Judicial independence was put to the test on May 11, 1896, after Tsuda Sanzō, a policeman assigned to guard the Russian crown prince (later Nicholas II), tried to kill his charge. Extreme political pressure was applied to the Supreme Court to ensure that Tsuda was executed under the provisions of the Penal Code that protected the Japanese imperial family (there was no death penalty for the attempted murder of other people). Kojima Iken, who was head of the Supreme Court (i.e., the Great Court of Cassation), convinced the trial judges to resist the government efforts to bend the law; instead of death Tsuda received life at hard labor.[31] This dramatic Ōtsu case clearly established that judges were independent of political pressure, if they wished to be. A leading Japanese legal scholar, Tanaka Hideo, states: "The Ōtsu judgement remains the most valuable tradition of the Japanese judiciary. Whatever their shortcomings, Japanese judges since then have scrupulously guarded their independence, and the nation has reposed implicit confidence in their integrity and their freedom from corruption, although of course not everyone always likes their decisions."[32] Ishii Ryōsuke notes that "the outcome of the case [The Ōtsu Incident] was . . . a shining example of the judiciary's independence of the executive and was tremendously significant *for having put just such an impression in the minds of the Japanese.*"[33] In a book published in 1976, I wrote:

> Judges, while they enjoyed judicial independence and were in theory free from outside pressure, were subject to manipulation by other justice officials, especially by those in Tokyo. The chief flaw in the court system's independence was that it was under the control of central administrators who could pressure recalcitrant judges in various ways, including demoting them to less desirable benches. An ambitious young judge would be inclined to make decisions with one eye cocked toward the minister. One specialist on Japanese law [Dan F. Henderson] acknowledges this situation but claims that "there is little evidence of interference in specific cases." While it is doubtful that a judge was ever ordered by the minister to "throw" a case, it is clear that pressure was exerted upon the bench in a number of important political trials. In this sense, the judicial independence so highly valued by the courts was breached again and again. However, few judges were able to stand rock-firm in the nationalistic flood that swept Japan.[34]

Research for later books has merely reenforced the above view.[35] Naturally, Meiji oligarchs, elected politicians, and Justice Ministry administrators pressured judges, sometimes successfully, and judges not infrequently adjusted rulings to fit in with the trend of the times. These facts, however, should not lead scholars to announce boldly that there was no independent judiciary.[36] Rather, the perception that judges were independent grew throughout the imperial era, especially when judges ruled against the government in sensitive political cases.[37] Dandō Shigemitsu, a giant in the field of criminal law, supports this argument that judges felt strongly that they were independent.[38] Most of the common people, it appears, also subscribed to the concept of independent courts. Although there are no public opinion surveys to support this conclusion, one can deduce from newspaper and magazine articles, which usually commented favorably on judges' independence, that the people believed that the courts dispensed equitable justice. Perception is important!

Procurators were another vital element of the court community. They first appeared in 1872, another of Etō Shinpei's suggestions. Etō viewed procurators as watchdogs over judges and as administrators for the judicial police; also, they could safeguard rights of litigants and watch over suspects under indictment. Although procurators had a right to demand a court judgment, they had no power to make one.[39] Nevertheless, procurators were in a strong position. They dominated police by giving advice in the handling of cases and the drafting of documents. They dominated preliminary examination judges whose duty it was to decide whether or not to send a case to open trial. Indeed, to a great extent, since judges used documents produced by procurators, the court experience was often a case of trial and conviction by procurators! At the open trial, procurators dressed like judges, sat above the courtroom with the judges, and identified themselves closely with the bench.[40] Moreover, procurators, because of their wide discretionary power to prosecute or not prosecute, became a political force in the pre-1945 era.[41]

Lawyers were another indispensable court community group. Their role in the justice process was limited, because they had no legal right to visit clients during the interrogation phase, which sometimes ran from one hundred to two hundred days. Thus, by the time lawyers conferred with clients, procurators had compiled a voluminous file of damaging evidence. Therefore, lawyers employed courtroom skills to obtain the lowest possible sentence for a client.[42] Their accepted role was to humbly note extenuating circumstances, beg leniency, and promise a reformed client.[43] On the whole, attorneys were regarded as the poor relations in the legal fraternity and looked down on by judges and procurators. Consequently, they developed an esprit de corps of their own and vigorously attacked legalists who worked for the government (i.e., procurators and judges).[44]

Although this book focuses on the above court community, police, naturally, played a role in the Teijin scandal investigation. Takagi Naomichi, a key suspect in the criminal investigation, accused police of brutality. It is doubtful that the public was surprised or shocked by this charge, because tales of police brutality were common fare in newspapers. I wrote in an earlier book: "Although these illegal actions were seldom officially blessed, they were unofficially encouraged by authorities who did not forcefully stop such practices. . . . Even among the less informed members of the public, these illegal actions and subsequent cover-ups were an open secret."[45] A former procurator notes: "The practice of forcing confessions became rather common among police; prisoners were kept incommunicado; the preliminary examination, which was kept secret from the public, became a sort of Star Chamber affair."[46]

Development of Personal Rights

The term *"jinken"* can be translated as "human rights" or "personal rights." I use "personal rights" (except for the postwar era), because that English term better reflects the reality of how rights were viewed by the government, legalists of the court community, and the general public. Most people did not think about rights in terms of inalienable human rights bestowed by heaven; instead they viewed rights as a gift from the emperor enshrined in the Meiji Constitution. Miyazawa Toshiyoshi, an expert on the Meiji Constitution, points out that the document guaranteed various rights to subjects granted by the emperor. "They were never thought of as something which existed before the constitution. They were regarded as the rights *of the subjects* but never as *human* rights, i.e., the rights that the people can claim *as human beings*."[47]

Limited rights under the constitution, however, were a giant step away from previous views on people's rights. One scholar of the Meiji civil code writes that the natural law idea of rights was not only "one of the most difficult concepts for Japanese to master" but "proved troublesome to translate" and "remained abstruse even after it had acquired Japanese dress." This was because Tokugawa law "acted in terms of justice for the polity and began not with the individual's rights but with his duty to superiors and to the group. Relations to others were defined in terms of responsibilities, not liberties; stressing private rights was in fact to infringe on the polity's rights to duty and loyalty."[48] The difficulty of introducing a legal concept of rights is illustrated by the efforts of Mitsukuri Rinshō to translate French law. After Mitsukuri completed parts of the Code Napoleon, a committee examined the translation. "These discussions often expanded into debate and sometimes into despair over the conceptual gulf between French and Japanese."[49] Mitsukuri coined the term *"kenri"* (power plus interest) for "rights." In Chinese and Japanese classics, however, this term meant something like thinking about making a profit, which Confucian norms characterized as vulgar behavior.[50] Another hotly debated term was *"droits civils,"* which he translated as *"minken"* (people's authority or people's power). Mitsukuri recalled: "There was an argument over what did I mean by saying that the people (*min*) have 'power' (*ken*). Even though I tried to justify it as hard as I could, there was an extremely furious argument. Fortunately, the chairman, Mr. Eto [Shinpei], supported me and finally the matter was ended."[51] Over twenty years passed, but the term *"kenri"* remained contentious. Itō Hirobumi, who oversaw the drafting of the Meiji Constitution, used "Rights and Duties of Subjects" for the heading of chapter 2. Education Minister and Privy Councilor Mori Arinori (American-educated) argued that this term was improper, because subjects should have nothing but duties in connection with the emperor. Itō replied that if the people were not given some rights, there was no purpose to making a constitution. Eventually the Privy Council approved Itō's choice.[52] Their approval, however, was not automatic; other privy councilors, like Mori, objected to extending "rights" to the people. Their solution was to change "Rights and Duties of Subjects" to "Responsibility of Subjects."[53]

Writing on civil rights twenty years after the promulgation of the constitution, George Uyehara states: "The Constitution of Japan provides no absolute guarantee in respect of civil rights and liberties; that is to say, it does not restrict the power of either the government or the Diet to make laws with regard to these privileges. . . . It can do anything constitutionally to restrict the rights and liberties of the people, provided it first enacts a law to that effect." Uyehara explains why Itō Hirobumi and other framers were satisfied with limited civil rights: "Under the feudal *régime* Japan had no civil code defining the rights and liberties of the people, except common law or custom. It seemed, therefore, to the constitutional framers a great advance for the civil rights and liberties of the people to be formulated, recognized, and guaranteed by law in the Constitution."[54]

During the Meiji era, people concerned with protecting the procedural rights of criminal suspects and the personal rights of prisoners badgered authorities. For example, the Osaka Municipal Assembly and the Osaka Bar Association condemned certain prison punishments in 1887, and the following year a reformer spearheaded a protest against outrageous working conditions at a prison sulphur mine in Hokkaido. At the turn of the century, dozens of lawyers donated their time to defend farmers who protested pollution of the Shimotsuke Plain (this is the first recorded pro bono publico service by Japanese lawyers). Violations of personal rights were discussed in the Diet (1912), and procurators were charged with abuse of power (1914); unsuccessful law bills were introduced to better protect criminal suspects. Outside the Diet, many lawyers defended workers and the poor who ran afoul of government regulations. The Japan Bar Association twice in 1918 created committees to investigate possible violations of personal rights. In one of these cases, the committee report charged that procurators abused personal rights and violated the law. Police received their share of negative publicity as well. For example, Fuse Tatsuji, who began a legalist career as a procurator (1904–1905), published, as an attorney, *A Theory on Reforming the Machinery of Justice (Shihō kikan kaizen ron)* in 1917. The book focuses on various illegal interrogation methods employed to force confessions. By 1920 a postwar depression produced a wave of labor demonstrations and strikes; lawyers like Fuse were kept busy defending workers. One particularly violent strike at the Kawasaki Dockyard in Kobe (1921) turned into a battlefield. Out of this terrible time emerged the Liberal Legal Association (Jiyū hōsō dan) (established in Tokyo in August 1921). The aim of the roughly forty lawyers who joined this group was to investigate personal rights abuses and to reform the legal system. In the face of harsh government suppression of the communist movement (e.g., the Peace Preservation Law of 1925), lawyers and others concerned about personal rights published in newspapers, magazines, and books information about violations by authorities. Allies in the Diet helped by quizzing cabinet ministers on this issue.[55]

Nevertheless, this effort to raise public awareness about the criminal justice system's abuses was handicapped by the fact that the public held little sympathy for communist suspects. Moreover, defense lawyers, who were sometimes ideological soulmates of communist clients, were in not a few cases also prosecuted under the provisions of the Peace Preservation Law.[56] In the Teijin scandal, however, civil libertarians were presented with a high-profile trial in which leftist ideology played no role. Hence, they stood a much better chance of convincing the public that some officials abused criminal suspects' legal rights.[57]

Tokyo Procurators

Tokyo procurators played a key role in the Teijin scandal indictments and trial. Oddly, sugar companies were involved both in the first prosecution that gained Tokyo procurators a seat at the political table and in the events that set off the Teijin prosecution (the former a bribery case; the latter, nonpayment of taxes). Also by coincidence, is Hiranuma Kiichirō was involved in both incidents (as head of the Criminal Affairs Bureau of the Justice Ministry in the former case; as former justice minister and a major political figure in the political intrigue surrounding the Teijin affair). In the first case, the public was provided with a detailed report on a bribery transaction between businessmen and politicians. The Greater Japan Sugar Refining Company, which was in financial difficulty and eager to sell out to the government, bribed politicians whom it hoped would pressure bureaucrats into approving a purchase. Although this was not the first time that rumors circulated about illegal business deals, it was the first time that the Tokyo procurators cracked down on the bribers and bribees. Before this sugar company case, procurators had been handicapped by a lack of investigative funds and poor police cooperation. Hiranuma, however, not only obtained money for the investigation, but also brokered a deal with Prime Minister Katsura Tarō to permit this sensitive investigation and prosecution. Seven businessmen were judged guilty of bribery on December 6, 1909, and out of twenty-two politicians sixteen were convicted. According to Hiranuma's memoir these convictions marked a watershed: the Tokyo procurators were becoming important players in the political world.

A second sensational bribery case, during the Ōkuma Shigenobu Cabinet (April 1914–October 1916), further expanded procuratorial political influence. In brief, Home Minister Ōura Kanetake, a leading figure in the Yamagata Aritomo clique, was caught bribing Diet members for votes and violating election law regulations. A compromise was negotiated between Hiranuma and the premier: procurators would issue a "suspension of indictment" (*kiso yūyo*) in exchange for which Ōura would withdraw from public life. Thus, beginning with the sugar bribery incident, procurators enlarged their investigative powers, and by the time the Ōura case was concluded, the usefulness of "suspension of indictment" had been demonstrated. Over the following years, the power of suspension of indictment became a sharp political sword in the hands of the Hiranuma clique, which could prosecute or not prosecute as it saw fit.[58] As for Hiranuma, after a record number of years as procurator general, he became justice minister in September 1923.

During the late 1920s Tokyo procurators not only were on the cutting edge of a large number of sensational corruption cases, but also were the leading force in the state's crusade to crush the Japanese Communist Party. Shiono Suehiko, one of Hiranuma's loyalist supporters, was chief of the elite Tokyo District Court procurators from October 2, 1927, until September 20, 1930. During this period, he presided over the Tokyo part of the massive roundup of communists on March 15, 1928 (nationwide about 1,600 communist suspects were apprehended). Thus, the busy Tokyo District Court bureau was involved in regular criminal cases, political bribery investigations, and ideological cases. According to Shiono's memoir, he ordered subordinates to strive to promote justice, and he encouraged them to pursue each investigation with vigor and to be unwilling to compromise their convictions. It was especially important, he felt, for the Tokyo bureau to excel, because it set the pace for procurators nationwide. Moreover, the successful prosecutions during his tenure increased the general prestige of the ministry.[59] Some scholars regard the Hiranuma clique as favoring the Seiyūkai. Although there is some truth in this viewpoint, Hiranuma's close follower Shiono's zeal to root out corruption spilled over political boundaries; he prosecuted politicians from both major parties. Indeed, the only state minister sent to prison, vice-president of the Seiyūkai and former justice minister Ogawa Heikichi, was indicted by Shiono's group.[60]

It was not necessary for procurators to beat the bushes to discover corruption cases; politicians and their allies were eager to supply information on this subject. Seiyūkai deputy leader Ogawa Heikichi saw the origin of the politics of mutual vilification in the early 1920s; it stemmed from the fact that the Seiyūkai under Prime Minister Hara Kei had such a huge legislative majority. Therefore, discrediting the government, in hopes of causing a cabinet change, became an opposition tactic. By the mid-1920s, charges of corruption flew back and forth among politicians. Ogawa thought that this intensification of the politics of mutual vilification resulted from the major parties having similar platforms and being of roughly equal strength, and an acceptance of the idea that a cabinet collapse would usher the attackers into positions of power.[61] That this vicious cycle of corruption accusations could be halted, at least temporarily, was illustrated during the Wakatsuki Cabinet (1926–1927). The three main party leaders (Tanaka Giichi of the Seiyūkai, Wakatsuki of the Kenseikai, and Tokonami Reijirō of the Seiyuhontō) made a political truce, agreeing to "cover up things that smell." Soon, however, the Kenseikai and the Seiyuhontō made a deal that excluded the Seiyūkai. The latter, joined by other opposition groups, began exposing scandals.[62] Reflecting on this situation, "Ogawa concluded that the politics of mutual vilification had produced a loss of trust in the parties, not only by the public but by other segments of the government as well, and that this loss of trust, most commonly expressed in the view that the parties were hopelessly corrupt, was a major contribution to the generation of a feeling of *hijōji* [emergency period] in the early 1930s."[63]

Thus, Shiono Suehiko became head of Tokyo procurators during an escalation of the mutual vilification political campaign; he was happy to accommodate informers who made corruption charges. Among the cases handled by this bureau were election law violations (the first general election under manhood suffrage was held in February 1928), a Tokyo City graft investigation, bribery in the sale of private railway companies to the government, and a bribery case against the governor-general of Korea. The indictments and trials resulted in convictions of several state ministers.[64] Shiono recalled in his memoir that these successful prosecutions "shocked the political world" and that justice officials "were covered with prestige." In these cases (plus some ideological prosecutions as well), procurators were the driving force, with police following their lead.[65] Corruption cases of this era were not limited to Tokyo. Indeed, as one scholar notes: "There were so many cases that it was like peak time of the flower blossoms. It went on all over Japan and it involved civilians and the military."[66]

Engaged with this upsurge of corruption cases, some of Shiono's procurators must have decided that the political and business worlds were permeated with corruption, that this corruption was seeping into the imperial bureaucracy, that communism and other radical ideas flourished in this corrupt atmosphere, and that it was the duty of procurators to clean out this sewer of corruption. The actions of procurators involved in the Teijin scandal case are better understood if this viewpoint is kept in mind. Both Kuroda Etsurō and Biwada Gensuke, who acted in turn as chief procurators during the Teijin investigation, were members of the Tokyo District Court bureau during Shiono Suehiko's anticorruption crusade.

Courts and Trials

Courts were divided into four classes: local (ward), district, appeals, and supreme. Besides these courts, there were army and navy courts, an administrative court, and family courts. Usually one judge was assigned to each local court. Cases brought before this court could not exceed a property value of one hundred yen or were in the category of police offenses (i.e., minor crimes). A district court, which was a collegiate bench, handled cases involving property valued at more than one hundred yen or crimes procurators regarded as serious enough for this level of judgment. An appeals court, which was a collegiate bench of second instance, reviewed cases decided by lower courts (it was the final appeal point for local court cases).

Either the prosecution or the defense could request a hearing by an appeals court. The Supreme Court reviewed writs of error.[67] A Supreme Court opinion on a point of law "was binding on the lower courts in all particulars of the action concerned."[68] The function of an appellate court was very different from that of an Anglo-American appellate court. It "could . . . examine witnesses who had already been examined by the lower court and receive new testimonial or documentary evidence. . . . The appellate court could rely both upon the recorded evidence of the first instance trial and upon new evidence produced at its own oral hearings. Considering the fact that about one third of prewar District Court cases disposed of by a formal judgement were appealed, one could say that a trial in the District Court was a sort of prelude to the trial process which terminated in the Court of Appeals."[69] The Supreme Court, as the final appellate court, was for the most part restricted to reviewing questions of law. Although Diet members and legal scholars sometimes argued against the constitutionality of statutes, Supreme Court judges did not take issue with the supremacy of the Diet's legislative power.[70]

Jury trials were held from October 1, 1928, for certain types of cases, but the Teijin trial was conducted by a three-judge panel (a chief judge and two associates) at the Tokyo District Criminal Court. A supplementary judge also attended trial sessions. The Teijin trial was no exception to the general rule that prewar trials were lengthy affairs. Indeed, the Teijin criminal trial, which ran from June 1935 until December 1937, lasted a record 265 sessions (excluding the final verdict session). Examination of defendants (June 1935–December 1936) was followed by the testimony of witnesses (beginning in February 1937). The prosecution's final statement began on August 6, 1937, and the last words of defense lawyers followed. The senior judge's domination of these proceedings can be likened to a ship captain's authority. Defendants, witnesses, lawyers, and procurators were his to command. As one judge puts it: "The prewar system maximized the responsibility of the trial judge and minimized that of the [defendants and lawyers]. . . . In sharp contrast to Anglo-American procedure, the trial judge had strong directive powers in the process of fixing issues and of proof taking, and a trial was conducted in piecemeal fashion with several successive hearings often separated by a substantial time interval."[71] Since discovering the "truth" rested solely with the judges, a lengthy piecemeal process was favored, because it permitted a thorough investigation of complicated cases.

There was, however, a compelling reason for the extraordinary length of the Teijin trial: legal training for judges was deficient in economic education (this remained the case in the early postwar era).[72] Moreover, elite

Tokyo procurators were deficient in this area as well (see the following chapters). Yazawa Makoto, professor of law at Tokyo University, writing on the fiduciary obligations of company directors, notes that "the lack of development of . . . standards seems related to the system of legal education, the training of judges, and the demonstration of justice. Career judges have never been engaged as lawyers in a business practice so as to gain a practical knowledge of corporate management." Furthermore, legal actions against company directors have been difficult to pursue "because of judicial unwillingness to invade the realm of business judgment and also because of the dearth of lawyers with the special skills and training needed in this area of law."[73]

The judiciary was one of the institutions most trusted by the public. Indeed, even in the midst of the budgetary crisis caused by the Great Depression and the searing ideological crusade to stamp out communism, "judicial independence remained intact and judges were considered the most trustworthy of all government officials."[74] This view is buttressed by a May 1932 newspaper editorial on governmental corruption: "There has never been any suggestion of corruption extending to the courts," writes the editor, "though justice has invariably erred on the side of leniency."[75] Former Chief Justice Hattori Takaaki (a judge from 1938) notes that judges had "a strong sense of professional integrity and consciousness of membership in a special professional group. The fact that there is not a single recorded instance of judicial corruption, while many bribery cases were reported in the legislative and executive branches . . . and the fact that the judiciary did not yield completely under militaristic and ultranationalistic pressure, even in the critical years of World War II, are further manifestations of this consciousness."[76] Hattori also notes that in general "it is accepted that prewar judges fulfilled their mission well and had judicious characters. They were perhaps the most reliable of the bureaucratic organizations in Japan."[77] The opinion that in general the pre-1945 public viewed judges as trustworthy is endorsed by the distinguished legal scholar Hirano Ryūichi: "Judges, with a sense of their special responsibility to adjudicate cases 'in the name of the emperor,' tried hard to keep their moral standards as high as those of priests. . . . People trusted judges partly because they believed that judges with such a mental attitude would act impartially, and partly because of their general respect for public officials serving the Emperor."[78]

CHAPTER 2

Background of the Scandal

SINCE THE TEIJIN SCANDAL and subsequent prosecution arose from a stock sale, a brief look at customary business practices, economic conditions, joint-stock companies, and "artificial silk" is called for. Furthermore, the state of business ethics, as judged by scholars and businessmen, is presented below in order to explain the press and public willingness to believe accusations of illegal acts by the purchasers of Teijin Company stocks.

Japanese capitalism was plagued with contradictions. Businessmen found it difficult to discuss profit incentives, as they claimed to work for the nation's advancement. Yet they praised private competition while eagerly taking state aid. After the end of the nineteenth century, the ideology of the managerial elite remained about the same as that of business pioneers, as business leaders asserted that national interests came before private ones. A new element, however, entered the picture in the late Meiji era: capitalists' concern over growing labor unrest. By the end of World War I, this concern was met by emphasizing cooperation between labor and business leaders. Some business leaders stressed harmony, and others claimed that managers, like workers, were in fact salaried employees.

Business ideology of the 1920s laid stress on cooperation and contribution to national goals; almost always successful businessmen lectured against selfish striving for material gains.[1] Dan Takuma, president of the Industrial Club, urged a group of young men, in 1924, to do their best no matter what their position was in an enterprise. "If you are successful in this and make some contribution to the Nation and your fellow countrymen, the sense of having contributed is your compensation. If you are fortunate, fame and wealth will be perhaps granted to you, but these compensations should come as natural by-products. They are not the ultimate aim."[2] After Dan Takuma was assassinated in 1932, his replacement as head of the National Federation of Industrial Organizations, Gō Seinosuke, noted that

Dan "loved his business as he did his children, and he devoted his life to it. Profit-making was of secondary importance to him."[3] Makino Motojirō, president of a bank and author of several books on business practices, also stressed the difference between Japanese and Western businessmen: "Those who will do nothing except for profit do not have the true spirit of a Japanese. They have the head of a foreigner. They are detestable."[4]

Although business leaders were criticized during the 1920s, widespread hostility first appeared during the world depression. In the early 1930s, civilian and military rightists targeted the *zaibatsu* together with the political parties; businessmen and politicians in a corrupt deal, they insisted, were subverting traditional morality and oppressing the people.[5] For example, during the investigation of the Blood Pact Group (Ketsumeidan), procurators reported this view of the defendants who killed Prime Minister Inukai Tsuyoshi (May 15, 1932): "Political parties, the *zaibatsu* and a small privileged group attached to the ruling class . . . [are] sunk in corruption. They conspire in parties to pursue their own egoistic interests and desires, to the neglect of national defense and to the confusion of government." Overseas national prestige is lost, "while at home the morale of the people collapses."[6] In this hostile climate, business leaders avoided explicit discussion of the profit motive more than ever.[7]

Newspapers and magazines, seeking to expand circulation, seldom missed opportunities to illustrate the harsh realities of capitalism or to illustrate the greed of capitalists. Big business, for instance, presented the media with a perfect example of greed in the dollar-buying scandal of 1931. After England left the gold standard, in late September 1931, the Japanese government delayed reimposing a gold embargo for about three months. *Zaibatsu* banks used the interim to purchase dollars with soon-to-be-devalued yen. It is estimated that Mitsui made fifty million dollars in this manner. Public opinion was outraged.[8]

Economic Conditions

During World War I, the economy enjoyed boom conditions accompanied by great structural changes. Nakamura Takafusa sums up this new situation concisely: "With the disappearance of European and American products from Asian and African trade, these extensive markets suddenly became wide open to Japanese products. Export volume and prices shot up. . . . A spate of new firms appeared in rapid succession; stock prices soared. . . . From its status as a debtor nation to the tune of ¥1.1 billion on the eve of war . . . [Japan] transformed itself into a creditor nation with a surplus exceeding ¥2 billion."[9]

Outstanding among the firms riding the economic wave crest was Suzuki shōten, which emerged rapidly as a new *zaibatsu*. Established by Suzuki Iwajirō in 1877 as a small Kobe sugar store, by 1902 it was a company capitalized at ¥500,000. Directed by Kaneko Naokichi, who replaced the deceased Suzuki, the company expanded rapidly into camphor, salt, oil, wheat, beer, tobacco, alcohol, rubber, fertilizer, metals, chemicals, and rayon. The company also branched out into shipping, heavy industry, storage, insurance, and banking. World War I accelerated the company's amazing expansion, to the point that Suzuki began to look as large as the huge Mitsui combine.[10] In a 1917 letter to the company's London branch head, Kaneko wrote: "Now Suzuki shōten is advancing with a 100 percent rate of success in whatever we plan to do."[11] Indeed, under Kaneko's brilliant leadership, "Suzuki staked out a world empire and boosted its transactions to more than a billion yen a year."[12]

Wartime boom conditions, however, were followed by a series of panics, beginning with a stock market crash in 1920. Moreover, agriculture, a mainstay in overall economic growth, declined throughout the 1920s. This grim situation reflected a growing excess of farm products worldwide. A catastrophic earthquake on September 1, 1923, which demolished the capital area, compounded the nation's woes. Although the Bank of Japan's "earthquake relief bills" (rediscounting commercial bills scheduled to be paid in the metropolitan area) averted a panic, the natural disaster caused an enormous financial loss estimated as high as ten billion yen. Furthermore, the nation's declining financial situation forced a delay in the planned return to the gold standard.[13]

Returning to the gold standard at prewar parity was the aim of all industrialized nations, and Japan was no exception. "It was perhaps unfortunate," one scholar writes, "that she missed the most opportune time right after the armistice to accomplish it, when she had accumulated a huge specie holdings abroad and still enjoyed the domestic prosperity. As time passed, it became increasingly difficult to achieve the goal."[14]

December 25, 1926, marked the beginning of the new Showa imperial era (1926–1989). Optimists who thought that the reign change would produce economic prosperity had a rude awakening within a few weeks. In fact, the cabinet of Wakatsuki Reijirō (January 1926–April 1927) was aware of the thin ice on which the economy rested. Finance Minister Kataoka Naoharu, for example, worried about the remaining earthquake relief bills, which he viewed as an economic cancer, because these bills, rediscounted by the Bank of Japan for companies and banks in the disaster area, represented mostly unrecoverable debts. The government tried to bail out unstable banks by persuading the House of Representatives to compensate banks holding earthquake relief bills. Fifty-one banks (about half were commercial banks and half were special banks) held over 3,400 bills worth nearly ¥207 million; the Bank of Taiwan controlled most of those held by special banks. Moreover, about 70 percent of those held by the Bank of Taiwan were issued originally by Suzuki shōten. Guided by Kaneko, the trading company expanded into a new *zaibatsu* during the war and deepened an already close relationship with the Bank of Taiwan and the Kenseikai (whose name changed later to the Minseitō) politicians. Eventually, the Bank of Taiwan loaned Suzuki so much money that it could not afford to let the trading company fail; in order to obtain funds for Suzuki, it borrowed from other banks backed by the Bank of Japan as a final line of credit.[15]

It is clear that the Bank of Taiwan and its Suzuki Trading Company debtor were already drifting onto an economic reef before the depression of 1920 and the devastating 1923 earthquake. Suzuki, which dealt in Taiwan's staple products, expanded rapidly, fed by generous Bank of Taiwan funding. When the boom collapsed, however, the Bank of Taiwan could not simply issue more notes to replenish its financial reservoir, because Suzuki's foreign trade debts had to be paid in hard money. A report by the Bank of Japan, after the earthquake, disclosed that Suzuki was the most indebted among the top five indebted firms and that, among the top ten banks holding earthquake relief bills, the Bank of Taiwan held over one-third of the total debt. Of this large debt, about 60 percent was owed to the bank by Suzuki.[16]

During a Diet debate about compensating banks, opponents of the law bills, led by the Seiyūkai, tried to defeat the legislation by exposing government corruption scandals. They also spotlighted the shaky financial condition of the Suzuki company and its special relationship with the Bank of Taiwan. An unexpected consequence of this exposure was a run on several banks. Finally, the Bank of Japan stopped supporting the Bank of Taiwan, which ceased making loans to Suzuki shōten on March 27, 1927. In early April Suzuki closed its Japan offices. Although the Wakatsuki government tried to save the Bank of Taiwan by issuing an emergency imperial ordinance, the Privy Council, on April 15, refused to supply funds. This not only produced widespread bank runs but brought down the cabinet on April 20. During an extraordinary Diet session in early May, however, financial relief measures were passed to reopen the Bank of Taiwan and certain other banks.[17] The reestablished Bank of Taiwan took over surviving assets of Suzuki shōten, including 225,233 shares of stock in Teikoku jinzō kenshi kabushiki-kaisha (Imperial Rayon Company, Ltd.) or Teijin, a Suzuki shōten subsidiary. As security for the Bank of Taiwan's indebtedness, 205,000 Teijin shares were deposited at the Bank of Japan, with the debtor bank obligated to sell all the shares within ten years to pay off its debt.[18] Furthermore, to protect its investment in Teijin stock shares, the Bank of Taiwan installed three employees as Teijin Company directors.[19]

Throughout the balance of the 1920s, government leaders moved toward joining the major powers on the gold standard, which was accomplished on January 11, 1930, by the Hamaguchi Cabinet (July 1929–April 1931). Unfortunately, this long-delayed move came at the worst possible time: the aftermath of the crash of the New York Stock Exchange on October 24, 1929, and the beginning of the worldwide depression. Optimism quickly changed to despair as specie flowed out of Japan and business stagnated. The Inukai Cabinet (December 1931–May 1932) responded by reimposing the gold embargo. Finance Minister Takahashi Korekiyo, who was known as the John M. Keynes of Japan, employed a policy of deficit financing to pull the nation out of the depression. Bonds issued by the Finance Ministry, purchased by the Bank of Japan, covered annual deficits. The economy, stimulated by military expenditures, a great surge of exports, the seizure of Manchuria, and fighting with China, recovered prosperity, growing out of the Great Depression more rapidly than most nations. Indeed, by 1935 the economy was near full employment.[20] One scholar describes Takahashi's economic policies as "one of the most successful combinations of fiscal, monetary, and foreign exchange note policies, in an adverse international environment, that the world had ever seen."[21]

Joint-Stock Companies

The sale of the Teijin Company stocks, which precipitated a criminal investigation and trial, should be viewed in the context of customary business practices. Japanese were attracted quickly to the joint-stock principle, a device for pooling savings under a unified leadership. Indeed, by 1930 about 40 percent of companies were joint-stock concerns, and they represented 80 percent of private capital.[22] Despite the rapid growth of this Western form of capitalism, Japanese joint-stock companies were "suffused with the spirit of the Japanese family system."[23] A January 1931 newspaper article analyzes what this "spirit" meant with regard to the performance of joint-stock companies. The article cites *Kabushiki-kaisha bōkoku ron* (Joint-Stock companies: ruination of the nation) by the well-known economist Takahashi Kamekichi. After tracing the historical development of Japanese companies, Takahashi opines: "Created and developed largely by bureaucrats and men of the former samurai class, as they have been, many of them are characterized by complete lack of business ability and prudence in their boards and their excessive dependence on the authorities." He points out that "directors and shareholders are too greedy. It is largely owing to the excessively high dividends and bonuses which are paid out of the capital instead of the profits that many companies have gone to the dogs, abruptly announcing an enormous loss which could no longer be kept secret." Next Takahashi cites examples, among even the soundest companies, of dividends and bonuses that ranged from 70 to 95 percent in 1928. In the United States the top figure would have to be closer to 50 percent, he notes. Takahashi concludes by reflecting on the many examples of fraudulent reports and accounts "drawn up so as to conceal financial defects. In fact, the untrustworthiness of the accounts is the main cause of the difficulty experienced by many companies in raising funds."[24] Given Takahashi's reputation as an authority on economics and the sad state of the economy in the early 1930s, his book would have been reviewed widely and read by many people. Takahashi also authored the book *Nihon shihonshugi no gōrika* (Rationalization of Japanese capitalism) in 1930, and a year after the appearance of the above newspaper article, he produced four volumes in a series on the growth of public finance and the economy plus a book on the changing nature of the business community.[25]

The newspaper article also spotlights the "blatant irresponsibility of directors": "It is no exaggeration to say that the failure of banks and companies . . . since 1920 has almost always been due to some glaring breach of trust on the part of the directors."[26] An article in the business journal *Diamond*, by Fukuzawa Momosuke, son of the famous Meiji era educator and founder of Keio University, made the point that company directors were not doing a proper job, were overpaid, and were sometimes corrupt. Furthermore, outside inspectors who are charged to watch directors, Fukuzawa wrote, in too many cases either were not doing their job properly or were ignored by directors.[27]

Professor Takahashi's book *Kabushiki-kaisha bōkoku ron*, cited in the above newspaper review, was in fact a secondary product of *Rationalization of Japanese Capitalism*. A book publisher persuaded Takahashi to write a popular version of parts of the earlier work. To do so, the publisher argued, would focus public attention on corrupt business practices and the professor's call for reform.[28] Takahashi pulls no punches in the popular version.

"Malicious intent on the part of managers and shareholders eats up corporations. In part this problem is caused by a lack of knowledge [about proper business ethics] among managers and stockholders who engage in rotten depravity."[29] Unfortunately, he writes, company managers concentrate on the present, neglecting a long-term viewpoint. Moreover, company managers do not keep proper financial records and in some cases falsify their books. Instead of using profits to strengthen the firms' foundations, to pay off debt, and for research, managers pay huge dividends. Shareholders' demands are also responsible for this situation, which undermines future growth.[30] Takahashi concludes: "Business morals have been abraded and antiproductive; false business practices are permitted openly."[31]

Japanese scholarship of the postwar era supports Takahashi's negative views on the state of business ethics during the 1920s and early 1930s: "In fact, the moral hazard of large stockholders colluding with managers was a serious social problem during this period. Not only was the level of dividends extremely high, but bonus payments to top managers quite frequently amounted to 5 to 10 percent of profits. Even if a company was in the red, dividends and bonuses were paid by means of false statements of settlements or sales of assets."[32]

The irrepressible businessman-politician Mutō Sanji, president of a splinter reform party, addressed a party general meeting in January 1931, at about the time the above newspaper article was published. Mutō charged that the government's proposed budget underestimated the seriousness of the economic slump and overestimated tax revenue. What the government was doing, he said, "will prove analogous to the evil practice of some private concerns which pay dividends out of capital."[33]

What the public thought about journalistic accounts of misfeasance, embezzlement, and bribery in the corporate world is unknowable, given the lack of public opinion polling in the early 1930s, but a continuing parade of such newspaper articles must have increased public distrust of financial elites in general and stockbrokers in particular. Some qualification of this statement is necessary, because the press had a practice of printing wild rumors and even untruthful accounts, and many newspaper readers must have been aware of this practice. As one close student of the press puts it: "So long as the gossip monger keeps free of touching on military, naval or diplomatic secrets and so long as he reveres the Imperial House, there is but slight restriction on his activities. . . . Even the most respectable newspapers yield to the temptation to print slander news of the most intimate nature."[34] Nevertheless, in their shotgun-style method, newspapers did expose illegal and unethical business practices.

The Tokyo Gas Company scandal, for instance, illuminated for public view corruption among joint-stock company officers and politicians. Press coverage of this affair sheds light on journalistic ethics. This scandal hit front pages about eight months before Kawai Yoshinari and others closed the Teijin Company stock deal.

According to Tokyo procurators, the Tokyo Gas Company planned to increase its capital by ¥100,000,000, and in June 1929 it offered ¥500,000 in bribes to various people as a guarantee that the city assembly would approve the application. Moreover, following the distribution of bribes, blackmailers squeezed the company for money. Names of very prominent people appeared in the first newspaper accounts of this affair: Privy Councilor Itō Miyoji, Governor-General of Korea Ugaki Kazushige, and former minister of Commerce and Industry Sakurauchi Yukio. As the investigation progressed, a growing name list of politicians was published, but the big names of Itō, Ugaki, and Sakurauchi disappeared. Thus, it appears that distinguished names were used to sell papers. Among the defendants sentenced in April 1934, at the Tokyo District Criminal Court, were the former executive director of the gas company, two former deputy mayors, and three former House of Representatives members (one of whom was the company executive director).[35]

Several months before this trial's conclusion, charges of illegal stock manipulation by the Banchōkai (i.e., the Teijin Company stock deal) surfaced in the press and on the Diet floor. Thus, the public was treated to a corruption scandal double feature.

From this review of customary business practices, one might conclude that many company directors and stockholders were greedy for short-term profit; inspectors were either ignored or drafted into the quick profit camp; fraudulent record keeping was common; misfeasance, bribery, and blackmail were not uncommon. No doubt many newspaper readers, who also must have concluded that corruption was rampant in the business world, were willing to accept uncritically prosecution charges of illegal acts in the Teijin Company stock transfer.

Rayon

Rayon (this name was coined in 1924) was created by European scientists in the nineteenth century, but commercial application did not begin until nearly 1900, when a proper spinneret appeared that could use viscose to produce a filament. Viscose is cellulose made viscous. Cellulose comes from plant cell walls (e.g., trees, hemp, flax, cotton). Wood pulp became the main source of viscose.[36]

Many Japanese leaders in the textile field saw rayon as a threat to silk production, but some entrepreneurs viewed the new product as a business opportunity. Among these progressive businessmen was Kaneko Naokichi, head of the Suzuki *zaibatsu*. Kaneko's first attempt to produce a salable product resulted in a joint venture with Mitsubishi, but the effort failed. Next Kaneko subsidized several years of research by Hata Itsuzō, who managed to make a salable rayon product. Encouraged by this development, Kaneko purchased an old silk factory in Yonezawa in which Hata could experiment with the new product. In 1916, Hata, hoping to learn the secret of producing a superior rayon product, visited the United States; the mission failed. Kaneko persisted, sending Kumura Seita, who succeeded in learning the secret. Based on this knowledge, Kaneko built a new factory in Hiroshima. This was the origin of the Teijin Company, which became a unit of Suzuki Trading Company on June 17, 1918. Within a few years Teijin became a leading firm in an important new industry.[37] Kaneko's intimate connection with the creation of Japan's rayon industry and the creation of the Teijin Company provides a vital clue in understanding his role in the 1933–1934 Teijin stock deal and scandal.

Teijin and other rayon producers swiftly learned advanced production technology. In 1926 Japan produced five million pounds of rayon and imported over 3,300,000; the next year domestic production was over ten million pounds (imports were about 800,000 pounds), and the year after over sixteen million pounds (imports were over 250,000 pounds). By 1932 domestic production was sixty-nine million pounds. The importance of rayon in Japan's export market, and its rapid overtaking of silk, is illustrated by the export figures for 1928 as compared with the figures for 1932: in the former year exported rayon was valued at ¥8,239,000 and silk at ¥124,736,000; in the latter year rayon was valued at ¥60,540,000 and silk at ¥50,288,000. Although the United States continued to be the leading producer of rayon, Japan by 1933 moved into second place, with Teijin Company as the largest domestic rayon producer.[38] The Mitsubishi Economic Research Bureau, commenting on the rapid rise of the new industry, noted: "The low production costs of rayon yarn and fabrics are unequaled anywhere else, which makes them formidable competitors on the world market."[39] The Mitsubishi research team added that by the end of 1931 the six established rayon companies were developing better manufacturing equipment, and new companies were formed "on account of the high profits then obtainable."[40] Thus, as viewed by investors, the rayon industry must have appeared as a bright beacon in a gloomy economic sea.

Banchōkai

The Banchōkai, an exclusive, informal group, grew out of the social meetings of three businessmen: Kawai Yoshinari (director of the Fukutoku and Nikka life insurance companies), Gotō Kunihiko (former president of Keisei Railroad), and Iwakura Tomomitsu (former vice-president of the Hankyū Department Store). Sometime during 1923, the group began monthly meetings, on the fourteenth of each month, at the home of Baron Gō Seinosuke, which was located in Koji-machi Ward, Banchō (hence the name Banchō Club). Holding the evening meetings at the baron's home came naturally, according to Kawai, because the three felt a close relationship to him and were, in a sense, his followers. Moreover, Gotō was the baron's private secretary. The group's three originators invited others to join but capped membership at about ten, because Gō treated them to a superb dinner at a large carved table that nicely seated that number of guests. Additional members were Shibusawa Masao (the next to the youngest son of the legendary businessman), Nakano Kinjirō (former president of a nationwide delivery service), Itō Chūbei (head of Marubeni and Itōchū trading companies), Haruta Shigemi (director of Sino-Japan Industries), Kaneko Kiyota (former president of the Asano Cement Company), Noda Shunsaku (a Seiyūkai politician and lower house member), Shōriki Matsutarō (president of the *Yomiuri Newspaper*), and Nagano Mamoru (director of the Yamakano Stock Brokerage Company).[41] Two well-known businessmen-politicians occasionally joined Gō's table group: Baron Nakajima Kumakichi (tied to the Furukawa *zaibatsu* and a state minister) and Kobayashi Ichizō (a railway company president and founder of the Takarazuka Girls' Opera Company).[42]

Besides furnishing a meeting place and a gourmet's meal, Baron Gō treated these younger men to frank accounts of youthful adventures in Germany; sometimes courtesans from Yoshiwara provided entertainment. Kawai emphasizes that these gatherings were for relaxation; if someone brought up a business topic, Gō would urge a change of subject to something more pleasant.[43]

By the early 1930s, Baron Gō was one of Japan's most active business leaders. Indeed, one scholar regards him as "perhaps the greatest sponsor-organizer since Shibusawa."[44] After the assassination in 1932 of Dan

Takuma, the baron headed the prestigious Economic Federation.[45] Since Gō was regarded widely as an agent for the Mitsui combine and since Mitsui favored the Seiyūkai, it is not surprising that the Banchōkai gave political contributions to Hatoyama Ichirō, a leading figure in that party.[46]

Baron Nakajima Kumakichi remembers the Banchōkai as a collection of people who had business connections with Baron Gō: Japan Industrial Club, *Yomiuri Newspaper*, Sino-Japan Industries, International Transportation, a share trading company, and so forth. In the beginning, people from these groups, who received favors from the baron, invited him to monthly gatherings, but, eventually, Gō transferred the meetings to his home. Nakajima, who attended these meetings once or twice per year, claims that they had no specific purpose. Unfortunately, he claims, some outsiders regarded these meetings as a gathering of people hatching plots.[47]

There is a difference of opinion about Nakajima's role in the Banchōkai. Arthur Tiedemann views him as a "member" and Ichihara Ryōhei (citing a prewar source) categorizes him as a "guest member."[48] Kawai Yoshinari, in both a prewar newspaper account and a postwar memoir, insists that Nakajima was simply a friend of Baron Gō's who attended the group's New Year party.[49] Probably Kawai's view is correct. Nakajima, however, was at the center of another group called the Kasuikai, whose membership overlapped with that of the Banchōkai (it is unclear how many people belonged to both groups).[50] It is also worth noting that Barons Nakajima and Gō were fellow members of the Yōkakai (a group of ten businessmen who met for dinner to exchange views with important political and bureaucratic figures). Frank discussions at this group's monthly meetings influenced national political-economic policies.[51]

Noda Yutaka published "The Banchōkai Went Underground" in *Kaizō* in March 1934 (it probably came out in February). After paying proper respect to Baron Gō's accomplishments (e.g., as member of the House of Peers and head of the Japan Economic Federation), Noda categorizes the baron as a bag carrier for Mitsui and Mitsubishi. Thus, in fact, writes Noda, the baron is a high-priced salaryman. As for Nakajima, he was pushed out of the second-class Furukawa combine and is not recognized by the big players in the financial field. Gotō and Kawai, too, were, until they recently lost their jobs, employees of another second-rate *zaibatsu* (Kawasaki). After completing the list of Banchōkai members, Noda concludes that outside of Baron Gō collectively the members held no more than mid-level status in the financial world. In fact, if they showed up at the Industrial Club, he concludes, they would be given seats at the foot of the dinner table.[52] Noda's assessment of the Banchōkai's status in the financial world is reinforced by comments made by member Nagano Mamoru years later. Nagano wrote that if Mitsui and Mitsubishi were considered *hatamoto* (direct retainers of the shogun), then the Banchōkai members should be regarded as high-ranking commoners. There was an advantage to being in this lower position, he added, because it caused them to feel less bound by tradition and engendered a spirit of innovation.[53]

Contemporary critics of the Banchōkai viewed its members (except for Baron Gō) as second-rate businessmen whose profit-seeking methods were not only illegal but harmful to the financial community. Moreover, these critics viewed the political maneuvering of Banchōkai members as part of a corrupt deal between the financial and political worlds.[54] Outstanding among those who held this view was newspaper publisher Mutō Sanji.

Teijin Stock

Of the approximately 225,000 Teijin Company stock shares that the Bank of Taiwan confiscated from the defunct Suzuki shōten, 205,000 were deposited with the Bank of Japan.[55] The Bank of Taiwan was obligated to sell Teijin stock in order to repay a Bank of Japan loan, but a simple, quick exchange of money for stocks was difficult, because a sale agreement involved the Bank of Taiwan, the Bank of Japan, and the Finance Ministry.[56] Moreover, forming a purchasing syndicate with enough cash (each share would cost somewhere between ¥120 and ¥150) would require superior negotiating skills. Furthermore, the rapid growth of Teijin Company increased the stocks' value, which drew the attention of rival investors.

It appears that the first attempt to purchase the stocks was made by Kaneko Naokichi, who managed the collapsed Suzuki Trading Company. One scholar attributes the firm's phenomenal profits during World War I, which raised it to the level of Sumitomo, Mitsui, and Mitsubishi trading companies, to Kaneko's "rare ability" as a speculator.[57] Indeed, among the many new firms enriched by the wartime boom, the most famous "was the new zaibatsu complex of Kaneko Naokichi, whose firms included Suzuki Trading, Kobe steel, Harima shipbuilding, Imperial Rayon (Teijin), Japan Flour Milling, Great Japan Celluloid, and Hōnen Refining."[58] Sometime during the early months of 1932, Kaneko conferred with Yano Ichirō and Ishizaka Taizō of the Daiichi Life Insurance Company, trying to pull together enough money to buy a substantial number of stock certificates.

Kaneko's rare speculative ability failed, however, because too much money was required.[59]

At about the same time, Fujita Kenichi, a former House of Peers member and former head of the Tokyo Chamber of Commerce and Industry who had a long connection with the defunct Suzuki shōten, tried to broker a Teijin stock deal. First, he approached the influential Mori Kaku, who was Premier Inukai's chief cabinet secretary. Mori introduced Fujita to Privy Councilor Itō Miyoji, who agreed to help and who directed Fujita to approach Finance Minister Takahashi Korekiyo; although it is unclear whether Fujita had a face-to-face meeting with the minister, it is clear that no further progress was made on this front. Subsequently, Fujita tried to enlist Baron Gō's aid. This approach, too, was unsuccessful, because Fujita was told by the baron that he would have to furnish at least a third of the purchase price. Besides Fujita's inability to attract investors, there are other possible reasons his effort failed: Count Itō was infamous as a blackmailer of government officials and businessmen; Fujita had gained notoriety as a defendant in an embezzlement and misfeasance case (he was also a defendant in a case involving the illegal purchase of an imperial decoration).[60] One scholar suggests that greed played a role: Fujita demanded too large a commission.[61]

Other businessmen cast an eye on Teijin Company shares. Attracted by the rising profits of Teijin Company (between 1927 and 1932 it declared dividends from 8 to 12 percent per year), brokerage houses Nomura shōten, Yamaichi shōten, and Osakaya asked the Bank of Taiwan to buy shares. The bank, which anticipated a rise in the shares' value, was not eager to sell. In December 1932, however, Tamura Komajirō, who was in the cotton material business in Osaka, was permitted to purchase 10,000 shares at ¥150 per share. Perhaps Tamura's good fortune came from picking the right go-between to deal with the Bank of Taiwan: Mori Kōjō, a director of the Yasuda Bank and a former director of the Bank of Taiwan. This was possible because Tamura was the son-in-law of the Yasuda Bank's founder.[62]

In the meantime, Nagano Mamoru and Kawai Yoshinari, members of the Banchōkai, tried their hand at getting the stocks. Actually, Nagano helped Fujita until he decided that Fujita's scheme was unworkable. Then, Nagano approached *Yomiuri Newspaper* president Shōriki Matsutarō (a former high police official and a member of the Banchōkai), who in turn talked with Education Minister Hatoyama Ichirō (who was part of the Suzuki Kisaburō–Mori Kaku faction in the Seiyūkai). Hatoyama was to urge officials in the Finance Ministry (e.g., Vice-Minister Kuroda Hideo) and the Bank of Japan (e.g., Hijikata Kyūchō) to pressure Bank of Taiwan officials to approve the sale. After Fujita left the scene, Nagano, Kawai, and Shōriki, aided by Kobayashi Ataru, and Nagasaki Eizō, began a skillful campaign to bring buyers and sellers together. This team of go-betweens faced a formidable task: gaining permission for the sale from bank and Finance Ministry bureaucrats; handling politicians whose help might be needed; finding enough money to cover such a big sale; and, finally, getting the stocks at a reasonable price. Such a large sum of money, the go-betweens decided, could be gotten by combining the purchasing power of life insurance companies and cotton merchants. Perhaps they ruled out approaching the *zaibatsu* because they reasoned that these conservative combines would be leery of politics involved in this deal. At any rate, they approached a number of life insurance directors and the heads of various cotton spinning firms. Also, Shōriki saw Minister of Commerce and Industry Nakajima Kumakichi, perhaps hoping that he would advise the insurance companies to purchase the shares. The go-betweens saw Mitsuchi Chūzō, a former financial minister as well, perhaps hoping that he would persuade key officials to approve their stock purchase plan.[63]

In February 1933, Kawai and Kobayashi discussed a sale of Teijin stock with Takagi Naomichi, a Bank of Taiwan director. Although Shimada Shigeru, the bank president, was kept informed, Takagi carried on the negotiations. On May 6, Kawai's group offered ¥117 per share for the first 100,000 shares or ¥122 per share if the sale took place immediately. The buyers expressed interest in a second unit of 100,000 shares but wanted the option of waiting a month to make a purchase decision. Kawai explained who the buyers were and that Minister Nakajima Kumakichi would decide on the stock division among the insurance companies. Takagi replied that, in light of Teijin Company's profitability, the offered price was too low. These discussions continued until May 25, when it was agreed that the buyers would purchase 100,000 shares for ¥125 each. Contracts were issued on May 30: Osaka cotton dealers ended up with 40 percent of the stock, and life insurance companies got 60 percent. Altogether ten companies were involved: six in Osaka and four in Tokyo. Several interesting conditions were attached to these contracts: Teijin Company was to increase its capital by ¥15,000,000, and shares were to be split (for holders of every three old shares two new shares were to be added); share dividends were to be increased; shares were to be listed for regular transaction on the Osaka and Tokyo stock exchanges; two people from the buyers' group were to be appointed Teijin Company directors. This stock sale caused little comment, but as news of these conditions leaked out, the market value of the shares shot up to about ¥150 per share by late June.[64]

After the stock transfer various commissions were paid and gifts exchanged. Reflecting his important role, Kawai's commission was one yen per share from both the buyers and the seller (for a total of ¥200,000). Kawai presented this entire amount to the others: ¥170,000 to Shōriki (¥105,000 of this was passed on to Fujita and Hatoyama), ¥15,000 to Murachi Kyūjirō (an Osaka stockbroker), and ¥15,000 to Nagano. The Bank of Taiwan also paid Murachi ¥40,000 and Nagano ¥60,000. Nagano and four others gave Nakajima a "political contribution" of ¥10,000: one of the conditions attached to the sale was taken care of at the June 26, 1933, Teijin Company shareholder meetings: Nagano became a company director and Kawai was elected executive controller and director. It appears that former finance minister Mitsuchi played a role in their appointments. Director Takagi was promoted to the presidency of the company.[65] Although Kawai received a large commission, the key go-between in this transaction was Nagano, who understood not only the importance of winning over specific politicians and bureaucrats, but also the crucial need to first pull together enough buyers to purchase the freed stocks (Fujita's failure was, no doubt, instructive). And behind Nagano, as he assembled this complicated deal, were the prestige and connections of Baron Gō.[66] As one scholar puts it: "Nagano was the brain behind all of this."[67]

Few businessmen or politicians would have found anything strange about this large stock transaction. As Harry E. Wildes explains in a 1934 book: "The institution of the middleman, while not unknown to the Western enterprise, is developed to a surprising degree. Because the maintenance of personal prestige is all important among a people trained for centuries to respect social status, and because bargaining is beneath the dignity of those accustomed to regard merchants as the lowest class, much preliminary arranging takes place through intermediaries. Brokerage becomes a business whose ramifications extend widely."[68] A postwar Japanese scholar, reflecting on this transaction, sees the roles of Nagano, Kawai, and Shōriki strictly as go-betweens (*nakagaisha*) who worked hard to put together this complex deal.[69] As for Kawai's commission of 2 percent, this was a moderate fee, especially in light of the amount of labor involved in this difficult enterprise. Chalmers Johnson, writing about Tanaka Kakuei's postwar political machine, states: "Informal discussions in Tokyo lead me to conclude that the usual commission charged . . . to get the bureaucracy to act . . . was three per cent of the value of the project."[70] Hans Baerwald, reminiscing about fundraising in Japan for a new building at the University of California, Los Angeles, discloses that "finders' fees" (money to those who located a benefactor and made the introduction) ran between 3.5 and 4.5 percent.[71] As for the exchange of gifts among people involved in this affair, one modern student of reciprocity notes that gift exchange has deep cultural roots: "Gift-giving is a minor institution . . . with complex rules defining who should give to whom, on what occasions he should give, what sort of gift is appropriate on any given occasion, and how the gift should be presented. The moral obligation to give, to receive, and to return gifts is as much a part of traditional Japan as it is of the archaic societies with which Marcel Mauss concerned himself in his famous essay on the gift."[72] Gift-giving customs in the general society naturally influenced businessmen, politicians, and bureaucrats, because the action of giving a gift acted as a cement that bonded society. Gift taking by politicians or bureaucrats could, depending on circumstances, be illegal. Nevertheless, for gifts not to be given in this huge stock transfer would never have entered the minds of participants, so ingrained were these practices of fulfilling a social norm. Furthermore, given the harsh nature of the business world in the early 1930s, these buyers probably thought in terms of tying each other and Minister Nakajima with bonds of social obligation that might be drawn upon in the future.

Mutō Sanji

Mutō Sanji supplied the spark that produced the political explosion termed the Teiji Incident. Mutō was the former president of the Kanegafuchi Spinning Company and a reformist politician. As a member of the House of Representatives from 1924, he condemned illegal deals between businessmen and politicians. Mutō's reputation as a staunch defender of capitalism and a crusader who exposed the rotten parts of the business world was widely known when he took over leadership of the *Jiji shinpō* (a famous newspaper begun in 1882 by Fukuzawa Yukichi) in May 1932. A two-month-long series of articles in *Jiji shinpō* on the Teijin stock sale and other business deals, which began in mid-January 1934, was Mutō's idea; he issued a printed statement vouching for the authenticity of the reports. Although exposé articles were common fare, Mutō's sterling reputation lent them credibility. These articles, which were mainly written by chief editor Morita Hisashi and general manager Wada Hidekichi, camouflaged by the pseudonym Ōmori Sanjin, appeared under sensational headlines such as "Banchōkai o abaku" (Exposing the Banchōkai). Since Mutō was a firm supporter of capitalism, these articles were likely intended to illustrate that there were only a few rotten apples in a barrel of mostly sound ones. Given the grim economic situation, however, many readers must have reached the opposite conclusion. Be that as it may, these sensational pieces were read eagerly by a public disgusted by a seemingly endless procession of corruption scandals.[73]

Mutō's comments were not the first. Not only had rumors circulated about the stock sale bonanza, but a printed comment appeared in the November 1933 issue of *Kaizō*, in which Kawai's large commission was spotlighted and in which Nagano was cited as his teammate. Their appointment as Teijin Company directors was also mentioned. Moreover, the article pointed out that they had made ¥400,000 in another stock deal and suggested that they were guilty of illegal conduct.[74] The angry Kaneko and Fujita, who failed to purchase Teijin Company stock, also promoted the idea that bribery was in the background of the successful stock transfer. Fingers were pointed at officials at the Bank of Taiwan, the Bank of Japan, and the Finance Ministry; also accused were Nakajima, Hatoyama, and Mitsuchi.[75]

The front page of the *Jiji shinpō* on January 17, 1934, featured "Japan's Tamanii: Exposing the Banchōkai" (Nihon no Tammani: Banchōkai o abaku).[76] Mutō wrote that the root of contemporary social evil, which produced the May 15, 1932, killing of Inukai and created the emergency era Saitō Cabinet, was generated by the collusion of political parties and businessmen. After the terrible events of 1932, the political-business conspirators had retracted their "fangs and claws" and waited quietly. Recently, however, the *Jiji* "had learned of the existence of a mystery behind the political and financial world; that is, the appearance of the Banchōkai. In short, the Banchōkai is an abode of demons (*fukumaden*), which is, in a style similar to past political parties and businessmen, like New York's Tammany, sucking blood and poisoning the fields of politics and finance." Continuing, Mutō made clear that the Banchōkai was working as an agent for evil forces, which illegally colluded to dominate the political-financial world. The Banchōkai has "a financial giant as its leader, and has a current state minister and a newspaper president." This group, he wrote, "using political power as an umbrella together with money power and pen power, is acting behind the scenes of the political-financial field in an intolerable manner." As part of their "extensive conspiracy," they took over the chamber of commerce. Moreover, they were recently involved in the selling of Kobe Steel Company shares and taking over the Teijin Company. "We must not ignore these immoral and illegal acts backed by power or permit them to overrun" the nation. To stop this sort of thing, Mutō wrote, the *Jiji*, relying on a well-informed person who knows about these deals, would expose "without reservation the recent plots carried out by this gang." Mutō closed this sensational piece by appealing to public opinion.[77]

On January 18, in his daily column titled "As I Think," Mutō explained why the Banchōkai was spotlighted. Mutō claimed that the Teijin stock deal alone did not trigger the newspaper's response but that it was the Kobe Steel Company stock deal that convinced the *Jiji* that for the public's sake the Banchōkai must be exposed. Moreover, the *Jiji* felt it was a public duty to investigate the Teijin stock sale, because these were not ordinary stock shares: they were shares owned by the Bank of Taiwan and held as collateral by the government (that is, they should be regarded as public property). "In short, these shares, when sold, even if for only one yen more per share, would lighten the damage to the national treasury. Therefore, the method of handling these shares should be open to the public. The Bank of Taiwan officials, however, did not follow this method. Moreover, why did the Bank of Japan permit them to do this? This is the point that must be explained." Mutō ended his column by pointing out that this share transaction was much more than a simple matter of people in the financial field making a profit.[78]

Daily articles on "Exposing the Banchōkai" ran from January 18 until March 13.[79] Among the topics covered were "Origin of the Hotbed of Corruption," "Seizing Control of the Chamber of Commerce," "The Drama of Combining Beer Companies," "Takeover of Teijin," and "Takeover of Kobe Steel." Featured players in this series were Baron Gō, Kawai, Nagano, Shōriki, and others in the Banchōkai. The *Jiji*'s merciless pen targeted Baron Nakajima and Hatoyama as well. Later articles from the series were republished in two pamphlets: *Exposing the Banchōkai: This Volume Deals with the Teijin Company* and *Exposing the Banchōkai: This Volume Deals with the Kobe Steel Company*.[80] According to one scholar, the Banchōkai series was well received by the public. Economists, journalists, retired government officials, and reform-minded military officers visited Mutō's office to encourage him in this crusade against corruption.[81] "I am merely fighting evil that is trying to destroy society" was Mutō's standard reply to well-wishers.[82] Mutō, no doubt, said this from the heart, because his favorite phrase was taken from Martin Luther: "I was born into this world to fight and destroy evil."[83]

In his business and political careers, Mutō's aim was to "do good—do well"; in business he felt that "morality and economic rationality coincided."[84] As a newspaper head, Mutō revived a declining newspaper, "making it pay its way and at the same time fight for political purity."[85]

Born a year before the Meiji Restoration, Mutō studied at Fukuzawa's Keiō gijuku and traveled to the United States. After a year at Mitsui Bank, he joined Kanegafuchi Spinning Company, a Mitsui subsidiary, becoming president of the company in 1921.[86] "At the time he joined it was not a very important concern and it was in a rather bad way," but, after he began to manage it, "the mill became the most important in Japan, and the best paying; what is more notable is that it also became Japan's model mill."[87] Mutō achieved high productivity at the main mill and its branches by subscribing to the idea of *onjōshugi* (doctrine of warmheartedness). By the mid-Taisho period this term referred to actions taken voluntarily by a company leader to improve employees' welfare; if employees demanded certain measures, then the change did not result from *onjōshugi*. This concept embraced a wide range of measures: housing, health, education, and so on. *Onjōshugi* was not pure beneficence; its supporters also saw it as a means of preventing labor disputes and increasing production. Under Mutō's direction, Kanegafuchi paid the highest wages, provided the best working conditions, and gave the most extensive benefits in the nation. Not surprisingly, production increased as did profits. Indeed, Mutō's management approach was so successful that it became a model of good practice, and Mutō was awarded a decoration in 1918 by a grateful government.[88] By retirement time in 1930, Mutō had become the "Cotton King"; the company rewarded his devotion with an unprecedented bonus of ¥3,000,000.[89]

As serious labor disputes arose after World War I, Mutō easily entered the public debate. As one scholar notes: "Public activity was second nature to him. As a young man just back from American [*sic*] he had founded Japan's first advertising agency; he had been active in a Meiji political movement; he wrote prolifically. . . . In other words, he was a man who appreciated the force of public opinion, and moreover, he was adept at influencing it."[90] Following his publication in September 1919 of an article in *Diamond* on how to solve the nation's labor problems, Mutō was challenged by Professor Kawakami Hajime of Kyoto Imperial University, the author of *Binbō monogatari* (Tale of poverty). Kawakami ridiculed Mutō's argument that *onjōshugi* was a national treasure deeply respected by domestic capitalists, in contrast to Western capitalists' practices. An angry Mutō wrote a letter, demanding an apology, which Kawakami refused. Professor Yoshino Sakuzō of Tokyo Imperial University also rejected Mutō's solutions to labor problems.[91] This national debate left Mutō "distressed by the 'arrogant' and 'unseemly' attitude of Japanese professors who 'read a few books and jumped into the labor problem.' " Mutō concluded that such "uninformed, self-indulgent argument of scholars only hampered progress."[92]

Commenting on Mutō's "very decided opinions," a newspaper editorial noted that at the International Labor Conference (Washington, D.C.,

1922) "there were some passages at arms between him and Mrs. Takao Tanaka which was rather regrettable. Mrs. Tanaka, who was a niece of Viscount Shibusawa, was chosen because of her sympathy with working women, among whom it might have been difficult or even impossible to find a suitable delegate. Her sympathy and a few visits to the mills were the lady's chief qualification, and Mr. Mutō dealt with her statements very brusquely. . . . This was an example, however, of Mr. Mutō's very defined views."[93]

Not confining himself to labor problems, Mutō commented on political questions. "High on his list was elimination of what he termed rampant collusion between rich businessmen and government officials."[94] Thus, Mutō's journalistic crusade launched in January 1934 was not at all out of character, and the target, corrupt deals between businessmen and government officials, was not new.

By 1923 Mutō had gained national attention through innovative management practices and by speaking out on numerous public issues, including the urgent need to return to the gold standard. After forming the Jitsugyō dōshikai in 1923, he won a seat in the House of Representatives in 1924. The party was reorganized in April 1929 under the name Kokumin dōshikai. With this elevated platform, Mutō became even more outspoken on financial and political issues.[95] A typical Mutō comment was made in early 1927, as the Wakatsuki Cabinet tried to push bills through the lower house to save unstable banks: "Seen from a businessman's point of view, the bills in question are simple and clear. In a word they penalize the honest and help the dishonest. . . . There is a tribe of 'political businessmen' who, when they make money put it in their own pockets, but when they lose, collude with politicians and accept relief in the form of state funds drawn from the lifeblood of the people."[96] One close student of business history explains that Mutō "wanted to cleanse the political world of professional politicians who, ignorant of Mutō's insights into basic economic principles, strived only to protect their political interests. . . . The minuscule size of the party did not dampen Mutō's enthusiasm. . . . Mutō consistently censured the timidity of the Finance Ministry from the floor of the Diet."[97] This harsh barrage of denunciation, while making good newspaper copy, must have made many enemies.

Mutō's public personage, as reflected in a roundtable conference on financial and administrative reforms held at the headquarters of the *Tokyo Asahi Newspaper* on June 2, 1931, was combative and intolerant of other views. One of the issues was whether or not the government should call a special session of the Diet to consider the anticipated financial shortfall.

Among the distinguished panelists were Professor Minobe Tatsukichi, Finance Minister Inoue Junnosuke, and Railway Minister Egi Tasuku. Mutō urged them to agree that calling a special session of the Diet to debate the contents of the revised budged would be a proper course of action. Inoue, however, wanted to drop the matter, and Minobe and Egi pointed out that redoing the budget was legally impossible. Mutō, dissatisfied with these replies, repeated his argument for a Diet budget debate. Egi, cutting him short, said that the matter was settled.[98] "Mr. Ogata, the editor of the *Tokyo Asahi*, who was in the chair, asked Mr. Mutō to discontinue further discussion on this subject. Mr. Mutō complied, though very reluctantly."[99]

Mutō's managerial style at the spinning mill, which worked well until the Great Depression struck, was reflected in his wider public life. In Mutō's managerial system, he was the beloved and trusted father figure of the company; in the wider world of business and politics, his benevolent paternalism did not fare so well. Such great success in the spinning mill business, over so many years, produced an intolerant Mutō who was morally certain that he knew best. No doubt some who ran into the Mutō buzzsaw regarded him as a zealot. One newspaper account, after Mutō's death, noted that he "was a man who could not live without a rival or an enemy. As a cotton spinner, he was constantly at daggers drawn with Mr. Wada of the Fuji Cotton Spinning Company. As a politician, the late Mr. Inoue Junnosuke was his eyesore, whom he treated as if he had been his personal enemy and whose gold policy he played a conspicuous part in overturning. As a journalist, it seems that he marked out Baron Nakajima . . . for his enemy, and *Yomiuri*, for the rival of his paper."[100] Nakajima and Shōriki, head of the *Yomiuri*, were targets of the Mutō-inspired series of articles attacking the Banchōkai. Kawai Yoshinari, who received Mutō's attention in the *Jiji shinpō* series, said, nearly four decades later, that Mutō was a distinguished person well known for his success in the spinning mill field and one of the top people in the financial realm as well. Although he was a really "righteous person," wrote Kawai, "it appears that one side of him was very narrowminded, and he did cause conflict and commotion in various areas."[101]

On March 9, 1934, Mutō was shot; he died the following day. The murderer was Fukushima Shinkichi, aged forty-one, who had been unemployed since the summer of 1932.[102] The reason for this murder, according to police, was a personal grudge held by Fukushima. In October 1931, Fukushima began a movement to transfer the management of Tokyo crematories from private hands to municipal authorities, because he viewed the business as a monopoly from which one company squeezed too much money. Armed with a letter of introduction from Nakano Seigō, a leader of the Kokumin dōmei, Fukushima visited Mutō to explain that the poor would be better served by a change in management. The text of their conversation is unknown, but Mutō did contribute thirty yen to Fukushima's crusade. Later, after the *Jiji shinpō* published an article on this subject, Fukushima felt that Mutō had stolen his reform idea.[103] "He visited Mr. Muto several times to censure him, and to demand ¥3,000, but he was refused interviews. This made him all the more angry, and eventually led to the attack."[104]

Commenting on Mutō's murder, the *Japan Weekly Chronicle* editorialized: "It seems to have been a case of private revenge . . . though on the other hand, it is stated that the police are investigating the possibility of there being some connection between the crime and a party of business men involved in a scandal which Mr. Mutō was castigating very severely in his newspaper. That is a matter which must await the results of the investigation, and it would be entirely improper to speculate upon it."[105] The *Jiji shinpō*, in contrast, was eager to comment, saying that Fukushima must have been motivated by more than a mere personal grudge; others must be behind this shocking murder. Authorities had a duty, opined the paper, to expose those in the background. Ōmori Sanjin wrote that, although he hoped that the Banchōkai had nothing to do with the murder, "there is a very disagreeable fact, which may mean much, that the assassin recently had an interview with Mr. Shimidzu [i.e., Shimizu], a barrister, who is legal adviser to the Banchōkai and who was present at every conference of the Banchōkai to discuss the measures to meet the *Jiji*'s attacks on the association. The interview took place on March 6th three days previous to the assassination, the assassin being introduced by Mr. Yohinari [*sic*] Kawai, a member of the Banchōkai."[106] A *Jiji* reporter learned about this meeting, wrote Ōmori, while visiting Naritomi, a lawyer who was involved in the crematorium problem. By mere accident the reporter talked on Naritomi's office telephone with Shimizu (Iku?), who mistook him for Naritomi. Shimizu told the reporter that Mutō was wounded and asked that he keep quiet about Shimizu's talk with Fukushima. When Naritomi returned, the reporter confronted the lawyer and got details about the meeting. The reporter next visited Kawai, who requested that his name not be mentioned. "After his return to the newspaper office, the reporter was rung up by Mr. Kawai, who repeated his request not to mention his name. The over-anxiety evinced by Messrs. Shimidzu and Kawai in attempting to keep their names from publication deepens suspicion of their connection," concluded Ōmori. Finally, Ōmori pointed out that the dispute between Mutō and Fukushima over the crematorium problem had been settled before the attack.[107]

If the reporter's tale is correct, it was an amazing bit of good fortune to be waiting in Naritomi's office just as Shimizu called about the attack on Mutō. For the *Jiji*, which was considered a respectable paper several pegs above the scandal sheets, to print this information in the midst of a police investigation is understandable in view of Mutō's shocking death. Kawai, the chief target at the time, recalls that the *Jiji* ran his photo and came very close to saying that he had participated in the murder.[108] The *Chronicle* editorial neatly straddled the ethical fence by refusing to speculate on people behind Fukushima while presenting Ōmori Sanjin's views.

Before taking over the *Jiji shinpo*, Mutō was determined not to sacrifice quality for circulation. Exposure to publishing realities, however, convinced him that the *Jiji* "should be converted into a popular, bright, sensational or even sentimental paper—a selling paper." Thus, until the financial basis of the journal had been solidified, Mutō saw not the *Asahi* but the *Yomiuri* as the *Jiji*'s rival.[109] The paper's managing editor, Itō Masanori, disagreed with him and left the paper."[110]

Mutō's brainstorm to expose the Banchōkai fit in neatly with his principle of "do good—do well." The paper's financial decline would be halted and another blow would be struck against corruption in business and politics. Chalmers Johnson writes: "It is unclear to this day whether Mutō sincerely believed what he wrote or whether his charges were part of a militarist plot to discredit the political parties and their capitalist supporters."[111] The idea of Mutō being part of a plot, militarist of otherwise, is farfetched. Mutō meant what he wrote! He marched to his own drumbeat.

CHAPTER 3
Saitō Cabinet

A PROPER UNDERSTANDING OF THE TEIJIN Company stock sale scandal, which destroyed the Saitō Cabinet, demands a close look at the cabinet's origins. Only by embedding the Teijin scandal in a "thick" history of politics can an observer gain proper insights into this complicated affair. The politics of the Saitō Cabinet era, like the politics of earlier years, was a battle to control the cabinet. Immediately after the formation of the Saitō Cabinet, the ceaseless power struggle resumed, with political foes maneuvering to topple the cabinet. Among the political weapons employed was the venerable one of corruption accusations. Cabinet Ministers Nagai Ryūtarō, Nakajima Kumakichi, and Hatoyama Ichirō were, one after another, targeted by political foes, who charged them with various corrupt acts. This political smear campaign resulted in Nakajima's and Hatoyama's resignations. Moreover, at the Sixty-Fifth Diet session, politicians demanded an investigation of the Bank of Taiwan's Teijin Company stock transaction. Furthermore, procurators, urged on by Diet speeches, newspaper reports, and citizens' formal complaints, began a criminal investigation. Within a few months Ministers Mitsuchi Chūzō and Nakajima were indicted, and the reputation of Justice Minister Koyama Matsukichi was tarnished.

Japan faced foreign and domestic crises during the early 1930s. Amidst the deepening world economic depression, establishment leaders confronted an upsurge of Chinese nationalism and a rising Russian military threat, which challenged Japan's continental interests. Naval armament disputes and trade friction with the Anglo-American powers further complicated the political situation. The economy, gripped by a deep, long agricultural depression, was shocked anew by the Hamaguchi Cabinet's ill-timed lifting of the gold embargo. Moreover, Hamaguchi's decision to reduce naval armament aroused opposition among frustrated military men and their civilian supporters, who launched movements to increase armaments, suppress political parties, and restore the emperor's personal rule. Another element was added to this volatile mix in late 1931, when disobedient army units seized Manchuria. The term "emergency period" began to appear in print, a reflection of a mounting sense of national danger. Although commentators on the many crises did not speak in one voice, many regarded the nation's problems as unprecedented.[1] Terrorists, in early 1932, reinforced this crisis atmosphere by assassinating former finance minister Inoue Junnosuke and the famous industrialist Dan Takuma, whom they viewed as symbols of the corrupt political-business elite. Then, on May 15, Prime Minister Inukai was murdered, in a failed coup attempt, by a group of naval cadets, army officers, and civilians.[2]

Recommending a new prime minister for imperial approval fell, as usual, to the venerable statesman Saionji Kinmochi. From Saionji's perspective the leaders of the two major political parties were unsuitable: Wakatsuki Reijirō's Minseitō held a minority of lower house seats and was unpopular; the Seiyūkai held a majority but was weakened by severe factional strife, which limited its effectiveness in solving national problems. Moreover, Seiyūkai leader Suzuki Kisaburō's extreme conservative views were repugnant to Saionji. Saionji, who viewed Suzuki and former justice minister Hiranuma Kiichirō as two sides of the same coin, rejected the nomination of Hiranuma as well.[3] Instead, Saionji recommended Admiral Saitō Makoto, widely known as a political moderate adept at working with politicians. The new coalition cabinet was hailed as a "national unity government" designed to solve serious domestic and foreign problems. The major parties, especially the Seiyūkai, were unhappy with the renewed appearance of a transcendental cabinet, but the Seiyūkai supplied five cabinet members. Party leaders reasoned that a cooperative policy with Saitō during the emergency era would hasten their return to power.[4]

In nominating Saitō, Saionji was responding to an imperial court concerned about the rising threat of rightist radicals who hoped to effect a "transfer of power to the military under the cloak of imperial rule." Indeed, the emperor "admonished Saionji to recommend a successor to Inukai who would oppose 'fascism,' uphold the constitution, and work for peace."[5] Saionji viewed Saitō's "national unity" government as an interim solution to solve the leadership problem; his cabinet would act as a firewall between the radical right and the civilian politicians, as the parties consolidated their forces. Saionji's choice was acceptable to the major parties, since they pictured Saitō as an interim prime minister.[6]

Gordon Berger, an authority on 1930s politics, argues persuasively that it is a mistake to view the suspension of party government as solely a struggle between the forces of militarism versus liberalism. Certainly, concerns about the danger to political stability posed by rightist terrorists and radical army officers entered Saionji's decision, but the crippled Minseitō, Seiyūkai factionalism, and Suzuki's political record weighed heavily as well. Saionji's task was to find a premier with whom the court, the Diet, the Privy Council, the bureaucracy, and the military could work in harmony; there was little elite support for Suzuki. Furthermore, most people regarded the Saitō Cabinet as a temporary bridge over a difficult spot in the political road, with a return to party-centered government in the future.[7]

Since power struggles were an inextricable part of political and bureaucratic life, the contest to control the cabinet did not cease with Saitō's appointment; political and bureaucratic cliques, each of whom had a favorite candidate for the prime ministership, maneuvered to increase their bargaining position the next time the position was open. Moreover, it was an accepted practice to speed up the process by pushing the incumbent out of office. Money scandals, particularly bribery cases, were a traditional weapon in the ceaseless battle for political power. An editorial spotlighted this political practice: "Ordinarily the members of the Diet earn very easy money. . . . Most of the time is occupied in fruitless impeachments. . . . Some remissness in ceremonial, or some official irregularity, is eagerly seized upon for the purpose of stirring up a storm. So little concern is felt for propriety that if the Opposition can find some excuse for declaring that the Government has not acted with the proper respect due to the Throne, it foams at the mouth in an entirely artificial frenzy."[8] Saitō's tenure was no exception to this general pattern.

Colonization Minister Nagai Ryūtarō was the first target. After taking office, Nagai replaced officials in Karafuto, Taiwan, and Manchuria. His choice of Kajiwara Nakaji for president of the South Manchurian Railway generated a strong protest; rumors circulated about a corrupt deal between Nagai and Kajiwara. They arose, it appears, from the fact that Nagai's parliamentary vice-minister took a large loan from Kajiwara's bank. Critics saw the railway presidency as a quid pro quo. Although a combination of Seiyūkai politicians and army personnel stopped Kajiwara's nomination, Nagai survived. Another attack came in early 1933, when Nagai was criticized by House of Peers Viscount Mimurodo Yukimitsu for attending the funeral of socialist Sakai Toshihiko, whose views were anathema to many conservatives. Nagai pointed out that Sakai was a former colleague at Waseda University, so it was reasonable to attend the ceremony.[9] These episodes were harbingers of coming attacks on other state ministers. Ironically, despite their eagerness to oust the Saitō Cabinet, Seiyūkai politicians appear to have spent as much energy vilifying each other as they did in attacking the cabinet.

Several Banchōkai members, fresh from their Teijin stock coup, became more deeply involved in the political power struggle. Faced with army officers eager to seize state control, some party politicians responded by promoting the idea of a party coalition government. In the case of the Seiyūkai's Hatoyama–Machida Chūji group, the movement for a coalition of major parties was supported by the Mitsui combine and the Banchōkai. This effort collapsed in early 1934, according to Gordon Berger, because of factional fighting among politicians coupled with an outside attack by civilian and army rightists.[10] Arthur Tiedemann writes of this effort to revive party cabinets:

> The idea grew that now was the time to force a return to party Cabinets by unifying the Seiyūkai and the Minseitō and launching an all-out attack on the military. A key role in this movement was played by the members of the *Banchōkai.* . . . Nakajima Kumakichi . . . took the lead in pushing the union of the parties. . . . On December 25, 1933 he actually reached the point of holding a meeting of leaders from both parties. Unfortunately, at this juncture the movement to unify the parties became involved with the famous Teijin case. . . . It completely discredited the parties and stopped in its tracks the movement to restore party Cabinets.[11]

Ichihara Ryōhei views leaders of Mitsui and other *zaibatsu* as the puppet masters in this political drama. These big businessmen, he writes, decided in 1933 to give more aid to political parties; state minister Nakajima cooperated in their effort, by acting as a go-between for the two major parties. At the December 25 meeting, Nakajima discussed military violence and army involvement in civilian politics. This dangerous situation, he said, must be met by cleaning up corruption in the parties and by reinforcing them in various ways. Exactly what role Baron Gō played is unclear, but it was common knowledge that Gō acted as an agent for Mitsui; indeed, he was sometimes called Mitsui's head clerk (*ōbanto*). As for Shōriki Matsutarō (president of the *Yomiuri Newspaper*), Ichihara states that he not only set up the December 25 conference, but was also a main promoter of Baron Nakajima's call for party unity. To document this conclusion, Ichihara cites Nakajima's postwar memoirs and the diary kept by Harada Kumao, the ubiquitous political agent for the elder statesman Saionji Kinmochi. Why would the huge Mitsui combine bring a small group, of what one political commentator referred to as second- and third-rate capitalists (excluding Baron Gō), into this plan to strengthen the major parties? Ichihara's answer is that the old *zaibatsu*, especially Mitsui, were worried over a negative reaction among the general public and the military if they directly gave funds to the parties. Hence, Ichihara views the Banchōkai's role as that of a funnel for political money. Among the possible reasons why Banchōkai members would allow themselves to be used in this manner (making them targets of antiparty forces), Ichihara points out that some members were promoting the idea of Nakajima as a future premier.[12] Ichihara's view that some Banchōkai members were willing to play Mitsui's game in order to further Nakajima's political prospects is supported by Kawai Yoshinari's postwar comment: "If this incident [the Teijin scandal and trial] had not occurred, a cabinet could have been born from this group [the Banchōkai]."[13]

Justice Officials

People expected a full measure of "justice" in the courts. They expected judges to be independent of business interests, immune from political pressure, and free of corruption. Following the promulgation of the Meiji Constitution in 1889, justice officials diligently spread the message that judges were independent and that procurators acted according to the law. Therefore, public exposure of examples that contradicted this myth of perfect justice under the benevolent imperial gaze called for an immediate response by the Justice Ministry. During the stressful early 1930s, for example, justice officials were forced to defend their ministry against charges that officials were unwilling to accept a salary cut and that "red" judges were on the bench.

In October 1932 Finance Minister Takahashi, faced with a large revenue deficit and increased military spending, urged each ministry to cut expenses. A call for financial retrenchment was not new; indeed, prior cabinets, under both major political parties, faced budgetary crises as the nation sank deeper into the worldwide depression. About eighteen months before Takahashi spoke, a committee studying officials' compensation recommended a salary cut of up to 10 percent. This announcement was followed by a rumor that judges opposed pay cuts, because their pay scale was lower than that of administrative officials and because their salaries could not be lowered without first amending Article 73 of the Court Organization Law (1890). The rumor, in fact, reflected the views of many judges, who opposed several cabinets' plans for pay decreases. By late May 1931, as the government prepared to announce a salary reduction schedule (cuts of 10 to 20 percent, depending on rank), the public speculated on whether or not judges would submit.[14]

Nationwide judges discussed the salary plan. For instance, 133 ward and Tokyo District Court judges, on May 30, agreed that salary reduction by imperial ordinance was illegal and stated that they would not accept the government's plan. More senior judges, however, urged junior colleagues to accept voluntary pay cuts. The Wakatsuki Cabinet, faced with many recalcitrant judges, modified its original plan by inserting an exceptional clause in favor of judges. The imperial ordinance, which was issued on May 27, was in effect from June 1, 1931.[15] Most judges, too, compromised: they would receive full pay but contribute the amount the cabinet had planned to deduct to the national treasury.[16] Thus, a constitutional crisis was avoided.

Perhaps more damaging to Justice Ministry prestige was the sensational revelation that "red" judges were dispensing justice. Ultranationalists, who for years had pursued "red professors," now condemned the Justice Ministry.[17] Other critics regarded this ominous discovery as a logical result of liberal higher education and urged the government to reindoctrinate every exposed official.[18] Joining the hysterical chorus, the *Asahi* opined that this was "a serious blot on the glorious history of Japanese courts of justice."[19]

"Reds" in the judiciary came to light as police, who were investigating a bank robbery in October 1932, discovered that Judge Ozaki Noboru, Tokyo District Court, and a judicial trainee, Sakamoto Chūsuke, were members of the communist movement. Judge Ozaki, a Waseda University graduate, also lectured there on criminal law.[20] As authorities investigated their case, three other judges and several court clerks who were friends of Ozaki were charged with giving money to the Communist Party. These defendants, except for one clerk, renounced communism before their trials; they received prison terms of from three to eight years (Ozaki), and the unrepentant clerk was given ten. On appeal the sentences were reduced by about two years for each defendant.[21]

Rightist radicals, who had long criticized the Justice Ministry's soft policy toward communist suspects, now accused the ministry of harboring procommunist officials; they demanded a thorough housecleaning of the ministry. To emphasize their views, they pressured the government with rallies, printed statements, visits to government offices, and demands for impeachment of officials. One group suggested that Koyama and Saitō take responsibility by killing themselves.[22]

At the annual Justice Ministry conference for high officials held in late April 1933, Justice Minister Koyama urged better supervision of subordinates and a firmer control of the communist movement. Thought currents were changing rapidly, he noted, and the judiciary was not exempt from this general trend. The exposure of young judges tainted by communism, he concluded, was certain to damage judiciary prestige and to erode public confidence.[23]

High justice officials had special reasons for being concerned about "prestige" and "public confidence." Their ministry, until recent years, was overshadowed by the key Finance Ministry and the powerful Home Ministry. Bright Tokyo Imperial University graduates were more likely to have entered one of those two prestigious bureaucracies. Public perception of the Justice Ministry's position in the state structure, however, was changing for the better, as viewed by justice officials. An outstanding figure behind this change was Hiranuma Kiichirō who, as head of the Criminal Affairs Bureau and later as procurator general (1912–1921), used the prosecution of political and bureaucratic scandals to increase Justice Ministry political power. Thus, by 1915 the Hiranuma clique was a significant factor in politics.[24] A second opportunity to expand Justice Ministry power occurred in the mid-1920s, as the state suppressed the new communist party. Justice officials played a key role in devising and interpreting the new laws and administrative techniques required for this crusade; procurators and judges became household names in the many arrests and trials of this era. Furthermore, an unusually large number of bribery and other scandals came to public notice during the late 1920s and early 1930s, further increasing the visibility of justice officials. Given the above developments, it is certain that Koyama, who was already an associate procurator at the Tokyo District Court before the High Treason Incident of 1910 and who could recall earlier public perceptions, was concerned deeply over any loss of hard-won prestige.

Since there are no early 1930s opinion polls on the public's view of judges and procurators, one can merely hypothesize. First of all, justice officials probably looked good in comparison with politicians, businessmen, and bureaucrats in the midst of the terrible depression and the aftermath of so many political scandals. By 1932 the failure of Minseitō economic policies was clear, as were the selfish actions of financiers and big business leaders in the debacle that followed the return to the gold embargo. Speculators made huge fortunes as common folk scrambled to survive. Indeed, many critics accused Mitsui together with the Seiyūkai of selling out the nation to make a profit. Moreover, incessant corruption charges and prosecution of businessmen, bureaucrats, and Diet members filled newspaper pages.[25] Prominently positioned above this cesspool of corruption were judges and procurators, who must have appeared as knights on white chargers—especially the judges, who could draw upon the ideal of impartial justice that rose from the Tokugawa era in the person of Ōoka Echizen-no-kami, whose official life stimulated many trial legends that circulated widely in early Showa. It is doubtful that the luster provided by this myth of perfect justice was much tarnished by the salary dispute; the "red" judges affair was perhaps more serious, but punishment was swift and sure once the case was discovered (the amended sentences also showed mercy). In sum, Koyama's concern is understandable, but no major damage was done to the Justice Ministry.

The Meiji Sugar Refining Company Case

In March 1932 rumors circulated about tax dodging by the Meiji Sugar Refining (Meiji seitō datsuzei) Company (or Meitō). The *Kobe shinbun* published details about taxes owed by Meitō and payoffs in 1930 to cabinet officers and Minseitō politicians, and a report on attempted blackmail of Meitō officials. During the blackmail investigation, according to the newspaper, procurators discovered the tax evasion. Several weeks later the *Yamato shinbun* reported that the tax dodging had originated in 1929 and bribes to buy silence followed in 1930.[26]

The first rumors about tax cheating, it appears, came from the Seiyūkai. Someone had obtained a bookkeeping record of a Meitō plant in Kawasaki (this record was in fact two sets of "books," one of which showed the actual amount of sugar refined and the other, a lower figure for tax purposes) and used it for blackmail. After the company refused to pay, someone passed the "books" to the Seiyūkai. Stimulated by rumors, Tax Bureau officials and Tokyo procurators began separate investigations. Tax officials, after discussions with subordinates from Yokohama and Kawasaki, concluded that tax officials who earlier visited the Kawasaki plant were unaware of the illegal activity. As for the procurators, they quickly had police bring in the president of Meitō, Sōma Hanji. This sensational arrest alerted journalists, which prevented a quiet resolution of the case. In the meantime, the Tax Bureau continued to investigate; on April 28 Ishiwata Sōtarō, chief of the National Tax Section of the Tax Bureau, visited officials at the Justice Ministry. Ishiwata explained to justice officials that tax inspectors used an old standard table that listed the amount of refined sugar that could be produced from a specific amount of unrefined sugar. Over time, however, since better machinery had been perfected, it became possible to make more refined sugar from the same amount of unrefined.

The Tax Bureau was, in fact, said Ishiwata, working with sugar industry people to solve this problem by establishing a higher standard that would prevent so much refined sugar from escaping taxation. Therefore, concluded Ishiwata, the Finance Ministry had agreed that the company should not be charged a back tax for this customary procedure. President Sōma was released from jail on May 11.[27]

Ironically, Meitō sabotaged tax officials' efforts to settle this problem. On May 26 a lawyer representing Meitō visited the Tax Bureau to pay tax on the Kawasaki plant's secretly refined sugar. Tax people were shocked! Tokyo procurators, who heard about his visit, reopened the case. On June 22 Procurator Kuroda Etsurō arrived at the Tax Bureau to talk with its head, Nakajima Teppei. Nakajima should ask procurators to enter the case, argued Kuroda, because Meitō might destroy evidence. Moreover, Nakajima should send the required formal complaint to Kuroda's office. Kuroda emphasized that his office had uncovered a very large tax evasion and wanted to submit documents to the Tokyo District Criminal Court. Nakajima, refusing to be pushed into a hasty decision, replied that the Tax Bureau would handle the matter; first they would investigate, and then they would decide whether to file charges. On June 24 Nakajima received Kuroda's written request for an investigation. That evening newspapers carried sensational reports about tax officials who were not watching big companies; some suggested a rotten connection between officials and business. Astute readers must have assumed that procurators had leaked this information.[28] At some point, a frustrated Kuroda went over Nakajima's head and contacted Finance Vice-Minister Kuroda Hideo. It is unclear whether their exchange of views on the Meitō case was via a telephone conversation or in person.[29]

Finance Ministry officials, worried about bad publicity, dropped the old "standard table" system and switched to a tax on the actual weight of refined sugar; sugar companies were informed on July 16 that the new policy would be effective on April 15, 1933.[30]

After investigating the Meitō case, Nakajima and a deputy visited Kimura Naotatsu, head of the Criminal Affairs Bureau of the Justice Ministry. Meitō, they said, would be fined ¥600,000 for the hidden Kawasaki plant production, plus an additional tax of ¥120,000. Later, on August 15, tax and justice officials agreed that the matter was closed; justice officials promised to halt the procurators' investigation. Newspaper reports on this decision featured the conflict between procurators and tax officials over the size of the fine (procurators demanded a higher one). Some newspapers accused tax officials of overprotecting capitalists; ultranationalists might be offended, they suggested.[31]

"Meiji Tax Swindle; Sugar Company Fined ¥600,000 instead of ¥34,430,000; and No Criminal Charge," read one headline.[32] The procurators, said the article,

who have spent several months investigating the case, were confident that criminal charges would be laid by the Tax Bureau, and are astonished at the Bureau's refusal to do so. They are also annoyed at the Finance Department's neglect to notify them direct of the decision reached by the Tax Bureau with regard to the fine. Mr. Miyagi [Chōgorō], chief of the Tokyo Procurator's Office, has taken the matter up with the Procurator General of the Supreme Court, but it appears that the procuratorial authorities are helpless, since the information necessary for a criminal charge must be laid by the Tax Bureau first. All the procurator's office can do is threaten to publish the full results of their investigation, in the hope that this will spur the Finance Department to order further steps to be taken. . . . [It is reported] that the division of opinion between the Procurators' office and the Finance Office will assume a serious phase, and be made a question in the coming Diet Session.[33]

A newspaper editorial noted that there was little political ammunition available to use against the cabinet but that the Seiyūkai was considering the Meitō scandal as a weapon.[34]

Newspapers, which reported rumors of plots against Finance Ministry officials, noted that Tokyo police had been alerted.[35] Ishiwata Sōtarō's memoirs mention that after Nakajima Teppei, head of the Tax Bureau, received threatening letters, his home was protected by police. This stressful situation caused Nakajima to develop a nervous disorder; he fled to Shuzenji (a temple in a resort area southwest of Tokyo) to recover. Thus, Ishiwata inherited Nakajima's job of explaining the Meitō case in the Diet.[36]

The sugar tax issue surfaced at the Budget Committee meeting of the lower house on August 29. Tsukumo Kunitoshi (Seiyūkai), after first complaining about the absence of Tax Bureau head Nakajima, quizzed Finance Minister Takahashi Korekiyo and other officials. Why, asked Tsukumo, was the tax evasion charge first denied and then later admitted? Ishiwata apologized for the imperfect investigation. Were some tax officials, including Nakajima (then head of Yokohama Customs), entertained by the sugar company? asked Tsukumo. Another Finance Ministry official replied that the matter was under investigation. Tsukumo pointed out that there were efforts to hush up this tax evasion and to minimize its seriousness. Continuing this interpellation, he asked why the expert tax inspectors naively accepted false company books. Ishiwata expressed regret over this mistake. Then, Tsukumo rebuked them for an imperfect investigation, asking if there was a secret deal with Meitō. Finance Minister Takahashi promised to establish an investigative committee to clarify the situation.[37]

One scholar notes that Ishiwata, who in everyday conversations stuttered slightly, presented a perfect performance at the Diet. Although Tsukumo treated him roughly, demanding "yes" or "no" replies, Ishiwata did not budge an inch as he skillfully presented the ministry's position. Perhaps Ishiwata's earlier visit with former finance minister Mitsuchi Chūzō helped prepare him for this tense interpellation. Mitsuchi told him that, if his colleagues were blameless, he must do an outstanding job to protect the reputation of the ministry. Ishiwata responded by giving what was probably his best bureaucratic performance.[38]

A committee of finance and justice officials, which met to discuss this tax case, announced a decision on January 20, 1933 (the cabinet had approved it two days earlier). There were two interpretations of Meitō's policies, concluded the committee: either the company evaded paying excise tax or the company merely followed a standard practice accepted by the Tax Bureau (this statement does not cover the secret production under the old standard, for which the company was fined ¥600,000). The report opined that the standard scale for judging the amount of refined sugar produced should be adjusted. According to a newspaper article, Tokyo procurators were unhappy about this decision.[39]

> [The procurators] seem far from satisfied with the conclusions. . . . They say that it is clearly laid down in the constitution that Japanese subjects have the duty to pay taxes according to the law. . . . At any rate, the committee has concurred in the view of the Procurator's Office in regarding it as an evasion of tax, and therefore the Procurator's Office can prosecute similar acts without hesitation in the future. It is regrettable that the committee's findings say nothing about the deceptive means adopted by the Sugar Company. It may also be argued that failure to punish an act which is deemed tax evasion constitutes a betrayal of trust on the part of authorities concerned, but as the committee's conclusions have already been affirmed by the Cabinet and responsibility is shifted to the Government, the Procurator's Office cannot press the point further.[40]

Although the Saitō Cabinet blessed the committee's decision, the hot tax debate was not over. Tsukumo, at the Budget Committee on January 31, demanded an explanation of this decision. Justice Minister Koyama replied that the company had not violated the Penal Code, because its actions were acceptable under the Tax Bureau's old system. Kimura, head of the Criminal Affairs Bureau, agreed with the minister.[41] Three days later, at the Budget Committee, Koyama Tanizō pointed out that government replies merely intensified public suspicion that something was amiss. The prime minister replied that the case had been handled properly. Representative Koyama then urged that procurators be permitted to indict without a complaint being issued by tax officials. Justice Minister Koyama dismissed the idea as improper, adding that the views of tax officials must be respected.[42]

Not unexpectedly, rightists' voices were heard. In late August 1932, one group that gathered at Sengakuji in Shinagawa, Tokyo, marched on the residence of the president of Meitō and passed out handbills condemning Sōma Hanji. Other members of this group, demanding that Meitō apologize to the nation, raided one of Meitō's plants in northern Kyushu. Sasakawa Ryōichi, head of Kokusui taishūtō (a rightist group founded in 1931), visited Tokyo procurators to make out formal complaints against Finance Minister Takahashi and Tax Bureau head Nakajima. Members of his party sought to draw attention by a hunger strike near the Imperial Palace.[43]

In a letter to members of the special committee investigating the Meitō case, Sasagawa urged them "to handle this affair unflinchingly since the public is doubting the sincerity of their intentions" and "any settlement of the matter by a so-called political solution may affect unfavorably the ideas of the public concerning the duty of taxpayers. The Meiji Company ought to pay millions more."[44]

One can only guess at the public impact of the Meiji Sugar Refining Company case, but probably newspaper readers concluded that wealthy businessmen, with friends in high places, were not paying their fair share of taxes during a time of severe economic distress. Editorial fingers of blame, moreover, pointed directly at Nakajima and other bureaucrats and, by extension, to the Saitō Cabinet, which certified the dispute settlement. Justice administrative officials, too, were probably seen as accomplices in a scheme to favor the rich over the poor. No doubt some readers viewed procurators as saviors and Representative Tsukumo as a hero; perhaps some were swayed enough to support Seiyūkai candidates in the next election. As for the ultranationalists, perhaps they won a few converts.

One important result of this tax case was the public clash between the Finance Ministry and the procurators. In a social milieu that placed a premium on compromise solutions to disputes and in which great effort was made to "save face," this public battle was bound to leave ugly scars.

Procurator Kuroda, whose name was spotlighted by journalists, must have felt anger not only toward tax officials but also toward higher Justice Ministry administrative officials, whom he felt had betrayed procurators. This anger is reflected in threats to publish the procurators' investigative report to force a policy change on tax officials (this threat was leaked to the press). Furthermore, even after the cabinet's decision, Tokyo procurators remained defiant, and they made sure the public was informed. Did Kuroda or a colleague tell a reporter that not punishing Meitō reflected "a betrayal of trust on the part of authorities concerned" (see above)? Given the procurators' views on this case, the press report is probably accurate.

One scholar notes that even before this dispute some procurators were antipathetic toward Finance Ministry officials. No details are supplied, but he does add that Finance Ministry personnel considered themselves to be superior to other imperial bureaucrats.[45] Tokyo bureau procurators, too, considered themselves superior. The two elite groups were caught up in a very public confrontation in which the finance bureaucrats bested the procurators. One could be certain, however, that some procurators eagerly anticipated a second round in this contest. Mutō Sanji's exposure of the Teijin stock deal presented them with such an opportunity.

The Sixty-Fifth Diet

On the opening day (January 23, 1934) of the Sixty-Fifth Imperial Diet, a newspaper editorial stated: "Nothing very exciting is expected of the Diet session which begins its annual labours to-day, but there are plentiful possibilities of excitement arising. There have been many attempts to start something, but none of them very successful."[46] In fact, lots of excitement arose during this fateful session, which witnessed multiple corruption accusations against state ministers. Political corruption was not the only subject on the minds of Diet members, who, like their constituents, were trying to understand the motivation behind the May 15, 1932, murder of Premier Inukai and the significance of the following army, navy, and civilian trials of the assassins. Consequently, cabinet officers were bombarded with critical questions and comments on the rise of "fascism" in Japan, the need to control dangerous rightist ideology, and the importance of protecting constitutional government.[47]

Throughout the Diet session the cabinet faced angry corruption scandal interpellations. An indication of the coming political storm was presented to Prime Minister Saitō on January 24, when Izawa Takio and

Kamiyama Mitsunoshin (both peers and both former Taiwan governors-general) inquired about some scandalous rumors in connection with the merger of various ironworks. They reminded Saitō that they had opposed the planned mergers, and they promised to bring up the subject in the Diet. Saitō replied that Minister Nakajima Kumakichi was in charge of the committee overseeing the proposed merger; he expressed confidence that the rumors were untrue. Kamiyama also referred to allegations against Nakajima in connection with the Bank of Taiwan's sale of Teijin Company stock shares and Kobe Steel Company shares. After their visit, they repeated to journalists their opposition to the ironworks merger. The prime minister, they added, appeared to be uninformed about the rumors of scandal, even though the cabinet had made a public pledge to enforce official discipline.[48] Rumors, however, became "facts" in the *Asahi shinbun*: "Many Peers suspect that irregularities which cannot be excused from the point of view of official discipline have been committed in the disposal by the Bank of Formosa [i.e., Bank of Taiwan] of Teikoku Rayon and Kobe Steel Foundry shares, and also in connection with the question of the amalgamation of ironworks. . . . The matter will be taken up vigorously . . . because of the alleged implication of two or three Ministers of the present Cabinet."[49]

The planned ironworks merger, about which Izawa and Kamiyama expressed concern, grew out of an industrial rationalization movement promoted by politicians, bureaucrats, and businessmen. Deteriorating economic conditions brought on by the deepening depression resulted in the creation of the Temporary Industrial Rationality Bureau (June 2, 1930), loosely attached to the Commerce and Industry Ministry (the minister was concurrently the bureau's director). Businessman Nakajima Kumakichi, who later headed this ministry, was one of the new bureau's most trusted outside advisors. Out of discussions by officials and businessmen evolved the idea that competition among businesses must be replaced by cooperation between various enterprises and between the government and private business.[50] Vice-Minister Yoshino Shinji, a key figure in this process of consolidating and strengthening business, wrote: "Modern industries attained their present development primarily through free competition. However . . . absolute freedom will not rescue the industrial world from its present disturbances. Industry needs a plan of comprehensive development and a measure of control."[51] Following a German example, the bureau promoted the Important Industries Control Law (effective from August 16, 1931), which legalized cartel agreements among industries. Control over production levels, prices, and marketing was to be exercised by each industrial group; members signed an agreement. In 1932 Nakajima switched from being Vice-Minister Yoshino's most trusted civilian associate to a more formal role as head of the Commerce and Industry Ministry. Since Nakajima and Yoshino were on good terms, the tradition of the vice-minister resigning upon the new minister's arrival was broken. Together the two men continued to promote the industrial rationalization plan. Based on the 1931 control law, cartels were created in twenty-six key industries, of which iron and steel was one.[52]

By 1934, however, as the economy quickened, some owners of private ironworks and other people had second thoughts and resisted the merger plan. Nevertheless, after an unpleasant battle in the press and the Diet, a partial amalgamation took place in January 1934; the Japan Steel Manufacturing Company was created via the fusion of a number of iron and steel companies with the state-owned Yawata works. The government held 70 percent of the new company's capital.[53] In sum, Nakajima, who as a businessman had worked with bureaucrats to devise plans for nationalizing enterprises, continued as state minister to push these plans to fruition.

At the Budget Committee, lower house, on February 2, 1934, Kazami Akira (Kokumin dōmei) demanded that Nakajima explain the ironworks merger to dispel public suspicion about possible corruption. The minister replied that he had done nothing wrong morally or legally. Kazami's political colleague, Nakamura Tsuguo, distributed a report that showed that the planned amalgamation resulted in a national treasury loss of ¥22,000,000 (Nakajima's report showed a gain of ¥97,000,000). Nakajima asked to examine the figures. Next, Nakamura noted that the second assessment in connection with the Yawata Ironworks showed a decrease of ¥21,000,000 compared with the first assessment. Moreover, in the case of private iron-works a second assessment showed an increase of ¥3,000,000. Why the big decrease for Yawata (the biggest and government-owned) and the increase for the smaller private ironworks? he asked. In the House of Peers, on the same day, Tsuda Jusha (Kenkyūkai) did not fault the proposed ironworks merger, but he questioned the procedure followed in evaluating the worth of various works, especially the too generous valuation of private companies and the undervaluation of Yawata.[54]

On February 2, in the House of Peers, Seki Naohiko (Dōwakai) point-ed out irregularities in the Bank of Taiwan's sale of the Teijin Company stock. These shares, which were sold for ¥125, had increased at one point to ¥200 in value, he noted. Moreover, people who acted as intermediaries in this deal received an enormous commission of ¥632,100. Seki was not prepared to charge the Bank of Taiwan president with dishonesty, but he insisted that the government investigate the matter and report to the upper house. Seki also interpellated the cabinet on the sale, by the Oriental Development Company, of about 45,000 shares of the Nanyō Kōhatsu Company at ¥55 per share. Why, when the ruling market price was ¥75, were these shares sold cheaply? Nagai Ryūtarō, minister for colonization, replied that Seki was mistaken: the shares were sold for ¥70. Therefore, nothing was irregular about the transaction.[55]

Nakajima replied to critics by pointing out that, when a large merger of ironworks was carried out in the United States, it was fairly easy to assess the value of each company's stock, because they were listed on a stock exchange. Unfortunately, this was not the situation in Japan, he said, which necessitated the adoption of a special method to judge company assets. Therefore, companies that joined the merger plan were required to submit an inventory. Once the inventories were submitted, experts and members of the Assessment Committee were dispatched to inspect each factory. Two methods of assessment were employed: one was connected with the value of a plant minus depreciation, and the other was based on earnings. The latter method did not work, however, because of the upsurge in the economy and the increased earnings of ironworks. Finally, the committee decided that average steel prices during a set period would become the standard. Next he explained how the depreciation part of the assessment was dovetailed with other evaluations. Nakajima concluded that the assessment methods used would benefit some companies more than others, but it could not be helped given the circumstances; the assessment was done as fairly as possible.[56]

Unfortunately for Nakajima, the explosive issue of imperial loyalty became intertwined with the ironworks merger controversy. At issue was his politically incorrect view of Ashikaga Takauji, who founded the Muromachi Shogunate in 1338. Briefly, the founder of the Ashikaga regime angered modern imperial loyalists, because after aiding Emperor Go-Daigo in crushing the Kamakura Shogunate, Ashikaga rebelled and the emperor fled to a mountainous area south of the capital. The Ashikaga clan leader then installed a figurehead emperor, who appointed him shogun while Go-Daigo established the Southern Court at Yoshino. This Northern and Southern Courts situation lasted until 1392. Over the following centuries many scholars cursed Takauji for fighting the rightful emperor.[57] During the late Meiji period, the heated scholarly debate over which court was legitimate spilled over into politics. Finally, the Meiji emperor, who descended from the Northern Court, declared that the Southern Court was legitimate. Textbook publishers adopted this standard.[58]

At a lower house Budget Committee meeting on February 3, Kurihara Hikosaburō (Kokumin dōmei) chastised Nakajima for writing an article in *Gendai* and demanded an explanation. There was no excuse, Kurihara said, for an article that praised Ashikaga Takauji's personality, especially in a popular magazine. The minister explained that the article had appeared a dozen years earlier in a literary magazine and was reprinted without permission. Besides expressing deepest regret for the appearance of the article, Nakajima said that his viewpoint on Takauji had changed completely.[59] Nakajima, in the 1921 article, wrote: "As his wooden statue bespeaks, Takauji, as an individual was a man of noble character. He was broadminded and magnanimous. His attitude was all-embracing like an ocean. I have, in truth, the highest opinion of Takauji. History refers to the struggle between the North and South Courts, but it was really a conflict between the Court nobles and the military clans."[60] The statue of Takauji was at Seikenji in Shizuoka Prefecture: the literary publication was *Akidori*.[61]

Heckling of Nakajima continued at the lower and upper house budget meetings on February 5 and 7.[62] Despite this savage attack, many political observers opined that, once Prime Minister Saitō presented a scheduled defense of Nakajima, the political storm would pass. Some peers, they wrote, viewed this outrage over Nakajima's article as merely an excuse to embarrass the government. Perhaps political pundits were correct, but Nakajima, citing health problems, resigned effective February 9.[63] Nakajima wrote, several decades later, that behind this sad affair there were army officers. Indeed, before resigning he told Saitō that the military was targeting the entire cabinet. Nakajima concluded that it was his mediation effort to unite the two major parties that sealed his own fate and that of the cabinet as well.[64]

On February 5, at the morning session of the House of Peers, Finance Minister Takahashi replied to Seki Naohiko's earlier interpellation: the disposal of Teijin shares was within the Bank of Taiwan's jurisdiction. The bank's only obligation was to obtain the approval of the Bank of Taiwan Commission (established in 1927). Therefore, said Takahashi, the sale of Teijin and Kobe Steel shares was done properly. Next, he introduced Ōkubo Teiji, director of the Banking Bureau, Finance Ministry, who supported Takahashi's viewpoint.[65]

Ōkubo explained:

There is no legal provision governing such sales. Although the Bank [of Taiwan] need not secure the approval of the Finance Department, it is, of course, important that the Bank authorities should make a careful choice of time and methods of disposal. Proper supervision is exercised over the Bank by the supervisor in the Finance Department, but this official is not in a position to interfere where veto or restraint of any kind is especially called for. As regards the deals in question, they were quite in order. Teikoku Rayon shares rose to ¥150 in the latter half of 1928 . . . and the price advanced even to ¥200. . . . The Bank was looking for suitable purchasers of such shares [when the price fell to ¥104]. . . . In spite of the rumour of the increase of capital, it did not rise above ¥112. . . . The Bank authorities fixed the sale price at ¥120 or over. . . . [When the sale was final] the ruling market price was around ¥122. The conclusion of these transactions whetted public interest in Teikoku Rayon shares, and there was a steady rise in price, the highest . . . being . . . ¥151 [in July 1933]. . . . This is a common market phenomenon. . . . Although the Bank . . . has sold 100,000 shares, it still holds 110,000 old shares and 70,000 new, and it may be said that by ensuring the marketable value of Teikoku Rayon shares generally, the Bank has enhanced the values of those shares still in its hands. According to usage in transactions of this sort, the commission paid by the Bank . . . cannot be regarded as too high.[66]

Next Ōkubo dealt with questions about the Kobe Steel Company shares, which he said were also purchased at a fair price. Seki Naohiko (Dōwakai) was dissatisfied with Ōkubo's and Takahashi's replies, which reminded him of lawyers defending a client in court. It appears, he complained, that they simply accepted the bank's report and repeated it. Unfortunately, they did not give the real views of the Finance Ministry.[67]

At the afternoon session, Seki grilled the cabinet again on the sale by the Oriental Development Company of Nanyō Kōhatsu Company shares. Minister Nagai's earlier reply was unsatisfactory, said Seki, because new Nanyō Kōhatsu shares carry a premium of ¥12, so the shares should have gone for ¥82. This loss affected not only the Oriental Development Company but the nation. Moreover, he noted, a rumor circulated that Kuhara Fusanosuke combine interests were given 25,000 shares. Why was this done? Were the middlemen government officials? Furthermore, it appears that the Nanyō Kōhatsu Company entered the sugar business and decided to purchase used manufacturing equipment from the South Manchurian Sugar Company for ¥500,000. Is this old machinery worth the price? These questions must be answered, concluded Seki.[68]

Opposition politicians did not neglect other embarrassing issues. Education Minister Hatoyama Ichirō, for example, was interpellated about charges of corruption among school administrators and teachers; he was also accused of bribery. Charges of corruption in the education system were an old story, but because of economic depression public concern was unusually acute. Among the illegal activities reported were bribery by school principals of school inspectors, bribery by teachers in order to get salary increases or to receive promotions, female teachers giving special favors to principals, and principals receiving bribes from textbook dealers.[69] Hatoyama, who was repeatedly quizzed by Diet members, apologized for the corruption problems and promised to enforce stricter supervision.[70] As for the personal bribery charge, it probably caught Hatoyama off guard, because it involved a demand for a reinvestigation of a closed case. In brief, while chief cabinet secretary in the Tanaka Giichi Cabinet (April 1927–July 1929), Hatoyama had accepted a ¥50,000 donation from the head of the Karafuto (Sakhalin) Industry Company. Procurators decided it was a legal political contribution (see below).

On February 8, at the lower house budget meeting, Okamoto Kazumi (Seiyūkai) charged Minister Nakajima and Bank of Taiwan officials with illegally selling Teijin stock. Ōkubo, head of the Banking Bureau, repeated his earlier statement to the House of Peers: the Bank of Taiwan had the legal right to sell the shares; the stock transaction was done in a proper manner; the share price was proper. Okamoto discounted this explanation as worthless, because Ōkubo was a party to the transaction. Okamoto also insisted that judicial officials investigate a minister (the audience understood he meant Hatoyama) who had distributed money in 1933 to over 130 house members.[71] Finally, Okamoto charged that two Seiyūkai colleagues were involved in the Teijin stock deal (i.e., Yoneda Kikuma and Hayashi Jōji). Yoneda was the private secretary of Railway Minister Mitsuchi Chūzō; Hayashi was the private secretary of Hatoyama. Both representatives denied Okamoto's accusation.[72] Okamoto's sensational accusations, however, forced the creation of a Committee of Inquiry; they also led to his expulsion from the party, not surprising, given Hatoyama's important party position and his brother-in-law relationship with the party president.[73]

Corruption accusations surfaced again on February 15. Tanihara Ko (Minseitō) said that Okamoto's charges made many people wonder about Yoneda's and Hayashi's sordid connection with the sale of Teijin shares. Etō Genkurō (Seiyūkai turned Independent) pointed out that Hatoyama and Mitsuchi were involved together with Nakajima. Therefore, it was the premier's duty to investigate and report to the lower house whether or not these ministers worked with political merchants. Continuing, Etō said that it was alleged that Hatoyama had discussed with the Bank of Japan governor a document that contained the stock sale terms. Moreover, it was rumored that Vice-Minister Kuroda Hideo (Finance Ministry) was throwing money around every night in the Tsukiji area. These facts, he said, together with the charge that money was distributed among Diet members, should be probed. Next Okamoto took the floor. He refused to accept the denials of Yoneda and Hayashi, suggesting that they were being manipulated by someone. Besides that, he stated that in May 1931 Hatoyama had requested aid in destroying evidence in the Karafuto Industry Company criminal case. Because of his help in this case, Okamoto said, procurators stopped investigating Hatoyama.[74]

The cabinet responded quickly. Hatoyama denied Okamoto's story: he had neither asked Okamoto for help nor met with him. Justice Minister Koyama reported that Okamoto's statement about the Karafuto Industry Company scandal was incorrect factually and that Hatoyama was not involved. Koyama stated that he had checked with procurators who handled the Karafuto Industry Company embezzlement case, which came to light during the investigation of the notorious Decorations Scandal case of 1929. During the investigation, as people with the Karafuto Industry Company were interrogated and company account books were checked, it was learned that the company's managing director had given Hatoyama ¥50,000. Procurators, however, decided that this was a straightforward political donation for Hatoyama's coming election campaign.[75]

Politicians targeted by Okamoto also refuted the charges. Indeed, Yoneda denied any contact with the Banchōkai and any connection with the stock sale. Hayashi echoed these comments. Mitsuchi, who was quoted by the *Asahi shinbun* as welcoming the creation of a Committee of Inquiry, explained that he did not profit from the Bank of Taiwan's sale of Kobe Steel Company shares. The truth, said Mitsuchi, was that the 114th Bank of Takamatsu, for which his brother worked, asked for his advice about buying Kobe Steel stock shares. Mitsuchi replied that they were not a good investment. As for Vice-Minister Kuroda, whom Etō Genkurō suggested was paid off, he admitted to dining out often. Charges that he received money from Banchōkai members, however, were absolutely false.[76]

The Committee of Inquiry, which was investigating Okamoto's allegations, consisted of members from the Seiyūkai (11), Minseitō (5), and Kokumin dōmei (2). Shimada Toshio (Seiyūkai) was chairman. The committee asked Okamoto to support his charges with evidence. When Hatoyama visited Kyoto, Okamoto replied, Hayashi arranged a meeting with Osaka businessman Nomura Tokuhichi. A rumor circulated that Nomura's group promised a reward of ¥2,000,000 if the Teijin stock sale succeeded. This meeting illustrated Hayashi's involvement. It is rumored, noted Okamoto, that Hayashi saw Yoneda and others in connection with this matter. Pressed for more conclusive proof, Okamoto could supply none. Asked about money from Fujita Kozaburō, who managed the Karafuto Industry Company, Okamoto said that at Hatoyama's request he had met Fujita at an office in Tokyo, where he was instructed to say, if anyone inquired about the money, that it was for election expenses. Following the meeting with Fujita, said Okamoto, he had visited Hatoyama's residence. Of course, no money was gotten from Fujita, since this was a sham meeting to cover up an entry in the Karafuto company's books and to throw procurators off Hatoyama's trail. Asked to prove that Hatoyama distributed money among 130 lower house members, Okamoto refused to furnish details except to state that Morita Masayoshi showed Inoue Riei a bundle of money, which was to be distributed at Hatoyama's order. Morita denounced Okamoto's statement as false. Justice Ministry records on the Karafuto Industry Company investigation were given to the committee on February 21.[77] In testimony given on November 7, 1929, to Procurator Biwada Gensuke at the Tokyo District Court, managing director Fujita said that he and Hatoyama were high school and university classmates. From 1926, he gave money to Hatoyama and the Seiyūkai. In late January 1928, Fujita stated, Okamoto was given ¥50,000 for Hatoyama's election expenses. Moreover, money was given to a former governor of Karafuto, to Yamamoto Teijirō (minister of agriculture and forestry), and to Prime Minister Hamaguchi Osachi. Although superiors did not give permission for these donations, Fujita thought that these gifts would someday benefit the company. They totaled ¥170,000.[78]

At the Committee of Inquiry final meeting (February 28), Etō Genkurō, who accused Hatoyama and Mitsuchi of colluding with political merchants during the Teijin stock sale, was questioned. Asked to produce evidence to substantiate these charges, Etō said that the information about Hatoyama came from an unnamed person involved in the stock sale. Pressed about Mitsuchi's involvement, Etō replied that the railway minister should be asked. Taketomi Sei (Minseitō) censured Etō for making serious accusations that he was unwilling to substantiate. Then Taketomi asked about rumors that a certain group was behind these corruption charges. Etō denied the allegation. At this same committee meeting, Hatoyama insisted that he had never asked Okamoto to do anything, had never received ¥50,000 from Fujita, and did not meddle in the stock transactions. When a committee member noted that Hatoyama had admitted to journalists that he got ¥50,000 from Fujita for election expenses, the minister denied making the statement. Finally, when asked why party colleague Okamoto made these accusations, Hatoyama responded that he had no idea.[79]

The committee met on March 2 to write a report. As expected, Seiyūkai members wanted Hatoyama, Mitsuchi, Yoneda, and Hayashi cleared of Okamoto's accusations, because no proof of wrongdoing had been discovered. Minseitō members, who were not certain that all charges were baseless, insisted on the right to produce a minority report. As for the Kokumin dōmei, it demanded not only Hatoyama's political head but the cabinet's resignation. Meanwhile, rumors circulated about Hatoyama's intention to resign. The *Asahi Newspaper* identified various fascist influences at work behind Okamoto.[80]

A lively debate on three versions of "truth" took place on March 3. Committee Chairman Shimada urged the house to accept the majority view that the accused were innocent. Sugiyama Motojirō (Labor), after commenting on the three versions of events, added that the general conclusion of the press was that a corrupt relationship existed between political parties and big financial interests. Did Shimada not think, he asked, that public opinion was ready to accept Okamoto's accusations? Tanihara Kō (Minseitō) complained about inadequate testimony and scanty documentation. For example, Ōkubo, head of the Banking Bureau, failed to appear before the committee. Hence, it was impossible to confirm or deny Okamoto's allegation. On the matter of money paid to Diet members, the charge was false, but the accusation that Hatoyama received ¥50,000 from Fujita appeared to be correct, he stated. Hamada Kunimatsu, commenting on Mitsuchi's involvement with Kobe Steel Company shares, noted that Mitsuchi was a well-known financial expert, so it was not surprising that a bank would ask for his advice. The viewpoint of Kokumin dōmei was voiced by Noda Bunichirō, who felt that there were irregularities in the sale of stock shares by the Bank of Taiwan. It appears, he said, that bank president Shimada, under the influence of powerful people, acted arbitrarily. Noda also hinted at Mitsuchi's involvement. As for Hatoyama, Noda said that his party accepted Okamoto's testimony. Put to a vote, the Seiyūkai version won 206 to 120 ballots. Later, asked by the presiding officer of the lower house to withdraw his charges, Okamoto agreed to withdraw the accusation that a minister had distributed money among Diet members but refused to withdraw the rest.[81]

Hatoyama put rumors to rest by resigning the same day the Committee of Inquiry voted. Interestingly, in a postwar autobiography, Hatoyama wrote: "In July 1934, the Saitō Cabinet fell because of the Teijin Incident."[82] Hatoyama said nothing about opening doors for Teijin stock buyers, nothing about his commission, nothing about paying off Diet members, and nothing about the ¥50,000!

The Kuhara Fusanosuke and Suzuki-Hatoyama factions were battling for control of the Seiyūkai. One scholar, in explaining Okamoto's actions, identifies him as "a Kuhara group man."[83] Another scholar sees behind Okamoto's actions a deal between the Hiranuma support group, a faction of the Seiyūkai, and the Kokumin dōmei, aimed at destroying the Saitō Cabinet.[84] Both views, up to a point, are correct, since the "outs" were trying to dislodge the "ins," in order to seize the premiership. To view Hiranuma as a puppet master manipulating the strings, however, is a mistake. In fact, there was no need for Hiranuma's direct involvement in sordid political machinations, because a small army of Hiranuma boosters labored ceaselessly, aiming to place him in the premiership.[85] It is unclear which "group" Taketomi Sei saw behind Okamoto's corruption charges, but it may have been the triple combination mentioned above. Comments about fascists at work appear to identify Hiranuma's support group, including military officers. These public comments were vague, as usual, and open to various interpretations. The always vocal Mutō Sanji, in a *Jiji* column titled "As I Think," complimented Okamoto and Etō for spotlighting the issue of corruption, which exposed the public to the true nature of politics. Although Mutō did not advocate a reward for Okamoto, he felt that expulsion from the Seiyūkai was unwarranted. Baron Harada Kumao, who was Prince Saionji's informant, records in his diary that Okamoto was a "hooligan" (*gorotsuki*) who worked first for Mori Kaku and then for Hatoyama. Harada opined that politicians who used such a terrible person invited the sort of problem Hatoyama faced.[86] In sum, Okamoto's actions are best viewed through the lens of the bitter power struggle between the Suzuki-Hatoyama and the Kuhara Seiyūkai factions. Somehow Kuhara supporters managed to turn Okamoto against Hatoyama, under whom Okamoto had enjoyed a subordinate relationship. Their aim was twofold: to undermine the Suzuki-Hatoyama party leadership and to destroy the Saitō Cabinet.

If the Sixty-Fifth Diet session is regarded as a play performed before a national audience, then it wore the label of a tragedy, from the Saitō Cabinet's perspective, with two ministers pushed out of office and one other under a darkening criminal cloud. That a farce intervened, as if scheduled on a playbill, seems only proper, because a farce was needed to lighten the national mood before the final act of the tragedy. It was appropriate for Okamoto Kazumi to be the producer, director, and costar of this absurd comedy; equally appropriate was his costar Justice Minister Koyama Matsukichi.

On February 5, 1934, Okamoto distributed among Diet members a pamphlet in which he accused Koyama of accepting bribes. In a formal complaint filed with authorities, Okamoto identified stockbrokers Numama Toshio and Kobayashi Takejirō as the bribers. Okamoto alleged that the two, between March and mid-June 1932, entertained the justice minister at various places. Okamoto pointed out that Kobayashi was arrested in 1929 for giving money and shelter to communists but that his punishment was unusually light. Indeed, argued Okamoto, Kobayashi paid a large sum of money to officials, with Numama acting as the go-between. Tokyo procurators replied to this charge by releasing details about the Kobayashi case. Kobayashi, a wealthy businessman, was arrested on November 21, 1928, on charges of sheltering communists; he was not accused of giving them money. A trial resulted in a six-month prison sentence. Judges, however, added a stay of execution, because Kobayashi was unaware that the house guests were communists. Justice Minister Koyama denied Okamoto's allegations: he had never met Kobayashi or Numama. Journalists, probing this affair, discovered that Kobayashi and Numama were friends of a lawyer Koyama, who was a former Yokohama District Court procurator. The *Asahi Newspaper* wrote that even though the lawyer and the justice minister bore the same surname, it was highly improbable that Okamoto could have confused the two.[87]

In the midst of this uproar, the lower house Disciplinary Committee voted a two-week suspension for Okamoto, who refused to withdraw some accusations made in the Diet. Moreover, in early April, Okamoto was arrested for slandering the justice minister. Police also detained the manager of an assignation house in Akasaka where the justice minister's reputed illegal dealings transpired; she was charged with giving false evidence. Nevertheless, rumors circulated that the minister planned to resign, because the incident injured the ministry's prestige.[88]

Commenting on the Diet session, the *Asahi* declared that those who felt that Admiral Saitō should resign were mistaken, since he was not responsible to any political party. "When it is remembered that the time is not ripe for the transfer of power to a party Cabinet, pure and simple, it can hardly be said that the mission of the Saitō Cabinet is over." As for political parties, the newspaper opined that early in the Diet session it seemed that they had improved, "but when the session was halfway over, the customary mud-flinging contest started, culminating in the resignation of Mr. Hatoyama. . . . Altogether, the tone of discussion fell even lower than in former sessions, and the credit of political parties among the people has suffered further. None of the parties cut even a tolerable figure. They are past praying for now as much as they were before."[89]

The Cabinet's Final Months

Even before the resignations of Nakajima and Hatoyama, political pundits concluded that the Saitō Cabinet would soon resign. The cabinet, despite its blessing of the army's Manchurian conquest, tried to stabilize international relations and to control state expenditure. For example, it made an agreement with the Chinese south of the Great Wall, and it avoided a military confrontation with the Soviet Union, which angered Army Minister Araki Sadao. Furthermore, in November and December 1933, Araki, who supported a proposed budget increase for more farm relief, was frustrated by Finance Minister Takahashi, who was determined to support the most productive parts of the economy. Railway Minister Mitsuchi played a role in this anti-Araki decision. Araki resigned from the cabinet.[90]

Despite the cabinet's numerous foreign and domestic problems, however, its downfall resulted not from budget battles with the military or political fights with the Diet but from the sensational exposure of the Teijin stock sale. During the Sixty-Fifth Diet session, the Procurator Bureau, Tokyo District Criminal Court, was investigating this transaction. Even before the Diet session began, procurators heard rumors about officials of the Bank of Taiwan, the Bank of Japan, and the Finance Ministry being bribed; Nakajima, Hatoyama, and Mitsuchi were identified as participants in this rumored crime. Behind these rumors were the angry Kaneko and Fujita, who had failed to purchase Teijin stocks.[91] What actually put procuratorial machinery into motion, however, was Mutō's series of articles, comments in the Diet, and several official complaints. Recall that the *Jiji shinpō* Banchōkai series began with an announcement in mid-January about the forthcoming exposure followed by two months of inflammatory articles. Mutō was shot on March 9, died on the tenth, and the series ended on the thirteenth.

During February, Miyagi Chōgorō, head of the district court procurators, received three complaints (one originated in Osaka; two came from Tokyo) about people involved in the Teijin stock sale. The Osaka complaint was written by Nakai Matsutarō, a Mutō supporter, who charged that Teijin Company president Takagi Naomichi (also a former director of the Bank of Taiwan), Kawai, Nagano, and others were guilty of embezzlement, misfeasance, and other crimes. One of the Tokyo complaints, submitted by Katō Noboru, was aimed at Shimada Shigeru (president of the Bank of Taiwan), who was charged with misfeasance, making fake documents, and receiving a bribe. The other Tokyo complaint, from Hasui Keitarō, an executive committee officer of the Dai Nippon kikusui minshū tō (a rightist organization), made similar charges against Kawai, Nagano, Shōriki, and Shimada. Miyagi picked Kuroda Etsurō, who was the bureau's financial expert, to head this investigation. Indeed, Kuroda was the bureau's point man for the earlier Meitō tax case. Kuroda picked Biwada Gensuke as his deputy. Once they decided that the crime of misfeasance could be proved, three other procurators joined them. It appears that up to this point (the three additional procurators came on board just after the Sixty-Fifth Diet closed) the investigation was fueled by Mutō's articles and Diet speeches, among which there were many factual errors.[92]

The *Jiji shinpō*'s ferocious attack angered Banchōkai members, with some urging a libel suit. They ruled out a lawsuit, however, because a drawn-out court case might play into Mutō's hands. Instead, they employed the pen to fight the pen: a reply to Mutō's daily bombardment appeared in a January 22 advertisement in all the Tokyo area newspapers; the second reply appeared in the March issue of *Keizai ōrai* (which came out on February 10). Although written by Kawai, the advertisement was signed by Gotō Kunihiko, as a club officer. In the advertisement, titled "About the Banchōkai," the group was depicted as a social organization centered on Baron Gō, which gathered monthly to discuss current events; a rule of the club was not to discuss money-making deals. Furthermore, reports that Baron Nakajima was closely connected with the club were mistaken. Because the two barons were friends, however, they did socialize at affairs like the club's New Year party. A newspaper, Kawai concluded, that claimed that three members of the club were connected with the Teijin and Kobe Steel Company stock deals was mistaken. Indeed, at the Banchōkai meetings these two topics were never discussed.[93]

It is understandable why the Banchōkai did not sue Mutō. Not only would the court action have been protracted, since courts were notorious for snail's pace judgments, but personal attacks in newspapers were commonplace. As one close student of the era's press put it: "The personal libels, the keyhole gossiping, the direct assaults upon the character of Japanese statesmen, business executives and other figures in the public eye are beyond belief. American tabloids are conservative by contrast."[94] True, there were antilibel regulations, but they were ineffective. The famous liberal politician Ozaki Yukio, who sat in the Diet from the first session in 1890, "declared that no amount of inducement could cause him to reply to any journalistic libel."[95] Not as understandable is Kawai's bold lie that no club member was connected with either stock sale. Given the number of people involved in the complicated Teijin stock transaction, and given the Mutō probing spotlight, how could he hope to keep their involvement secret?

Kawai used the *Keizai ōrai* to hit hard, writing that something was wrong with Mr. Mutō. What, he asked, are these "Exposing the Banchōkai" articles all about? Why did Mutō use pejorative terms for the club, like "a hotbed of political and economic corruption," when in fact proper businessmen were Banchōkai members? "Where are the improper acts, Mr. Mutō?" By misinforming the public in these articles, Mutō was abusing his position. "Your righteousness is distorted," wrote Kawai. "Has the series of articles increased the *Jiji shinpō*'s circulation?" Kawai pointed out that one *zaibatsu* head said that it was ironic that Mutō, who used to be so angry over journalistic personal attacks, began to make similar attacks on others once he took over the newspaper.[96]

And so it went during January, February, and into March, with the Banchōkai and the stock deals being discussed in newspapers and in the Diet. After weeks of rumors and attacks on the Saitō Cabinet, the Tokyo procurators imposed a press ban on the Teijin stock sale topic on March 25.[97] A short time later, Chief Procurator Miyagi was ordered to report to the Nagasaki Appeals Court; his replacement was Iwamura Michiyo, who was chief at the Nagoya District Court. Officially, Iwamura took over the Tokyo position on April 2, but, since he was still in Nagoya on April 3, it is clear that the transfer was delayed. Miyagi agreed with Kuroda that this case was to be handled as misfeasance.[98] Before departing, Miyagi ordered Kuroda and his colleagues "not to charge any of the Bank of Japan directors with misfeasance, because this would touch on the matter of international trust."[99] Thus, they were to limit the investigation to the Bank of Taiwan and the Finance Ministry. On April 3, Procurators Biwada and Nagao Takeo, who were on their way to Osaka to begin the search, seizure, and interrogation phase of the case, stopped off in Nagoya to inform Iwamura. After hearing their report, Iwamura replied that concentrating solely on proving that Bank of Taiwan officials committed misfeasance was insufficient to win conviction. By addition of the crime of bribery, he emphasized, they would win. The procurators took this advice to heart and shifted the investigation's focus toward proving the crime of bribery.[100]

On April 5 procurators in Tokyo and Osaka carried out raids simultaneously on Bank of Taiwan offices, Teijin Company offices, and private residences. Documents were seized as evidence, with so many taken from just the Teijin Company headquarters that they filled a truck. President Takagi was arrested in Tokyo and taken by detectives to Osaka. During the following days other people were arrested: Okazaki Akira, a Teijin director, who was also escorted to Osaka (April 11); Nagasaki Eizō (president of the Asahi Oil Company), Nagano, and Kawai (April 18); and so on. By May 19 the arrests reached Finance Ministry Vice-Minister Kuroda Hideo. Four of his colleagues followed: Ōno Ryūta, head of the Special Bank Section; Aida Iwao, bank inspector; Shidomoto Jirō, retired bank inspector (May 20); Ōkubo Teiji, head of the Banking Bureau (May 21). Two large papers, the *Nichinichi* and the *Asahi*, violated the press ban by selling special editions (*gōgai*) on the street. This sensational story sold out.[101]

How did Finance Ministry officials react to the sensational arrests of colleagues? Aoki Kazuo, who was chief of the Foreign Currency Section, wrote in a postwar memoir that officials were proud of the ministry's spotless record: no bribed officials. The unexpected arrests, therefore, were shocking. From the moment he heard about the accusation of bribery, however, Aoki was certain of his colleagues' innocence. Once the suspects were jailed, Aoki got permission from a superior to address ministry personnel. This was a strange case, he said, and the arrest was improper. Eventually, the ministry suspects would be found not guilty. In the meantime, he urged ministry officials to remain calm and to continue to perform their duties. That evening he visited Finance Minister Takahashi's private residence. Although the minister criticized Aoki for the speech, fearing that it might cause a collision between the finance and justice ministries, he agreed with Aoki that the five could not be guilty. Moreover, Takahashi confided that, when Justice Minister Koyama had discussed the case with the cabinet, the finance minister could not understand what it was all about. Aoki explained to Takahashi that conversations with defense lawyers suggested that the prosecution's case was based on some self-confessions. On hearing Aoki's report, Takahashi appeared relieved. Before departing, Aoki assured him that there would be no clash between the ministries.[102]

By late May, newspapers were speculating over the next premier's identity. Journalists gave former prime minister Kiyoura Keigo and governor-general of Korea Ugaki Kazushige the best odds. Seiyūkai supporters, who had rejected these candidates, pushed for a coalition of the two major parties under the leadership of Suzuki Kisaburō.[103] The Kokumin dōmei demanded Saitō's resignation:

> The Premier tries to stick to power on the pretense that the whole truth of the case is not yet known, but it is more than probable that he knows exactly how matters stand, as he must have received a detailed report of the case from the Minister of Justice. Nor is it conceivable that the Procurator's Office prosecuted a man of Mr. Kuroda's position without irrefutable evidence. Failure of the Government to take responsibility and resign quickly makes the public suspect that it is bringing secret pressure to bear upon the

judiciary. There is also room for suspicion that it is contriving to prevent a former Minister and a present Minister, whose implication is rumoured, from possible prosecution.[104]

While political circles pondered, the press speculated, and rumors circulated, the procurators' investigation ground on. It appears that procurators told police to stay away from the Teijin scandal investigation. Fujinuma Shōhei, chief of the Metropolitan Police Board, recalled that the Tokyo procurators launched this case but ran into obstacles. Kuroda then appealed for help to the head of the Criminal Affairs Section, who informed the chief that subordinates were too angry with the procurators to cooperate. Nevertheless, Fujinuma ordered police to help. Kuroda, in an effort to smooth over the rift, made a pilgrimage to police headquarters: he apologized and requested help.[105] Fujinuma's account is probably correct, but for procurators to keep police in the dark about a sensitive investigation was not unusual, and for them to take the lead in a case was also common by the early 1930s. In a normal criminal case, police detected a possible crime and a suspect was arrested, at which point a procurator would become involved. In sensitive cases, like the mass arrests of communists (e.g., March 15, 1928, and April 16, 1929) and the various corruption scandals of the late 1920s, procurators, who worried about information leaks, sometimes were less than open with police. During these years, as Tokyo procurators became more important (e.g., in handling thousands of communist suspects), their feeling of self-importance increased with the bureau's increased stature. In sum, conflict with the capital's police headquarters over jurisdiction and leadership was not a new development.[106]

From the prosecution viewpoint, the key development was President Takagi Naomichi's confession, which implicated other people. Takagi confessed that Nagasaki gave 1,300 Teijin shares to Bank of Taiwan directors, who in turn gave shares to Vice-Minister Kuroda, Banking Bureau Director Ōkubo, Railway Minister Mitsuchi, and Commerce and Industry Minister Nakajima. Leftover shares were converted to cash and given to Finance Ministry officials Shidomoto, Aida, and Ōno. Bank directors Takagi, Okazaki Akira, Koshifuji Tsunekichi, and Yanagida Naokichi kept the leftover money.[107] Chief Procurator Iwamura said that, on hearing about Takagi's confession, he told procurators that the entire case would stand or fall on Takagi's deposition; if he repudiated it, the prosecution would collapse. Therefore, he ordered a thorough review of Takagi's deposition. This was done by Biwada and other procurators, who confirmed all of Takagi's original statements. With this supposedly solid base established, the prosecution moved on to other aspects of the case.[108] The next important event was a so-called petition written by Kuroda to Chief Procurator Iwamura about a month after his arrest in which the vice-minister explained what happened to the four hundred shares (i.e., money received after the shares were converted to cash) he received from Nagasaki: ¥10,000 went to Ōyama Hisamaro (a friend in the lower house); ¥10,000 went to Mitsuchi; ¥10,000 or ¥20,000 was given to the Seiyūkai; a ¥30,000 loan went to the son of Finance Minister Takahashi: the balance was invested by a financier at Yamaichi shōken.[109]

Why did Takagi, whose confession was crucial for the procurators, cooperate so quickly? Suzuki Yoshio, his trial lawyer, stated that, after being arrested on April 5, Takagi was taken to Osaka and questioned by Biwada on the sixth. The following morning a policeman threw him to the toilet's concrete floor and kicked him. Policemen continued to handle him roughly, and he was kept in a very small cell (in slang termed a "pigpen") with ten vagrants, who swarmed with lice. Moreover, the interrogating procurators repeatedly called him a corrupt person. Suzuki felt that Takagi was psychologically and physically unable to withstand this treatment. Gradually, under procurators' incessant insistence that he was bribed for his stock deal role, Takagi bent to their will. On the fourth or fifth day of the ordeal, he began to agree with procurators that he had accepted Teijin shares. Lawyer Suzuki said that Takagi mistakenly assumed that a confession would allow him to return home. Instead he was sent to jail in Tokyo.[110] Although he withstood similar living conditions and incessant quizzing longer than Takagi, Vice-Minister Kuroda also confessed. Fellow defendant Kawai Yoshinari suggested another compelling reason for this confession: Kuroda was a heavy *sake* drinker who suffered severe withdrawal agony.[111]

Kawai Yoshinari presents a graphic picture of Procurator Kuroda, who emerges as a national reformer, a kindred spirit of the so-called revisionist bureaucrats. The primary characteristic of these bureaucrats was "their determination to change the existing order—political, social, economic, or all three—for the purpose of increasing the nation's spiritual and military strength."[112] During an interrogation session on May 2, 1934, Kawai claimed that Kuroda had said that society was rotten, including the Finance Ministry; only the university professors and the procurators had escaped the infection. It was the duty of procurators, said Kuroda, to clean up things. He added that he wanted to become procurator general in order to do a thorough housecleaning job. Displaying some warmth, the procurator said that he felt sorry for Kawai but added that the cleaning process would not hurt him too much. Anyway, it could not be helped, and Kawai should regard the ordeal as a sacrifice to reform society.[113]

That procurators' humiliation by Finance Ministry officials was not forgotten is indicated by a remark reported by suspect Nagano Mamoru. One procurator said, as he urged Nagano to confess, that businessmen corrupted officials and politicians; the action taken by finance officials in connection with the Meiji Sugar Company tax case was improper. Nagano's recollection of this interrogation session, published in a newspaper after his release on bail, does not identify which procurator made this comment, but it was probably Kuroda.[114]

Former minister Nakajima, who was next to the last to be interrogated (July 4), provides an insight into the procurators' camp as well. In a postwar autobiography, Nakajima wrote that, before he was interrogated, an attorney friend introduced him to lawyer Akiyama Kosaburō, a former procurator who knew Chief Procurator Iwamura. Moreover, Akiyama knew Biwada and was his senior before retirement. Akiyama used these professional contacts to discover what the prosecution side was thinking and reported back to Nakajima. The case, said the lawyer, involved bribery to get to the Teijin stock shares. When Nakajima asked why bribes were needed, Akiyama replied that the procurators were not clear on that matter but that they were investigating cabinet members. It appeared that the Banchōkai gave either shares or money to Mitsuchi and Nakajima. Akiyama concluded that the only thing to do was to wait for the completed examination. As Nakajima heard this report, he felt that this was a political plot by procurators to destroy the cabinet. It was also clear that Akiyama considered him guilty and had no intention of mounting a strong defense. In fact, the lawyer wanted Nakajima to confess and be rewarded by the court with the lightest possible sentence.[115] Nakajima concluded this section of the autobiography: "Akiyama did act on this assumption [of Nakajima's guilt]. . . . His actions caused my role in the Teijin Incident to become very complicated and caused trouble for my friends and the public. I apologize for this."[116]

Leaks to journalists by Justice Ministry personnel hinted that Saitō's decision to resign would be informed by politics. "The present scandal has very far-reaching effects on the political situation, and therefore there is no doubt that Dr. Koyama . . . had reported the nature of the case to the premier and Mr. Takahashi . . . before he gave permission for the prosecution of Mr. Kuroda. . . . Imperial sanction was also required for his prosecution [Kuroda held an imperial appointment and an imperial decoration], and this procedure of securing imperial sanction was, no doubt, taken with the approval of the Cabinet." Thus, opined the newspaper, "Admiral Saito and Mr. Takahashi are well aware of the nature of the scandal. Of the subsequent progress of judicial examination also they must have been kept informed by the minister of justice. . . . The whole circumstance leads judicial officials to suspect that political considerations [i.e., choosing another premier] largely enter into the premier's 'watchful waiting.' " This same source emphasized: "It is absolutely impossible . . . for Mr. Kuroda and others to be found not guilty, for this is a case which was prosecuted with Imperial sanction. The procuratorial authorities would not have prosecuted him without very strong reasons."[117]

Unexpectedly, procurator Kuroda Etsurō was removed from the investigation. One newspaper report read: "Procurator Kuroda, who is in charge of the examination of the Finance Department affair, was seized by cholelithiasis [gallbladder problem] on the 24th instant [June] and entered the Hino Hospital . . . for treatment. It is now reported that his condition is making favorable progress and that unless complications arise, he will be able to leave hospital in a week or so. In the meantime, Procurator Biwada . . . will take charge of the examination of the case. It is hoped that Procurator Kuroda's illness will in no way impede the progress of the judicial examination."[118] Encouraging early signs were wrong: Kuroda died on July 23 at age forty-three (the funeral was on the twenty-fifth). Kuroda's death did not go unnoticed: the head of Tokyo's Military Police Unit gave an oration, and another military police commander sent flowers. Businessman Fujita Kenichi gave one thousand yen to establish an educational fund for Kuroda's children.[119] Imamura Rikisaburō, a defense lawyer for Teijin Incident suspects, made an interesting comment about Fujita's donation. As readers will recall, Fujita, who was assisted by Nagano, failed to work out a deal to purchase Teijin stocks. Following the failure, Nagano, Kawai, and others were successful. Even though a token payment percolated down to him (Shōriki passed on ¥105,000 to Fujita and Hatoyama), Imamura states that Fujita was angry and bore a grudge against Nagano and Kawai. Contributing the education fund money was part of the process of getting even.[120]

At a conference on June 29 with Prime Minister Saitō, Justice Minister Koyama, relying heavily on former vice-minister Kuroda's so-called petition, reported on the Teijin case. Procurators had evidence to prosecute the five finance officials, Koyama said. Moreover, a current minister and a former one were involved. Koyama apologized to Takahashi, because his son's name appeared in Vice-Minister Kuroda's statement. The cabinet, which was teetering on the edge of political oblivion, was pushed over the precipice by Kuroda's confession. The cabinet resigned on July 3, 1934. The following day Admiral Okada Keisuke, another political moderate, was ordered to form a cabinet.[121]

Saitō's government, which marched onward in a hail of political stones during April, May, and June, collapsed quickly upon receiving Koyama's report. The decision to resign, however, was not triggered only by the vice-minister's confession, but also because the "petition" identified Finance Minister Takahashi's son, Koresaka, as the recipient of a large loan from Kuroda. According to Railway Minister Mitsuchi Chūzō, after the resignation he asked Saitō and Home Minister Yamamoto Tatsuo about the contents of Kuroda's "petition." Neither one had read it, they replied, but they instead relied on Koyama's oral report. After the preliminary court investigation was completed, Mitsuchi took a copy of the "petition" to Saitō. Mitsuchi discovered that Saitō was well informed about the investigation and had concluded that the procurators' case was a web of lies; seeing the "petition" merely illustrated that Koyama's oral presentation was based on very weak evidence. Hearing the former premier condemn not only Koyama but also the criminal justice system, Mitsuchi pointed out that Saitō had picked Koyama. Saitō replied that it was a terrible mistake. Finally, Saitō told Mitsuchi that what had pushed the cabinet over the edge was Koyama's statement that Takahashi's son would soon be interrogated by the procurators and that Nakajima would be as well.[122]

Who Destroyed the Saitō Cabinet?

Stimulated by the crisis with China and growing diplomatic isolation, concerned over the deepening depression and the lack of a clear consensus on national goals, many politicians, businessmen, bureaucrats, and military officers in the 1930s were seeking new ways to solve national problems. In general, between 1932 and 1936 "[political] parties ceased to function as agencies for the reconciliation of conflicting elite viewpoints and ambitions, and power shifted quickly toward the civilian and military bureaucracies."[123] During this emergency era, however, factionalism and sectionalism, which were endemic in the political power structure, more than before undermined the ideal goal of stable elite rule. Political parties, as they attempted to recover their former position in the plural elite, were faced by a politicized military, which had as its goal a monopoly of political power. Party response to politically ambitious army officers and to "new bureaucrats," who often had little use for traditional-style politicians, was mixed. On the one hand, mainstream leaders in the major parties saw a return to power in the near future; long-practiced political strategies need not be modified. Money would come from big business, local supporters would bring in votes, and contacts with the bureaucracy and military would be maintained. There were, on the other hand, antimainstream factions within the parties that favored the creation of a one-party system or the creation of a new party by a combination of antimainstream forces. Following either path, it was hoped, would restore politicians to their rightful place in the power structure. Among these antimainstream groups there were politicians willing to form alliances with revisionist bureaucrats and the military. Unlike the mainstream factions, which looked to the traditional *zaibatsu* for money, the antimainstream relied on the so-called new *zaibatsu*, which were thriving on defense spending.[124]

Faced with the Saitō national unity cabinet, the Minseitō and the Seiyūkai went along with the political current, but by late 1933 politicians from both parties were maneuvering to create a coalition to retake the premiership. These attempts, however, were defeated not only by antiparty forces but by party faction fights. Leadership of the largest party, the Seiyūkai, was in the hands of Suzuki and Hatoyama; the Minseitō was headed by the venerable Wakatsuki Reijirō, but Machida Chūji was the party's driving force. In the coalition movement, Hatoyama and Machida represented the mainstream of each party. The antimainstream coalition was led by Kuhara Fusanosuke (Seiyūkai) and Tomita Kōjirō (Minseitō). The Hatoyama-Machida group, which aimed at creating an old fashioned coalition within the two-party system, was supported by the Mitsui *zaibatsu* and the Banchōkai. The other group, which aimed at creating a new single-party system and which planned to cooperate closely with the military, depended on Kuhara's new *zaibatsu* for funds.[125] "Early in 1934, the coalition movement finally disintegrated under the pressure of the tensions between these two competing alignments and the attacks on the mainstream leadership (and its financial backers) from the right wing and the Army."[126]

According to Arthur E. Tiedemann, Ikeda Seihin, a senior Mitsui executive, was involved in the effort in late 1933 to counter army dominance by reviving party cabinets. This effort was stimulated by the army's public demand for more arms at the expense of hungry farmers. "The idea grew that now was a time to force a return to party Cabinets by unifying the Seiyūkai and the Minseitō and launching an all-out attack on the military. A key role in this movement was played by the members of the *Banchō-kai*. . . . Since Baron Gō was commonly regarded as a Mitsui agent, it was thought that Ikeda [Seihin] was behind the movement. One member of the *Banchō-kai*,

Nakajima Kumakichi . . . took the lead in pushing the union of the parties. . . . On December 25, 1933, he actually reached the point of holding a meeting of leaders from both parties."[127] After mentioning the Teijin Company stock sale and the corruption charges that followed, Tiedemann goes on to state that the "aim of the procurators seems to have been to demonstrate the utter corruption of the business world and the political parties. . . . It completely discredited the parties and stopped in its tracks the movement to restore party Cabinets."[128]

According to Ōuchi Tsutomu, frustrated military officers were behind the attack on the Saitō Cabinet. Finance Minister Takahashi, supported by the premier, resisted rising military expenses. Moreover, the army was unhappy over Foreign Minister Hirota Kōki's attempt to slow down expansion into North China and his conciliatory approach to Great Britain. Furthermore, Army Minister Araki, who resigned in January 1934, was replaced by the more moderate General Hayashi Senjūrō. At that point, the army's Kōdōha (Imperial Way Faction) began working to destroy the cabinet. Among the groups opposing an enhanced army political role, notes Ōuchi, was the Banchōkai; Kawai, Nagano, Gō, and others urged the Seiyūkai and the Minseitō to cooperate in order to protect the Diet system. Even though these groups had some success (e.g., open attacks on the military in the Sixty-Fifth Diet), the major parties were too disunified to succeed; too many power-hungry individuals were willing to make deals with the forces of "fascism." Thus, during the same Diet session, the savage attacks on Nakajima and Hatoyama occurred. Behind these attacks, Ōuchi sees the Seiyūkai antimainstream leader Kuhara and farther back in the shadows the "great villain" Hiranuma Kiichirō. Hiranuma was angry, opines Ōuchi, because Saitō joined forces with Saionji and others to block his elevation to the Privy Council presidency. Therefore, Hiranuma cooperated with Kuhara.[129] Ōuchi states: "It has been said that Hiranuma instigated the attacks on Nakajima and Hatoyama. Furthermore, the coming Teijin Incident was a great play produced by Hiranuma, who was the prosecution boss."[130] In regard to Mutō Sanji's attack on the Banchōkai, Ōuchi writes: "The reason why Mutō decided to publish these articles is not necessarily clear." It is certain, though, he wanted to "impeach them with his pen," and perhaps the articles were meant to increase the paper's circulation.[131] These articles produced the Teijin Incident, "which was a political deal designed to knock out the cabinet. The main person behind this was Hiranuma who used Shiono Suehiko, a big shot in the prosecution and a member of the National Foundation Society (Kokuhonsha) [of which Hiranuma was president]. Using Shiono, Hiranuma fabricated this incident."[132] Ōuchi concludes that, with Kuhara's support, Hiranuma expected to gain the premiership.[133]

Eguchi Keiichi mostly follows Ōuchi's thesis that Hiranuma planned to cooperate with the military in order to reform the political system. Unlike Ōuchi, however, Eiguchi does not charge Hiranuma with manipulating Shiono to "fabricate" the Teijin affair. Instead, he sees rightist groups centered on Hiranuma using the growing scandal as a weapon against the Saitō Cabinet.[134]

Ichihara Ryōhei summarizes the Teijin affair this way. In late 1933, the *zaibatsu*, acting through Nakajima and the Banchōkai, tried to promote interparty cooperation. As the Banchōkai became active in the party unification effort, it attracted the attention of the anti-*zaibatsu* "fascist" forces. The civilian bureaucratic fascists were under Hiranuma's influence, and the military fascists were clustered around General Araki.[135] "Under the conditions of the time," writes Ichihara, "it was clear that if one stone was thrown, it would cause ten thousand waves. The stone thrown was the January 1934 article 'Exposing the Banchōkai' in Mutō Sanji's *Jiji shinpō*."[136] Procurators Kuroda and Biwada supplied the "fascist power" that turned the Banchōkai exposure affair into the Teijin Incident.[137] Behind them, concludes Ichihara, was "the influence of Hiranuma's ominous star."[138]

Nakamura Kikuo, in *Shōwa seiji shi* (A political history of Showa), views the Teijin scandal as "a plot to knock out the cabinet, which was planned within the judiciary (*shōhōbunai*)." Various anti–Saitō Cabinet forces "expanded the incident" until the "anti-Saitō forces prevailed."[139] Ōshima Kiyoshi, a biographer of Takahashi Korekiyo, sees the Suzuki mainstream Seiyūkai group, aided by procurators, as the driving force behind the Teijin affair. As the incident expanded, other anticabinet groups joined the attack.[140]

Political journalist Aritake Shūji sees Shiono Suehiko behind the Teijin Incident. He notes that procurator Kuroda was very knowledgeable about the stock market, because he had dealt in shares as a university student. In fact, says Aritake, Kuroda was dealing in Meitō shares at the time of the tax-dodging scandal. Moreover, Shiono, head of the Criminal Affairs Bureau, knew about these stock transactions and prodded Kuroda to prosecute the Banchōkai members. Unfortunately, Aritake's source for this "fact" was a rumor. Aritake also cites the postwar memoir of Fujinuma Shōhei, former head of the Tokyo police, who writes that Shiono, who knew about Kuroda's stock transactions, used this knowledge about

Kuroda's less than ethical activity (i.e., trading in the shares of the company he was investigating) to push Kuroda into investigating the Teijin stock transaction. This manipulation of Kuroda's weak point, says Fujinuma, was no secret among well-informed people. The former chief even claims that procurator Kuroda mentioned this fact to Teijin case defendant Nagasaki Eizō.[141] Aritake also points out that Fujinuma saw Shiono's and Kuroda's actions as part of a plot to install Hiranuma as premier.[142]

Another biographer of Finance Minister Takahashi Korekiyo sees the Teijin affair arising from a plot by reform elements eager to knock out the Saitō Cabinet. Procurators, who dominated the Justice Ministry, "became the advance party in the attack."[143] Mitsuchi, one of the two indicted state ministers, stated in open court that the indictment was caused by the political maneuvering of "a couple of low-ranking procurators."[144] Nakajima, the other state minister defendant, says in his memoir that the Ashikaga article exposé was promoted by the military.[145] As for the Teijin Incident, he writes that "it was clearly a new political plot by the procurators who aimed at knocking down the Saitō Cabinet."[146]

Christopher Szpilman writes that the cabinet, from its formation, was under attack by National Foundation Society members and other people who wanted a Hiranuma Cabinet. "Hiranuma and the Kokuhonsha unleashed a vilification campaign against a [*sic*] cabinet. They, along with the media, suspected Saionji's ploy to perpetuate some form of party politics under the guise of Saitō's transcendental 'national unity' cabinet."[147] Kokuhonsha members helped uncover the scandals that plagued the Saitō government. "In January 1934, Tokyo Chief District Procurator, Iwamura Michiyo [in fact, Iwamura was in Nagoya until early April] (a Kokuhonsha member) directed the district procurators to investigate transactions in the stock of Teijin." In the Diet, Szpilman notes, the attack was directed at Nakajima, who was trying along with Machida to organize a coalition to resist the military, and at Hatoyama. Szpilman continues with the arrest of Finance Ministry officials who "disclosed alleged financial transgressions by Education Minister Hatoyama Ichirō [he confuses Hatoyama with either Nakajima or Mitsuchi]." In conclusion, he writes: "Kokuhonsha officials and Kokuhonsha publications played a major role in forcing Admiral Saitō's resignation, but they did not accomplish their main political goal."[148]

To summarize these views, first, several groups in the political elite were eager to seize the premiership. Second, people within these groups were willing to make deals to achieve power, which resulted in some odd combinations. Third, Baron Hiranuma was supported by a small army of admirers who viewed him as a perfect leader for a troubled time. Fourth, some people regarded Hiranuma as an evil political influence, guiding the nation down the path to "fascism." Fifth, the military combined with Hiranuma to destroy Saitō's government. In these accounts procurators receive pride of place, with good reason, because they investigated, indicted, and prosecuted the Teijin trial defendants. What does this add up to? About the only thing that was abnormal in this swirling current of political intrigue was the determination of some army officers, together with "new bureaucrat" allies, to seize the cabinet. Attacks on Nakajima and Hatoyama, and even the savaging of the Banchōkai, fell within the boundaries of normal political practice. During an era of so-called party government (1918–1932), it was normal for politicians and their supporters to engage in an orgy of mutual vilification, with opposition politicians using nearly any tactic to discredit cabinet officers. Hence, there was nothing odd about the attacks on Nakajima and Hatoyama. The attack on the Banchōkai by Mutō Sanji, however, was somewhat different. Mutō was a genuine business and political muckraker. He was not manipulated by outside forces, except to the extent that a hot topic increased *Jiji shinpō* sales, because Mutō stubbornly pursued his own goals. Ōuchi Tsutomu states that the origins of Mutō's actions are "unclear." Actually, they are very clear, in light of his career before taking over the *Jiji*. It is the actions of Procurator Kuroda Etsurō that are open to various interpretations, but even in his case some clarification is possible. Supposedly, Kuroda acted as part of a plot hatched by Hiranuma supporters. This fact cannot be documented. Even Ōuchi, eager to impale Hiranuma with his pen, can do no better than to write, "It is said that Hiranuma. . . ." Journalist Aritake's similar view also rests on rumors and a strange tale of professional blackmail told by Procurator Kuroda to defendant Nagasaki, who mentioned it to someone else. It is unclear in Fujinuma's memoirs whether he was the "someone else" or whether he heard the story from subordinates. There are accounts of Kuroda by defendants he interrogated, which appear in newspapers, open trial statements, and memoirs. The multiple accounts, which reinforce each other, have a ring of truth. Kuroda is pictured as a zealous reformer, angry at corrupt businessmen and politicians, eager to clean out the sewers. Given the sensational corruption cases that passed through the Tokyo office during the late 1920s and early 1930s, it is hardly surprising that Kuroda had contempt for these lawbreakers, which expanded to include finance officials during the Meitō investigation. Doubtless, he was also contemptuous of senior Justice Ministry officials' willingness to compromise. Those who criticize Kuroda and his colleagues find fault with the manner in which the interrogations were carried out and the alleged fabrication of evidence. Moreover, they see a political purpose behind Kuroda's action: the overthrow of the Saitō Cabinet. The Teijin Incident, however, is better understood by disconnecting Kuroda's actions from a grand conspiracy concept centered on Hiranuma. Put briefly, Kuroda was publicly humiliated by officials in the Finance Ministry during the Meitō tax affair. Tokyo procurators, alerted to the Teijin Company stock sale by newspaper comments and Diet speeches, were stimulated by three complaints to investigate. Kuroda, as the resident financial expert, was the key investigator. One can imagine him nodding, saying, "Well, well!!!" as he was presented this opportunity to revisit his Finance Ministry "friends." Perhaps Shiono whispered in his ear, but, in fact, a whisper was not necessary. As Kuroda began this investigation, he probably saw it as just another in a series of similar cases; the only difference was the possible involvement of highly placed Finance Ministry officials. Imamura Rikisaburō, a veteran political trials lawyer during the Meiji, Taisho, and Showa eras, who was also the senior lawyer at the Teijin trial, wrote that "ever since the Meitō Incident, the Tokyo procurators had an arrow in their bowstring aimed at the Finance Ministry."[149] The Tejin case presented an opportunity to release the arrow. It is doubtful, therefore, that Kuroda began this investigation intent on overthrowing the cabinet or elevating Hiranuma to the premiership. Since he died in July 1934, he did not live to see how others would use this case in the political arena. The alleged fabrication of evidence, which will be discussed later, is best explained by Kuroda's intense desire to implicate despised Finance Ministry officials and to punish crooked businessmen and politicians. As the interrogations continued, however, Kuroda and his colleagues realized that the investigation could produce a political explosion. At the end of December 1934, after the March press ban was raised, newspapers printed procurator-supplied details about the investigation. One account says that, on his return to Tokyo from Osaka (April 16), Biwada reported to Chief Procurator Iwamura. The next day all procurators involved in the investigation met, and "it was seen that the case held the possibility of critical political development."[150]

In sum, various individuals and groups pushed Tokyo procurators to investigate the Teijin stock sale. Procurator Kuroda used this investigation to pursue his goal of clean government and, in his overzealousness, broke regulations and laws. Colleagues were caught up in this effort as well. Finally, Justice Minister Koyama's report to Premier Saitō caused the cabinet to fall. It is a mistake to view the actions of Tokyo procurators and Justice Minister Koyama as part of a grand conspiracy aimed at destroying the cabinet, because Kuroda had no need to become a conspirator to act as he did.

CHAPTER 4

Preparation for the Trial

NEITHER KURODA'S DEATH NOR a cabinet change stopped Tokyo procurators' preparations for preliminary court hearings. Former minister Nakajima was interrogated by procurators after the Saitō Cabinet fell and was indicted; former minister Mitsuchi was questioned in August but not indicted until September. As suspects were arrested, between April 28 and September 13, 1934, procurators indicted them for various crimes. In brief, procurators decided that Teijin stock shares were sold at below fair market price, so the sellers were charged with misfeasance. Finance Ministry personnel and Nakajima, who were connected with the sale, were charged with bribery; Mitsuchi was accused of perjury. Out of seventeen suspects twelve confessed to various crimes during the course of the investigation; one was dropped (Takanashi Hiroji, a bank inspector with the Kawasaki Daihyaku Bank) during the preliminary court hearing. Mitsuchi and three Finance Ministry officials (Ōno, Aida, and Shidomoto) denied guilt throughout the investigation.[1]

The main charge against former government officials was bribery. Vice-Minister Kuroda, in his "petition" to Chief Procurator Iwamura, confessed to receiving 400 Teijin stock shares. Ōkubo Teiji, who was named in Takagi's confession, was accused of receiving 100 shares from Okazaki Akira, his brother-in-law, who was a Bank of Taiwan director. After his arrest on May 21, Ōkubo denied receiving shares, but on May 23 he confessed to receiving 100 shares. Later he repudiated the confession.[2] Ōno was charged with accepting ¥7,000, at the Finance Ministry, from Bank of Taiwan president Shimada. Shimada confessed this act; Ōno denied it. Aida was accused of receiving ¥5,000 from Takagi at the Bank of Taiwan Tokyo branch office. This he denied. Shidomoto, who denied the charge, was accused of accepting ¥2,000 from Shimada. Procurators said that Nakajima received 200 shares on June 26, 1933, from Shimada and

Takagi, at his official office. Before the preliminary court Nakajima confessed to receiving stock shares, but he repudiated this confession at the
open trial. Also charged with receiving a ¥10,000 bribe from Nagano,
Nakajima confessed at the preliminary court, but at the trial he insisted
that the money was a political contribution. Mitsuchi was charged with
perjury after he refused to cooperate with procurators as a witness against
Nakajima. Throughout the investigation and trials, Mitsuchi steadfastly
insisted that he did not get 300 shares from Takagi; he did not receive 200
shares from Nakajima to convert to cash; he did not give money to
Nakajima. Unfortunately for Mitsuchi, Takagi, at the preliminary court,
said repeatedly that he gave the shares to Mitsuchi at the railway minister's
official office. Shimada's and Yanagida's testimony supported Takagi's.[3]

The Problem of Mitsuchi

Mitsuchi Chūzō, the last of the defendants indicted, presented a special
problem for procurators and justice administrators. First, he was a venerable politician. Second, his patron was Finance Minister Takahashi.
Mitsuchi was linked with Takahashi in a mutually dependent relationship,
in which Takahashi assumed the status of parent (*oyabun*) and Mitsuchi, the
status of child (*kobun*). Although their kinship was ritual in nature, they
appear to have regarded it more as a blood tie. Indeed, Takahashi's biographer says that, when the finance minister heard that Mitsuchi was under
investigation, he decided to resign from the cabinet, because Mitsuchi was
a very close supporter.[4] As for Mitsuchi, writing in 1937, after Takahashi's
assassination in the army mutiny of February 26, 1936, he recalled that, for
over twenty years in both public and private life, they had a very close relationship.[5] Mitsuchi, then, benefited from the protection of a former prime
minister (the Takahashi Cabinet, November 1921–June 1922), former
finance minister (many times), and former viscount (renounced title in
1924). Takahashi became finance minister again in November 1934.
Moreover, Mitsuchi, too, had held many important posts: chief cabinet
secretary (with Premier Takahashi), finance minister (Tanaka Cabinet,
April 1927–July 1929), communications minister (Inukai Cabinet,
December 1931–May 1932). Thus, before becoming railway minister,
Mitsuchi's career was distinguished. Topping off this imposing background, Mitsuchi, who already held high imperial decorations (he was list-
ed in the First Order of Merit class), was scheduled to receive the Grand
Cordon of the Rising Sun in April 1934.[6] Because of this impressive vita,

Mitsuchi was probably the best known among the defendants and was a focus of press and public speculation. According to the Osaka *Mainichi*, Mitsuchi criticized procuratorial officials for leaking embarrassing information that implicated him in the expanding Teijin scandal. These leaks, noted Mitsuchi, emanated from the top procuratorial ranks. Declaring that he was not involved in the scandal, he challenged procurators to substantiate these leaks.[7]

Procurators wanted to use Mitsuchi as a witness against Baron Nakajima, who first talked "voluntarily" with procurators in early July and then met with them during the next several weeks. The *Asahi* reported that the interrogation of July 21 by Chief Procurator Biwada was lengthy and severe. That evening, Baron Nakajima was sent to Ichigaya Prison. During Biwada's interrogation, another procurator and a judge searched the baron's Tokyo home; other procurators visited his Hayama beachside retreat.[8] About a week later, a newspaper reported that, after Premier Okada returned from Ise Grand Shrine, Nakajima would be indicted. The article concluded that another former minister (i.e., Mitsuchi) would probably be interrogated.[9] Since the baron held a Second Order of Merit (one grade below Mitsuchi's) and was a peer, justice officials had to notify the Board of Chamberlains at the imperial palace. Once the palace suspended Nakajima's peerage status, the legal case could proceed. The press reported as certain fact that Nakajima received ¥10,000 in cash and three hundred stock shares.[10]

Mitsuchi appeared "voluntarily" at the Tokyo District Court on August 21. Examined first by Chief Procurator Iwamura, he was next interrogated by Biwada.[11] "It is alleged," wrote a journalist, "that he is deeply involved in the scandal. . . . During his examination he is said to have been confronted with Baron Nakajima and other accused now in prison. Mr. Mitsuchi is said to have stubbornly denied all charges imputed to him." The article concluded: "According to one report, although he was rewarded handsomely for his efforts in facilitating certain transactions, his action does not constitute a legal crime, as he was then Railway Minister and there was no question of his abuse of his official post."[12] At the Tokyo District Court on August 29, according to the press, Mitsuchi faced preliminary judge Morozumi Seiichi. "He was subjected to a strict examination and confronted with two men now in prison. . . . In view of the fact that Mr. Mitsuchi has made false statements right from the beginning thereby complicating the examination, the judicial authorities' attitude seems to have become strong, and his arrest is deemed to be likely."[13] The press, again, assumed Mitsuchi's guilt.

Mitsuchi appeared before the preliminary court on August 21, 28, and 29; he refused to admit guilt.[14] During September he was called before procurators again but refused to alter his statement. Procurators said, according to journalists, there would be no criminal charge if he would confess to receiving money and aiding Nakajima. Mitsuchi, however, refused to make his statement dovetail neatly with confessions obtained painstakingly by procurators.[15] Therefore, exasperated procurators indicted him on September 13 for perjury. Several factors should be considered. Procurators usually had overwhelming evidence before issuing an indictment. Confession was considered the queen of evidence, although under the Meiji codes it was illegal to force one. Nevertheless, police and procurators were obsessed with obtaining confessions, and, when they were certain of guilt, they were very intolerant of recalcitrant suspects. Therefore, Mitsuchi's stubborn refusal to bend to procurators' pressure would have angered them more than a little, especially since they had removed the threat of a bribery charge. Also, the press, supplied with information by justice officials, assumed Mitsuchi's guilt.

A movement to save Mitsuchi arose within the Admiral Okada Cabinet. This movement is especially interesting, because the new cabinet was identified publicly as anti–political party and pro–new bureaucrats.[16] Gotō Fumio, a leading figure among the new bureaucrats, played a key role in the formation of the cabinet and was rewarded with the post of home minister, a post equated with that of deputy premier.[17] By the time all cabinet posts were filled, however, three senior Seiyūkai politicians held ministerships. Moreover, in late November, the indispensable Takahashi, former Seiyūkai president, was recalled to the post of finance minister.[18]

The origin of the movement to save Mitsuchi is unclear. On the one hand, three of Mitsuchi's Seiyūkai colleagues were ministers, and his patron Takahashi joined them in the Okada Cabinet four months later. On the other hand, it could have been Premier Okada's idea, because he was navy minister in the Tanaka Cabinet when Mitsuchi was finance minister (Takahashi, April–June 1927, and Mitsuchi, June 1927–July 1929, served in this post). Also, Okada was the first of two navy ministers in the former Saitō Cabinet. Since finance and navy ministers were normally part of the inner cabinet of all cabinets, these men had an opportunity to create personal bonds. At any rate, the new prime minister talked with the new justice minister (Ohara was promoted from vice-minister) about saving Mitsuchi the embarrassment of being stripped of his court honors and being formally indicted. Could not something be done, Okada asked, besides a normal prosecution? Please consider this possibility, said Okada.

Ohara understood that Okada was thinking along the lines of a "suspension of indictment." One scholar states that Ohara asked Kimura Naotatsu, head of the Criminal Affairs Bureau, to examine thoroughly the Mitsuchi case documents, but, after reading Kimura's report, Ohara concluded that the indictment had to go forward.[19] Year later, Ohara reflected: "Thinking back on the handling of Mr. Mitsuchi, I wonder if there was not a better way to handle that matter."[20]

A procurator in any criminal case (including a case in which there was no doubt that a crime was committed) had the authority to indict or not indict. No justice minister had authority to command a procurator directly, but a minister could go through the procurator general to issue an order. When this was done it caused people to complain, but it could be done. Moreover, there was a precedent for saving the face of a powerful state minister, and it had occurred less than twenty years earlier. The suspension of indictment solution was used to soften the humiliation of Home Minister Ōura Kanetake in 1915. Ōura was guilty of widespread bribery and election regulation violations. Justice Minister Ozaki Yukio, with Prime Minister Ōkuma Shigenobu's blessing, worked out a suspension of indictment deal with Procurator General Hiranuma Kiichirō and Justice Vice-Minister Suzuki Kisaburō. In return for the suspension of indictment, Ōura withdrew from public life.[21] This was not "justice" but a reasonable political solution for a very difficult problem. It is certain that Ohara remembered this case well. Ohara was justice minister at a time when the procurator general (Hayashi Raisaburō) might have been willing to stop the Mitsuchi prosecution. Ohara and Hayashi were not part of the Hiranuma clique, which was rumored to be behind the Teijin Incident prosecution. Ohara, however, did not interfere. Perhaps he did not relish a fight with elite Tokyo procurators and their supporters.

Procedures for Arrest and Preliminary Trial

Procurators responded to a formal written complaint. Once a complaint was received at the court having jurisdiction, procurators began an investigation. The need for an official complaint is illustrated in the Meiji Sugar Refining Company affair. Procurator Kuroda, who was unable to pressure Finance Ministry officials into issuing a complaint, was unable to prosecute.

Police were obligated to aid procurators in an investigation. From early in the Meiji era, police were divided into regular police (their duty was to prevent crime) and justice police (their duty was to investigate suspected crime and obtain evidence). Both these police units belonged to the same organization (in Tokyo they were under control of the Metropolitan Police Board). During the course of an investigation, however, justice police were subordinate legally to procurators. Nonetheless, they were not in the Justice Ministry, an arrangement that sometimes led to split allegiances.[22] Procurator Kuroda's cold reception at Tokyo police headquarters mirrors this tension (see Chapter 3).

According to the law, arresting officers were to carry warrants signed by a judge, but it appears that in numerous cases, except when accompanied by procurators or judges, police skipped this formality.[23] During interrogation, police strove to obtain a confession. Based on interrogation, police drafted two documents: a Written Report of a Criminal Investigation and a set of Police Notes. Police paperwork went to the procurators, who could, at their discretion, either prosecute or drop the case in question. If prosecution was chosen, the procurators cited the laws violated and got a preliminary judge's order to detain the suspect for interrogation. Some of this formal procedure could be skipped, at least temporarily, if a suspect "voluntarily" talked with procurators. For example, one newspaper reported in early July 1934 that Baron Nakajima "voluntarily presented himself at the Procurator's Office on Friday afternoon, and upon meeting Chief Procurator Biwada, explained in detail about certain letters exchanged with Matsutaro Masariki and others."[24] After interrogation of a suspect, procurators produced another Written Report of a Criminal Investigation. Like police, procurators were intent on securing a confession. Furthermore, it appears that it was not uncommon for procurators, once they felt they had determined the "truth," to insist that a suspect agree to their version in the report. Recalcitrant suspects could expect many long sessions with procurators; if irritated by an uncooperative attitude, procurators might send a suspect back for another session with the police, who, outside of procurators' view, might "encourage" a suspect to sign a confession. A suspect was not indicted until the end of the procurators' examination. Since there was no habeas corpus procedure and since suspects were not permitted lawyers until after indictment, they were at the mercy of jail guards and procurators. Once procurators were satisfied, their report, which contained basic statements of fact and a statement by the suspect, was sent to a preliminary judge. This judge, who decided if a law was violated, played a role similar to that of a grand jury investigation in the United States. This part of a criminal investigation could be lengthy "if the accused is obdurate in maintaining his innocence of the offense charged, since it is the object of the state, represented by the procurator,

to obtain a confession before the case is tried."[25] At this stage of the investigation, procurators and preliminary judges usually worked together as a
team. For example, a procurator and a judge searched Nakajima's Tokyo
residence, seeking documentary evidence.[26] Mitsuchi, who resisted accepting the procurators' version of the "truth," was called before the procurators and the preliminary court several times.[27] Hence, long interrogations
were not unusual. Nabeyama Sadachika's examination by a preliminary
judge determined to uncover facts, in the 1929 case of a suspected communist, for example, stretched out to forty-three sessions.[28] In this sense,
then, the Teijin case investigation was not exceptional. Takagi's chief
lawyer, Suzuki Yoshio, wrote that the defendants spent between one hundred and just over two hundred days in detention.[29] Kawai Yoshinari stated that Takagi, who cooperated with procurators, spent 207 days in
detention and was hospitalized for an ulcer.[30] Criminal suspects reacted dif-
ferently. Some of the Teijin affair suspects complained of ill-treatment at
the hands of procurators and miserable living conditions. In contrast, Vice-
Minister Satake Sango, who was suspected of bribery in the sale of a private railway to the government and who was released from detention at
Ichigaya Prison in February 1930, said that during his seventy-eight days
in custody he was delighted to be called from the cold cell for an examination by procurators.[31]

After preliminary judges (usually, a three-judge bench) mastered the
facts of a case, they could release a suspect or send him or her to an open
trial. Two documents were produced during the preliminary trial: the
Preliminary Examination Record (the minutes of the proceedings) and the
Final Written Decision of a Preliminary Examination. The first document
was the only legal proof at the trial. The final written decision of a preliminary examination (*Yoshin shūketsu kettei*, hereafter *Yoshin*) contained the
facts of the case, the reason for the crime, and the laws violated.[32]

The Law

Basically, this trial was about the price of stock shares, which, according to
procurators, were sold at below their proper market value. Moreover,
according to the prosecution, officers of the Bank of Taiwan, who engaged
in this illegal transaction, accepted and gave bribes; Finance Ministry officials were charged with accepting bribes. Therefore politicians, businessmen, and Finance Ministry officials were indicted for misfeasance, bribery,
and perjury. Preliminary Judge Morozumi listed the following violations

of the penal code: misfeasance (Art. 247), offering a bribe to a public official (Art. 198), a public official receiving a bribe (Art. 197), perjury (Art. 169), concurrent crimes (Art. 45), consecutive crimes (Art. 55), complicity (Art. 60), and being an accomplice (Arts. 62 and 65). Kawai was charged with the single crime of misfeasance and Mitsuchi, with perjury. Those accused of receiving a bribe were Nakajima, Kuroda, Ōkubo, Ōno, Aida, and Shidomoto. Charged with misfeasance and giving bribes were Shimada, Yanagida, Koshifuji, Takagi, Okazaki, Nagano, Nagasaki, and Kobayashi.³³ *Hainin* (misfeasance or breach of trust) was covered in Penal Code Article 247: "Every person who in managing a business for another person has, with intent to promote his (her) own interest or that of a third person or to cause damage to his (her) principal, performed an act in violation of his duties and caused pecuniary damage to the principal shall be punished with penal servitude not exceeding five years or fined not more than Yen 1000."³⁴ One Supreme Court decision opined that "when a person managing a business for another person has performed an act contrary to his duties and caused damage to his principal, his act is not criminal if done with an intention of promoting the principal's interest." Another stated that when a manager running "a business for another person does an act contrary to his duties and with knowledge that he is thereby promoting his own interests at his principal's expense, he is guilty of breach of trust if the foreseeable damage to his principal has resulted."³⁵ A third noted: "Knowledge of pecuniary damage essential to a criminal breach of trust need not be definite. It suffices if it is foreseen that damage is likely to arise."³⁶ According to a legal dictionary, the core concept of Article 247 is an illegal action by a manager that turns him (or her) a profit and simultaneously damages the interest of those whose property he manages.³⁷ Thus, the task of Tokyo procurators was to convince a three-judge panel that the Bank of Taiwan directors and others conspired to enrich themselves at the expense of the bank by selling the Teijin shares at below the proper market price. As one newspaper neatly put it in July 1935: "The crux of the case centers on the possibility of predicting a price rise of Teijin shares on the eve of the sale."³⁸

Bribery (*zōshūwai*) was covered in Articles 197 and 198 of the Penal Code. According to the former article, every public official "who in connection with his duty has received, demanded or agreed to receive a bribe shall be punished with penal servitude not exceeding three years. If in consequence thereof he has committed an improper act or has failed to perform a required act, he shall be punished with penal servitude for not less than one year nor more than ten years."³⁹ The latter article stated in part:

"Every person who has given, offered, or agreed to give a bribe to a public official or arbitrator shall be punished with penal servitude not exceeding three years or fined more than Yen 300."[40] Because the Bank of Taiwan was a semigovernmental organization, its officers were under the jurisdiction of these articles.

Perjury (*gishō*) was covered by Article 169 of the Penal Code: "Every witness who has been legally sworn and has given false testimony shall be punished with penal servitude not less than three months nor more than ten years."[41] One Supreme Court decision illustrates the legal quicksand surrounding this article: "It is not essential for the formation of the crime of perjury that testimony be untrue. A witness is guilty of perjury if he deliberately gives testimony contrary to his memory even though his testimony may be in accord with the truth or at any rate it cannot be proven to be untrue."[42] Ironically, the one defendant charged with violation of Article 169 was not charged with lying about details of the Teijin stock deal but with refusing to cooperate with procurators; Mitsuchi told them he had no knowledge of the particular aspect of the deal about which they insisted he provide information.

Articles 194 and 195 of the Penal Code played an unexpected and prominent role in the Teijin trial. Unexpectedly, as viewed from the procurators' side of the courtroom, these articles quickly became a central issue. Indeed, more than in any pre-1945 case, this trial focused public attention on violations of suspects' procedural rights, which the press and defendants' supporters described as "personal rights" (*jinken*). Article 194 stated: "Every person exercising or assisting in judicial, prosecuting, or police functions who in abuse of his power has arrested or imprisoned a person shall be punished with penal servitude or imprisonment for not less than six months nor more than seven years." Article 195 said: "Every person exercising or assisting in judicial, prosecuting, or police functions who in the performance of his duties has committed an act of violence or cruelty against a criminally accused or other person shall be punished with penal servitude or imprisonment not exceeding three years."[43] Ironically, these articles were in chapter 25 of the Penal Code under the title of "Crimes of Official Corruption" (*Tokushoku no tsumi*) next to the articles covering bribery. If most lay people would have been unaware of this juxtaposition, the procurators certainly were not! Besides the above Penal Code provisions, Article 254 of the Criminal Procedure Code was cited during the trial by lawyers who claimed that procurators violated suspects' procedural rights. Procurators also cited this article to justify their actions. Article 254 permitted any "necessary interrogation for an investigation" but prohibited the application of coercion.[44]

Finally, the crime of bribery deserves special mention. It was difficult to prove bribery, because prosecutors had to prove that the official accepted money, that the official was in a position to do a favor for the briber, and that the recipient of the bribe understood that it was a bribe. Then, there was the cultural norm of gift giving, in which the hairline boundary between an illegal bribe and acceptable etiquette was often unclear. Especially in the case of politicians, whose world demanded continual reciprocity, the boundary between legal and illegal was blurred. If challenged by a procurator, a politician could say that the "gift" was merely an election fund contribution.[45]

Lawyers

Given the politically and financially distinguished men among the sixteen suspects, it is not surprising that they were defended by outstanding lawyers, and, given the serious nature of the criminal charges, it is not surprising that the number of lawyers exceeded fifty. One authoritative source puts the grand total of defense lawyers, during the trial, at fifty-three (this total does not include lawyers who acted as special defenders at one stage or another of the trial; Baron Hozumi Shigetō is the outstanding example in this category).[46]

Each of the sixteen suspects was defended by more than one lawyer. For example Nagano was supported by twelve, Nagasaki by ten, and Kawai by nine. Aida and Shidomoto, however, retained two apiece. As for the lawyers, thirty-two focused on a single client, with the balance defending more than one client. If one judges professional reputation based on the number of clients, then Shimizu Iku and Nagano Teruo were ranked highly by defendants, because each defended seven. The famous lawyer Imamura Rikisaburō, who acted as a kind of field marshal for the defense team, handled six clients. Interestingly, five of his clients were former employees of the Bank of Taiwan.[47] The effort made to save Finance Ministry officers is indicative of the legal and moral support high-class defendants received. Mentioned earlier was Aoki Kazuo's rallying of ministry colleagues, as he proclaimed the charges against his colleagues false. "This clearly was an improper arrest. Therefore, absolutely, we will fight through."[48] Aoki created a support committee for his colleagues, which kept in close contact with defense lawyers. The creation of Ōkubo Teiji's defense team is an example of the importance of personal networks and the special aid given to high-class defendants. Ōkubo was represented by six lawyers, including the famous Uzawa Sōmei. More important, however, Ōkubo was a classmate (1908, School of Law, Tokyo Imperial University) of Baron Hozumi Shigetō. This distinguished professor of law took Ōkubo's case not only because of old boy ties but because 268 people wrote strong support letters in which they insisted that Ōkubo could never have accepted a bribe. These letters, which were printed, persuaded Hozumi to become a special defender.[49] Baron Hozumi was the son of Hozumi Nobushige and the nephew of Hozumi Yatsuka, both famous legalists at Tokyo Imperial University. Indeed, it would have been difficult to locate even a moderately educated person who had not heard of the three Hozumi! Because of their status as scholars with high rank, the two brothers married the eldest daughters of the two most prominent families in the Meiji business world (Shibusawa Eiichi and Asano Sōichirō).[50]

Ōno Ryūta benefited not only from Finance Ministry support but also because of his marriage to former justice minister Hara Yoshimichi's daughter. Hara was a famous attorney long before becoming a minister. Two of Ōno's lawyers were members of Hara's original law firm: Arima Chūzaburō and Gujō Korekazu. In fact, when Hara became minister, Arima began to manage the firm, using Hara's desk.[51] Arima represented only Ōno; Gujō also defended Aida, who was Ōno's ministry colleague.

Personal and political ties are clear in two of the four clients defended by politician and lawyer Nagawa Kanichi (he defended former ministers Mitsuchi and Kuroda and businessmen Nagano and Nagasaki).[52] Nagawa, who as a young judicial official caught the eye of Suzuki Kisaburō, departed the Justice Ministry, became a lawyer, and entered the Seiyūkai. When Suzuki became home minister (Tanaka Cabinet), Nagawa became a parliamentary councilor. After the Seiyūkai gained power during the Inukai Cabinet, he again worked right under Suzuki as a judiciary councilor (after Inukai's murder on May 15, 1932, Suzuki became the party's president). During the Saitō Cabinet, Nagawa was parliamentary vice-minister in Mitsuchi's Railway Ministry. Mitsuchi was a powerful faction leader in Nagawa's party.[53] Former vice-minister Kuroda had close ties with the Seiyūkai and Mitsuchi.

Horie Senichirō stands out among Nagano's twelve lawyers because of his reason for accepting the case. Nagano was married to the daughter of a resident of Hiroshima, which was Horie's hometown. As a young man Horie received help from the daughter's father. Thus, Horie took this case to express gratitude to his benefactor. For three and one-half years he rejected all other cases in favor of intense work on Nagano's defense. Not only did Horie attend all the open trial sessions, but he refused to accept any payment, including expenses for trips to Osaka. After the trial, however, Nagano donated funds to Horie's Hiroshima school.[54] Since Nagano, too, came from Hiroshima, perhaps it was his old school as well.

At first glance, Imamura appears to be the defense team's linchpin, but a closer examination illustrates that Nagawa Kanichi probably deserves that designation. Nagawa, a Seiyūkai politician, former judge, and assistant to Mitsuchi, lost no opportunity to attack the procurators' view of the Teijin stock sale. In the Diet, at the preliminary court, and at the open trial, Nagawa denied that the crime of bribery had occurred. Nagawa's key role is recognized by scholars publishing the papers of attorney Imamura: "In general, inside and outside of court, Nagawa led the defending activities. Such a person's activities, in some ways, were more important than those of Imamura."[55]

Sixty-Sixth Diet

The sixty-sixth diet session opened on November 28, 1934. Cabinet officers, especially Justice Minister Ohara Naoshi, expected to be questioned about the treatment of distinguished Teijin scandal suspects. They were not disappointed. Ohara was interpellated by Dr. Iwata Chūzō, a professor of law and advisor to the Bank of Taiwan. On December 1, in the House of Peers, Iwata (Dōwakai) asked why prominent people were detained when there was no danger of flight. Was the long period of detention used to extract confessions? Why were some of the suspects kept manacled for days at a time? Why were some kept in half-mat (about three feet by three feet) waiting rooms all day without being interrogated? Suspects who were manacled, pointed out Iwata, were defenseless against attacks by swarms of mosquitoes. This kind of treatment was a violation of personal rights. Furthermore, Iwata found it strange that distinguished financial officials were indicted months before anyone was charged with bribery. Finally, why was Baron Nakajima permitted to meet Mr. Mitsuchi? Ohara replied that it was not unusual for bribees to be indicted before bribers; no one was detained in order to force a confession; manacles were used for some suspects who appeared suicidal. Suspects were kept all day in waiting rooms, he agreed, but this was not done to pressure confessions; it happened because procurators were busy with other interrogations. Nakajima's meeting with Mitsuchi, Ohara emphasized, occurred together with Chief Procurator Iwamura and was held with Preliminary Judge Morozumi's permission. Iwata challenged Ohara's explanations. Lawyers who met Procurator General Hayashi Raisaburō, Iwata noted, were assured that authorities did not regard any suspect as suicidal. As for Nakajima, it was a violation of investigative procedure for him to meet an outsider, even with the preliminary judge's permission.[56] Moreover, if the prosecution "took the truth of Baron Nakashima's evidence for granted, Mr. Mitsuchi's summons as a witness was meaningless. The step may easily be interpreted as a deliberate attempt to indict Mr. Mitsuchi on a charge of giving false evidence. On the other hand, if the accused and the witness were brought together for the express purpose of securing agreed evidence, it would be difficult to trust the results of the examination."[57]

Newspaper reports may have undermined public trust in the Justice Ministry's handling of the case. For example, the Tokyo *Jiji* opined:

> The present scandal is quite unprecedented in that it includes among the accused many distinguished men in political and financial circles. If they really committed the crimes . . . the sordid transactions of which they were capable are simply astounding. . . . It is, of course, hasty to assume their guilt pending their public trial. . . . Rumour was set afoot the other day that some accused were subjected to virtual torture and that they were forced to make groundless "confessions" under physical pain. . . . Although the Minister of Justice categorically denied the accusation, the public is still in doubt as to what to believe. . . . [Since] the preliminary examination gave rise to charges of infringement of personal rights to the detriment of the prestige of the judiciary, it is sincerely to be hoped that public hearings will be quickly held in order to dispel all public misgivings. . . . As the details of the case have long been kept secret, many harmful rumours have been set afoot. . . . It was even rumoured that political plotting was at the bottom of the whole business.[58]

The Osaka *Jiji* printed a rumor that the preliminary judges saw flaws in the procurators' case but, suspicious of some defendants' actions, decided to recommend a public trial. Procurator General Hayashi, however, refuted this rumor. This paper also reported a growing estrangement between Finance and Justice Ministry officials. Finance officials, who were establishing a support committee for defendants, were confident that their colleagues were innocent, noted the newspaper. On December 28, 1934, Aoki Kazuo, director of the Financial Bureau, who investigated the Teijin stock sale, reported that the charges were groundless. Vice-Minister Tsushima Jūichi supported his view. Justice officials, said the paper, resented their attitude strongly and were contemplating a new bill that would subject such statements to contempt of court charges.[59]

Procurators lifted the March 25 Teijin case press ban on December 27, 1934. Perhaps, in the face of mounting Diet and press criticism, procurators deemed it wise to circulate their version of the case.[60] They might also have been responding to a *Yomiuri Newspaper* charge of overly rigorous news suppression.[61] The *Japan Weekly Chronicle*'s account of the Teijin scandal, like other newspaper accounts, was based on Judge Morozumi's preliminary examination report, leaks to the press by government officials, comments made by defendants and their supporters, and the views of the defendants' enemies. Not surprisingly, the *Chronicle* echoed the official viewpoint presented in the *Yoshin*. The reason for this bias is understandable, because most journalists took for granted that procurators and judges, in a case involving such important people, would neither fabricate evidence nor make major errors.

The *Chronicle* headlined the article "Full Story of the Scandal . . . Over ¥300,000 in Bribes," followed by the names of former ministers. After naming bribers, the paper supplied information on the Suzuki Trading Company, the Bank of Taiwan, the Teijin Company, and the stock sale. Spotlighting the role of high officials who used their influence with Finance Ministry and Bank of Japan personnel, the article claimed that this unsavory deal resulted in a loss of ¥1,600,000. This was an illegal sale, claimed the editor, because bribery was employed to lubricate the transaction. The article concluded with details about Mitsuchi's involvement in the transaction, searches of the homes and offices by the authorities, and information on the Banchōkai. There is little in this article with which procurators would have disagreed; indeed, although the newspaper used the term "accused," the article was written in such a manner as to leave readers with one conclusion: the sixteen suspects had committed the crimes charged in the *Yoshin*.[62]

One newspaper opined that at the Diet Justice Minister Ohara would be bombarded with questions about infringement of personal rights. At the Cabinet Council meeting on January 8, the article noted, several ministers asked Ohara about the treatment of Teijin suspects. Ohara replied that suspects were treated properly. Suspect Kuroda, he noted, had even written a letter to thank authorities for the manner in which he was examined.[63] On the eve of the Diet opening, one newspaper predicted a hostile session, with interpellators charging procurators with violations of personal rights. Many Seiyūkai members believe that the defendants are innocent, concluded the paper, because of the prosecution's weak evidence on the sources of the shares and the money.[64]

In the lower house on January 22, Ohara replied to Shimada Toshio's (Seiyūkai) questions about the violations of personal rights by declaring that an investigation of misconduct by procurators was unwarranted.[65] The following day, Dr. Minobe Tatsukichi, a famous legal scholar (emeritus of Tokyo Imperial University), questioned Ohara about violations of personal rights. Article 194 of the Penal Code, Minobe noted, made it a crime to mistreat criminal suspects or to force confessions. In the past, Minobe said, he had heard rumors about mistreatment of suspects, but he had been inclined to discredit them. After hearing Iwata Chūzō speak late in 1934, however, and after hearing other things as well, Minobe had concluded that, if only half these things were true, the prestige of the Justice Ministry would be damaged. Did procurators abuse their authority when they arrested and detained people? Did they use force or torture when they interrogated people? According to the memoir of Okazaki Akira, said Minobe, the suspect was summoned to the Osaka City police headquarters on April 11, 1934. The police called this a "voluntary" appearance. At the police station, Okazaki was kept with seven other inmates in a dirty two-and-one-half-mat room. One week after the arrest, an ill Okazaki was sent off to Tokyo, again in the form of "voluntary" appearance. Finally, in Tokyo a formal arrest writ was issued. In fact, Okazaki, until the writ was issued, was detained illegally. After all, said the professor, who would voluntarily remain in such a filthy place? As for the excuse that suspects were held to preserve evidence, Minobe noted that it was unnecessary and improper, because widespread domiciliary searches were completed. There are, he said, many facts that point to the conclusion that Okazaki's treatment was designed to extract a confession. Also, said Minobe, searches were sometimes too extensive; indeed, so much was seized at the Teijin Company headquarters that business was impaired. Moreover, some procurators examined suspects without a preliminary judge's consent. Justice Minister Ohara said, Minobe recalled, that several suspects were handcuffed to prevent suicide. Minobe was inclined to think, however, that in one case farewell letters were written not because of suicidal thoughts, but because the suspect feared dying from an illness. Minobe concluded that handcuffing was most likely done to cause physical pain. Furthermore, it appeared that suspects were handcuffed on orders from procurators. Besides Okazaki's memoir, Minobe drew on that of Nagano, who was tormented so severely by bugs in his cell that he appealed to the preliminary judge. And it was not just Nagano who was improperly cared for, because several other people were ill.[66] "If officials tortured the accused deliberately," said Minobe, "they deserve severe punishment, and the Minister of Justice could best maintain the prestige of the judiciary by dealing severely with such officials." These problems have one common origin, stressed

Minobe: "procuratorial authorities attach undue importance to 'confessions.'" Instead, said Minobe, "they should try to establish guilt by scientific means. It is not enough for the Minister of Justice to question the procurators concerned; he must also hear what the accused have to say in order to probe the matter to the bottom."[67]

Ohara replied that behind most of the criticism was a notion that the Teijin scandal was fabricated by procurators. Although investigative details could not be released until the trial, the minister assured legislators that strong evidence triggered prosecution. Thus it was inconceivable that procurators would base indictments on fabricated evidence. Replying to Minobe's charge that the Teijin Company documents were seized illegally, Ohara claimed that the procurators merely borrowed the company's documents (i.e., "provisional holding"). Indeed, said Ohara, all searches in the case were done with circumspection. As for "voluntary" appearance, procurators used no force. This method of summons, the minister noted, was a long-established practice. Regarding Okazaki's case, Ohara promised to investigate and announce the results. True, said Ohara, much evidence was seized, but authorities feared destruction of evidence, and, indeed, there were attempts to destroy evidence. Detention should be as short as possible, agreed Ohara. It is possible that a procurator may sometimes use harsh language, he conceded, but an interrogation does not become illegal for that reason. Therefore, charges of torture were false. Nevertheless, any official who employs torture, said Ohara, will be punished. Discussing the handcuffs, the minister stuck to the earlier fear of suicide argument. Moreover, he insisted that it was the prison governor who had ordered their use. Procurators merely pointed out to the prison governor the suspects' agitated condition. No procurator or judge, concluded Ohara, would place a suspect in a bug-infested cell as punishment. Therefore, if a suspect was put in such a place, it was by accident.[68]

Justice Minister Ohara tried to quiet protest over infringement of personal rights by agreeing to a lower house request for Teijin case documents. Among the papers submitted was the first part of former vice-minister Kuroda's "petition" written on June 22, 1934. It was presented to legislators as an example of a "thank you note" from a suspect to the procurators.[69] Kuroda addressed Chief Procurator Iwamura as "excellency," begging his pardon, with moist eyes, for the trouble he caused. "I have been imprisoned for over a month," he wrote. "Day after day each procurator is interrogating me in a sympathetic manner, which I very much appreciate. From time to time, Procurator Kuroda tells me that your excellency is very concerned about me. I am overwhelmed by your concern. Of course, from the beginning of the interrogation it has been my duty to tell the truth without causing trouble for everyone [i.e., for the authorities]."[70] The full text of Kuroda's petition, which was not introduced to the public until October 22, 1936, at the trial, was included in the procurators' final report and then incorporated in the preliminary judges' formal record. Releasing this self-serving fragment of it did not quiet Justice Ministry critics.

On January 29, Iwata Chūzō resumed a sharp interpellation on suspects' personal rights. Was it true that procurators said that businessmen were responsible for corrupt politicians?[71] According to one memoir, procurators said: "In their desire to feather their own nests, they bribe statesmen and politicians who are thirsty for money. The action taken by the Finance Department in connection with the Meiji Sugar Company affair was improper. We hold you, accused, of no account. It is the bigger ones, lurking in the background we want to bring to justice. Our object is to carry out a bloodless *coup d'etat* in order to purify society." Perhaps the procurators were prompted by good motives, said Iwata, but such statements "naturally give rise to a complaint of 'judicial Facism.' "[72] Iwata recalled that some of the accused in the shocking May 15 affair also were inspired by pure motives. While the military men used pistols to attain their objective, Teijin procurators abused prosecution power for a similar purpose. Therefore, their methods were equally illegal. Iwata noted that under the Criminal Procedure Code procurators had wide powers, but in fact they had expanded that power beyond the code's intention.[73] A procurator can "practically make the preliminary judge issue such orders as he likes. It rarely happens that the preliminary judge refuses the procurator's requests." Until judicial reforms were enacted, said Iwata, it would be impossible to stop "the practice of exacting 'confessions' from the accused."[74]

Iwata and Minobe drew on Nagano's memoir published in the *Kobe Newspaper*. Procurators were rude and brutal, Nagano wrote. "They never allowed him to say anything except the words admitting the charge that he had given 1,300 shares as bribes. The instant he attempted to deny the charge, they thundered out, 'Don't talk nonsense!' They rushed at him, ordered him to stand up, and then gripping both his arms, forced his face up with their fists. He was pushed to the wall behind, and his forehead and jaw were then pushed so that the back of his head was knocked against the wall." Nagano claimed that "a running fire of scathing questions by one of these procurators" grew worse after the arrest of Nakajima. One procurator said: "A fellow like you had better die. But then, perhaps you have not sufficient pluck to take your own life. If you do not know how to kill your-self, I will tell you. Knock your head against the wall, that's the way. Come on do it!"[75] Nagano reported that soon after arrest he was handcuffed. One day, after returning to prison from a preliminary examination, jailers who put on leather manacles inquired what he had done to anger the procura-tors. He replied that he had done nothing, but they refused to believe him. Fleas and mosquitoes were terrible pests, since he could not use his hands to fight them. It was even impossible to wash his face. From one jailer, Nagano heard that handcuffing of suspects was done to punish the unco-operative. Later, when he refused to cooperate, a procurator threatened to handcuff him again. Nevertheless, Nagano proclaimed his innocence; on July 10 he was moved to a new cell, where swarms of vermin robbed him of sleep. All night fights with biting bugs lasted about a month, as he kept appealing to Preliminary Judge Yoshida Hajime. Finally, he showed the judge one night's catch of fifty bugs. Judge Yoshida, after discussing the matter with the procurator, had him moved to a new cell. The procurator, however, told Nagano that if he refused to cooperate, he would be given a worse cell.[76]

Justice Minister Ohara, replying to Minobe and Iwata on January 30, defended procurators. On April 5, 1934, he said, when two procurators seized Teijin Company documents, it was with the consent of the compa-ny directors. Moreover, company books, which were necessary for busi-ness purposes, were returned soon after. As for Okazaki's "voluntary" appearance, the examination in Osaka, from April 5 to 11, was insufficient, so procurators asked him to accompany them to Tokyo.[77] "At first, he refused, and an arrangement was made . . . for the issue of a preliminary judge's writ for his arrest, but as this might compromise his honour, an understanding was finally reached that he should 'voluntarily' present him-self."[78] Looking at Iwata, the minister declared that charges of illegal actions by procurators were groundless. Of the Teijin affair suspects, thir-teen were kept in provisional cells in the court, he said. The fact that they were put into these provisional cells does not prove that authorities were forcing confessions. Indeed, noted Ohara, since Okazaki was ill when arrested, procurators, prison authorities, and the court provided special treatment. To handle the ill Takagi, Ichigaya Prison used its best cell. Although Takagi was examined one day for ten hours by a preliminary judge, he was permitted to remain in bed; blankets covered him, a stove heated the cell, and meal breaks were taken. Thus, charges of ill-treatment were unfounded, concluded Ohara. Ohara also dismissed Iwata's charges of "judicial fascism," demanding proof to support his statement. The suspects' memoirs were not proof, said Ohara, because they were replete with exaggerated accounts. Finally, Ohara said that Iwata's claim that procurators unduly influenced preliminary judges illustrated ignorance of the actual workings of the criminal justice system; judges maintain their independence. Iwata, concluded Ohara, should reflect on his remarks impugning the reputation and honor of preliminary judges and procurators.[79] Responding to Ohara, Iwata said that it was impossible to believe that the suspects' memoirs were pure fabrication, because these men still had to face the open trial. The comments about preliminary judges were meant merely to point out a flaw "in the judicial system which long practice has engendered." He wanted the authorities "to discard the usual practice of glossing over manifest evils, and earnestly endeavor to achieve the reform of the judicial system, with the cooperation of the Bar."[80]

That the matter of alleged ill-treatment came up was not surprising, opined one editor. "For one thing, several counsel briefed in the case have seats in the Diet, and the opportunity to heckle the Minister of Justice, and to strike a blow for their clients' case, is obviously too good to be missed. Yet it will not do to dismiss the interpellations as an ingenious device whereby counsel are preparing a favorable background for the actual trial." These complaints arose, in fact, because of "a serious suspicion that certain judicial officials have, to put it bluntly, third degreed the defendants. The charges are plain, and in certain important respects are not disputed." Defendants were placed in bug-infested cells and kept manacled for up to forty-eight hours; they were treated in a manner that was "calculated to break down their resistance and produce the much needed confession which is so peculiar a feature of Japanese criminal procedure. The replies of the Minister of Justice to these charges have not been exactly convincing." The editor noted that the Japanese procedure was similar to the French in that the investigators began with the assumption that a suspect was probably guilty. Nevertheless, "it is still possible for a defendant to receive a more or less fair trial. But when brow-beating is added to prolonged detention, when the examination is conducted in absolute secrecy and the accused held *incommunicado*, the opportunities for abuse are rather obvious." It is understandable, wrote the editor, why a full investigation of this case cannot be carried out until after the open trial, but, in the meantime, the Justice Ministry "could institute its own departmental inquiry." Besides the Teijin case, added the editor, there were "disturbing accusations arising from other cases.... Every now and again the press carries a brief story of the death of some unfortunate prisoner from which it is all too clear that the police have little hesitation in resorting to torture when they are particularly anxious to extract information."[81]

At a Budget Committee meeting on February 1, Okamoto Kazumi (Independent), who was removed from the Seiyūkai for making unproven bribery accusations, criticized Seiyūkai members who were lawyers for Teijin trial defendants. They were, he said, disclosing details of the preliminary examination in order to put political pressure on justice officials. He asked Justice Minister Ohara why such conduct was tolerated. Ohara replied that he would resist such pressure.[82] The reader is reminded that in early 1934 Okamoto accused Justice Minister Koyama of corruption; Okamoto was arrested for slander. Eventually procurators charged perjury against Okamoto, Sanekawa Tokijirō (president of the Great Asia Communications Company), and Mrs. Andō Teru (commonly called Okoi). The Tokyo District Court's sentence was eighteen months for Okamoto, one year for Sanekawa, and probation for Andō.[83] Given Okamoto's earlier actions, perhaps concern over lawyers' ethical conduct was not the primary reason for criticizing former political colleagues. Since his conviction was probably under appeal, perhaps he hoped support for justice officials might influence the judges reviewing his case (i.e., he might be granted a stay of execution instead of a prison term).

The Diet's outrage over infringement of personal rights illustrates the unequal nature of justice. While high social rank did not always insure proper treatment for suspects, it did insure a loud protest from friends and lawyers. Procurators who forgot that the legal system favored the upper classes were sharply reminded in the Sixty-Sixth Diet session. Indeed, upper-class supporters of the Teijin suspects pushed so hard against Justice Minister Ohara that he agreed during February 1935 "with the Diet that confinement and manacling should not be resorted to when men of obvious substance are concerned."[84] Professor Minobe Tatsukichi also reflected a class bias. Although a strong critic of illegal police actions and a foe of the 1925 Peace Preservation Law, Minobe had a blind spot when it came to extending full legal protection to the lower classes and communists.[85] In his January 23, 1935, maiden speech, Minobe said: "The speaker has often heard rumours that procuratorial authorities have overstepped the proper limits in arresting persons . . . but he has hitherto been inclined to discount them." What prompted Minobe to make the issue of procedural abuses the centerpiece of this speech? The surface issue was facts that illustrated violations; an unspoken reason was the class status of defendants.[86]

On February 1, 1935, the Zaikai shinbunsha (Financial World Newspaper Company) published a book on the Teijin scandal, which began with a reprinted editorial from the paper's January 15 edition. Reading the *Yoshin*, wrote the editor, made it obvious that the prosecution's case rests on confessions with little supporting physical evidence; the suspects repudiated the confessions, claiming they confessed to escape torture and terrible prison conditions.[87] Indeed, one suspect calls this case "a castle in the air built from torture."[88] Continuing, the editor noted that many writers in the legal, financial, and literary worlds had pointed to the thinness of physical evidence in this case. These views raised the issue of fairness on the part of procurators. After urging justice authorities to conduct an impartial trial, the editor concluded that it was the duty of his newspaper to point out questionable actions by authorities.[89]

Senior editor Sekimoto Masuo, in a piece written for the Zaikai shinbunsha book, analyzed the procurators' indictment: Procurators claimed that suspects violated Penal Code Article 247 by making an undeserved profit on the sale of Teijin Company stock. Was this really so? Sekimoto argued that it was obvious that defendants did not manipulate the market in order to raise the price of Teijin shares. After contesting procurators' claim that Finance Ministry officials accepted bribes, Sekimoto looked at the issue of the 1,300 shares, noting the significant fact that these were signed share certificates. Therefore, if they were moved to a new owner or converted into cash, there would be a paper record of the transactions. There was, he emphasized, no such record. Moreover, the government's claim that Kobayashi stole the 1,300 shares from his company's safe and together with Nagasaki used the shares as bribes, and then returned them to the safe, said Sekimoto, defies common sense. If Kobayashi planned bribery, why go through such a painful process? Why not simply use cash? Furthermore, it is difficult to discern a motive behind Nagasaki's giving out 1,300 shares to various people. One should also note that if Kobayashi repurchased 1,300 shares, he would have required a large sum of money; there was no paper record of Kobayashi obtaining such a sum.[90] Sekimoto concluded: "The Teijin Incident [investigation] has no physical evidence, even though the case has been under investigation for such a long time. Common sense says that something is wrong. . . . Thus, it is not difficult to see that the most controversial point [at the trial] will be over lack of physical evidence."[91] Sekimoto's comments were squarely on target: the lack of physical evidence presented defense attorneys their greatest advantage and presented procurators their greatest challenge.

The Financial World Newspaper Company book also contains excerpts from the Sixty-Fifth Diet session, the course of the procurators' investigation, Preliminary Judge Morozumi's list of laws defendants violated, a brief vita of each defendant, comments by several suspects, a history of the Bank of Taiwan, and the background of the Teijin Company.

Defendant Mitsuchi's views are reprinted from the *Tokyo Nichinichi Newspaper* (December 27, 1934) under the title "Where I Stand on the Teijin Incident."[92] Mitsuchi recalled his surprise and puzzlement as the investigation unfolded; things became clearer on August 27, 1934, when he was called before Preliminary Judge Morozumi. At that point, Mitsuchi realized that this was a trumped-up case fabricated by procurators who relied on information supplied by angry would-be purchasers of Teijin stock. On top of that, said Mitsuchi, some people (Mutō Sanji?) who were interested in gaining fame investigated the stock deal story. The entire case rests, noted Mitsuchi, on a confession by a weak, frightened Takagi, who wanted to escape jail conditions. Besides noting the weakness of Takagi and others who had confessed, Mitsuchi condemned overzealous procurators who employed improper methods. Like editor Sekimoto, Mitsuchi disputed the government's contention that 1,300 Teijin shares were offered as bribes. What happened to the 1,300 shares? Despite months of careful investigation, noted Mitsuchi, authorities were unable to offer a convincing explanation of how these shares were used as bribes. In fact, Mitsuchi concluded, the government case really rested on suspects' confessions, which in some cases were in conflict.[93]

"Extreme Abuse and Ill-Treatment" was dictated by a bed-ridden Okazaki (October 22–30, 1934), who had tuberculosis.[94] This document, which was sent to Preliminary Judge Morozumi, detailed the pressures applied by Procurator Biwada and explained why Okazaki gave in and confessed.[95] Kawai's contribution to this book was "I Only Followed the Proper Path of Business Practices."[96] Insisting that all his actions during the stock share transactions were proper and legal, Kawai wrote that his conscience was clear.[97] An anonymous (Nagano?) contribution to this volume is "A Castle in the Sky Built on Leather Handcuffs."[98] The defendant who wrote this essay viewed the use of leather handcuffs as a form of torture. Other abuses, such as being pushed into walls, standing for long periods, waiting all day in small, dark, smelly rooms, and being held in cells infested with bedbugs, were recorded. This sort of treatment continued for months, recalled the defendant, until procurators were satisfied with suspects' statements.[99]

The Public

What did the reading public make of the conflicting accounts in newspapers? Were newspaper accounts of infringement of personal rights correct? How did the public view the acrimonious exchanges in the Diet? Did the information released by the Justice Ministry accurately portray customary business practices? Since the Teijin scandal investigation was a major news item, it must have stimulated readers to ponder these and related questions.

It is doubtful that accusations of ill-treatment by police and procurators shocked most readers; newspaper stories about police brutality and even torture were not uncommon, as were stories about police administration and justice officials issuing orders that suspects' rights must not be violated. Suspects "voluntarily" accompanying police or "voluntarily" appearing at the procurator's office were also old news, so it is unlikely that this long-practiced but illegal method shocked many people. As for jail conditions, which were sometimes very bad, they also fall under the heading of stale news. Prisons, including Ichigaya, where some of the Teijin suspects were kept, were better maintained than jails, but most people, no doubt, had read or heard stories about dirty jails and detention houses filled with biting bugs, skin diseases, and illnesses contracted during prolonged confinement.[100] The use of leather handcuffs, however, may have struck some readers as unusual punishment. Those who knew about normal detention house procedure would probably have rejected Justice Minister Ohara's justification for their use. Imamura Rikisaburō, perhaps the nation's most famous criminal defense lawyer, recalled only one case in which they had been used (that of Nanba Daisuke, who tried to kill the crown prince regent on December 27, 1923). In the Teijin case, five suspects were restrained with leather cuffs.[101]

Despite a press ban, newspapers reported details about the investigative process. Therefore, it is apparent that some justice officials were seeking to manage the news; perhaps they were concerned about the ministry's prestige. Indeed, one newspaper article suggests that Diet interpellations hit a sensitive nerve. Under the chairmanship of Procurator General Hayashi, said the article, an inquiry committee was established in February 1935 to discuss methods for improving criminal prosecution. The committee, which was to meet weekly, planned to clarify criminal search policy, to consider appointing more procurators, and to enlarge procurators' offices in several large cities. According to the article, the committee saw a connection between complaints about infringement of personal rights and the vague nature of parts of the Code of Criminal Procedure. Besides modification of the code, the committee would consider an increase in the number of procurators.[102] "Under existing conditions," noted the article, "one procurator is often called upon to examine a dozen of the accused and witnesses in a day. In such circumstances, the idea of shortening the period of detention is impossible, nor can the personality of the accused and witnesses be adequately respected." The article concluded: "The pressure of business naturally makes the procurator nervous and more excitable, with the result that he sometimes uses rude language to the accused. The procurators office . . . must be made more commodious."[103] This committee, created by Justice Minister Ohara, completed its labors in June 1935, the same month in which the open trial began and issued a report in two sections: one section designed for beginning procurators and one aimed at all procurators. The report's main objective, it appeared, was to eliminate public criticism of procurators.[104] Obviously, public opinion, as reflected in the Diet and newspaper offices, had influenced Justice Minister Ohara. Moreover, the timing of this reform project must have suggested to many newspaper readers that suspects' charges of mistreatment were true.

One scholar notes that there was a strong anticapitalist current at the time and that the two-month attack by the *Jiji shinpō* stirred up public anger.[105] No doubt, these sensational articles must have angered some people, especially those suffering economic hardship, but it is difficult to imagine well-informed people being surprised by the unmasking of shadowy deal making portrayed in the *Jiji* or later in leaks to the press. Although some people may have been surprised at the amount of money that changed hands in the Teijin Company stock transaction, others would have seen nothing unusual in actions of Kawai Yoshinari and others; commissions, gifts, and payoffs were part of customary business methods. The only difference was the larger than normal size of the transaction. Furthermore, the public's capacity for being shocked or angry must have diminished in the aftermath of a series of sensational corruption scandals during the late 1920s and early 1930s, which featured wholesale bribery between businessmen and state ministers. Indeed, the appeal process of former justice minister Ogawa Heikichi stretched out until June 1937.[106] Still, the long-playing Teijin Incident did rip off the mask of the business world, permitting anyone with the price of a newspaper to view business reality. What people saw was not the myth of unselfish businessmen promoting national goals but a naked display of greed.

At first glance, most unusual in the Teijin case was the involvement of Finance Ministry officials. After all, writes one scholar, this ministry had a proud tradition of never having a bribery case.[107] Nevertheless, a wider perspective somewhat changes this picture, since there were cases of bribed bank inspectors and tax officials. Therefore, many newspaper readers may have concluded that the Finance Ministry was also rampant with corruption. In June 1933, for example, a newspaper reported that three bank inspectors were under investigation by Tokyo police "on a charge of receiving bribes from the Shiritsu Mutual Financing Association, whose officials are under examination on charges of negligence leading to the loss of ¥800,000." The inspectors, said the article, who were charged "to examine the books . . . deliberately overlooked certain facts, and made a false report to their senior officials, it is alleged."[108] This case appeared in Tokyo newspapers, so it must have been known widely. Since no high-ranking officials were involved, it was a minor blemish on the ministry record. However, in the midst of the Teijin trial a major tax scandal exploded in Osaka, which by January 1936 involved every tax office in the city.[109] At the trial of one tax official, Miyoshi Yoshio, the procurator suggested to the judges that a light sentence would be appropriate, because the defendant was suffering greatly. Furthermore, since "in Osaka in particular money is considered 'almighty' . . . dealing with such crimes in Osaka . . . the judicial authorities ought to punish the bribers more severely than the recipients." At the end of this article, another tax scandal, involving the former section head of the Kobe Tax Office, was reported.[110] Ironically, on the same newspaper page, Finance Minister Baba Eiichi is quoted: "Tax officials are inadequately paid in comparison with other officials. . . . I am of the opinion that an increase in their salaries is imperative to stop the scandals."[111] A possible solution, but one wonders what the public thought!

Newspaper readers were also entertained by a corruption case involving a former Osaka District Court procurator. The case of Mitani Ginzō appeared in the press in early June 1934. Mitani, a lawyer in Osaka, was suspected of accepting bribes from 1928 to 1932 while a procurator. At the trial, beginning on November 29, 1935, Mitani admitted receiving "loans" from a number of criminal suspects and convicts. The court sentence was three years' imprisonment and a fine of ¥12,400.[112] Thus, during the investigative stage of the Teijin case and into the early open trial phase, newspaper readers were generally offered a choice: procurators Kuroda and Biwada, as heroic figures holding up justice, or a Mitani taking bribes. While such newspapers portrayed Kuroda and Biwada as earnest officials exposing corruption, others saw them as violators of personal rights. Indeed, over the course of the investigation and trial many newspapers probably presented both views, as the exposure of procurators' methods and the failure to convict damaged the procuratorial camp's public image.

In the light of damning newspaper articles and years of sensational bribery trials, many readers probably decided that corruption permeated the worlds of businessmen, politicians, and government bureaucrats; military personnel, in contrast, must have looked incorruptible. Those who held that view, however, were due for a shock in July 1936 (the Teijin trial had passed the one-year mark in late June), as papers reported the alleged corruption of Lieutenant-General Uemura Haruhiko, director of the Board of Ordinance, who was suspected of taking bribes from manufacturing companies and contractors. A great public sensation ensued, since Uehara was a three-star general. In fact, there were not enough ranking active duty officers for a jury, so an imperial ordinance was issued that permitted the army minister to use reserve list generals. The court martial procurator charged the general with taking bribes from 1928 until 1934; the court's sentence was thirty months in prison and a fine of ¥43,070. No appeal was permitted.[113]

What conclusion would newspaper readers draw from these examples? Deeper thinkers, no doubt, concluded that every apple barrel contained some bad fruit, but others could easily decide that in the worlds of business, government, and the military, corruption was rampant. Press articles on various civilian and military rightist groups that during these years demanded a Showa Restoration must have reinforced this feeling. Without fail these reform groups cited corruption among the ruling elite as one compelling reason for reform; at trials of rightists arrested for illegal actions, an anticorruption element was always part of the defense. Furthermore, during the early and mid-1930s, so-called revisionist bureaucrats in the Home Ministry launched a purification crusade to cleanse the political world. Just before the fall of the Saitō Cabinet, the Reformed House of Representatives Members Election Law went into effect. The open purpose of this law was to punish violators of election regulations more harshly and to purify the election process; the unsaid purpose was to destroy the alliance between local elites and Diet members.[114] Newspaper articles on this law and its application during the September 1935 prefectural election and the February 1936 general election were a constant reminder that corruption was pervasive. Against this background the drama of the long-playing Teijin scandal trial unfolded—one act after another.

CHAPTER 5

Trial

THE TRIAL BEGAN ON JUNE 22, 1935, and ended on October 5, 1937. Judges issued a verdict on December 16. Thus, the Teijin scandal resulted in the longest district criminal court trial in pre-1945 Japan; it continued for a record-setting 265 sessions, excluding the day the verdict was issued. There were criminal cases that lasted longer, but they involved appeals to higher courts. Fujii Goichirō, who presided over the sensational Blood Pact Group trial (the defendants were convicted of killing Dan Takuma and Inoue Junnosuke in 1932), was the chief judge. His assistants were Ishida Kazuto and Okazaki Tōichi. Kishi Seiichirō was the supplementary judge. Procurator Biwada together with colleagues faced a reinforced platoon of defense lawyers (fifty-one on opening day) coordinated by Imamura Rikisaburō, a famous criminal lawyer. Among the sixteen defendants were four who had never signed a confession: Ōno, Aida, Shidomoto (Finance Ministry), and former minister Mitsuchi.

Judge Fujii, who had visited Meiji jingū (Emperor Meiji's shrine) early that morning, opened the court at 8:30 A.M. Procurator Hirata Susumu, for about one and one-half hours, outlined the prosecution's indictment, which focused on three crimes: misfeasance (*hainin*), bribery (*zōshūwai*), and perjury (*gishō*). Although eight defendants faced multiple charges, the prosecution mainly aimed the misfeasance charge at Bank of Taiwan officials (Shimada, Takagi, Yanagida, and Okazaki) and the bribery charge at former minister Nakajima and the five Finance Ministry officials (Kuroda, Ōkubo, Ōno, Aida, and Shidomoto). Former minister Mitsuchi was charged with perjury. Bank of Taiwan officials, said the prosecution, were guilty of misfeasance, because they sold the shares well below the proper price. Moreover, they received a bribe in the form of 1,300 Teijin Company shares, and they in turn used some of the shares to bribe others. These 1,300 shares, in 100-share units (i.e., thirteen share certificates) were received from Nagasaki on about June 19, 1933. Furthermore, the prosecution claimed that Shimada wrote a memo in which he outlined the division of 1,000 shares (300 shares were already deducted for use by Shimada, Takagi, and Yanagida): Kuroda (400), Mitsuchi (300), Nakajima (200), and Ōkubo (100).[1]

Next, Procurator Hirata explained the Teijin stock deal and analyzed the motive for giving the 1,300 shares. Besides the money made by brokering the deal (Kawai was paid a one-yen commission by each side for a total of ¥200,000), Nagano and his colleagues (Kawai, Kobayashi, and Nagasaki) made a handsome profit of ¥100,000 on a joint purchase of 5,000 shares of Teijin stock (this was part of the 100,000 shares); the 5,000 shares were listed under the name of Sekihara Kenji, Kawai's secretary. This profit, noted Hirata, resulted from the rapid rise in the worth of Teijin stock during mid-June. The group of four delegated Nagano to express their appreciation to the Bank of Taiwan directors. Their decision fit neatly with Nagano's ambition to move up in the business world. Hirata then traced Nagano's background, his aid to Fujita Kenichi, and the encouragement he received from Baron Gō. From stockbroker Nagano's perspective, said Hirata, this Teijin stock deal represented a ladder he could climb into a prestigious company directorship, perhaps even with the Teijin Company. With an eye on future needs, Nagano decided to expand the gift giving to Ministers Nakajima and Mitsuchi, and to the Finance Ministry people who helped with the stock transfer. For the gifts, Nagano turned to Kobayashi, who was manager of the Fukoku Chōhei Insurance Company (the joint-purchased 5,000 shares were in this company's safe as security for a loan of ¥625,000), asking him to borrow 1,300 shares. Furthermore, Nagano decided that Bank of Taiwan officials should distribute gift shares to the ministers and the finance officials; this, he reasoned, would place more people under obligation than if he simply gave them directly. As this plan progressed, Takagi got Nagasaki to convert 300 shares (out of the 1,300 received) into cash at ¥140 per share (total, ¥42,000). Some of this cash was kept by Bank of Taiwan officials, and the balance went to finance officials Ōno, Aida, and Shiomoto. Shimada and Takagi personally handed over this money, said Hirata.[2]

As for the two ministers, noted Hirata, Nakajima received 200 shares and ¥10,000 in cash from Nagano and others. The shares were presented to Nakajima by Shimada and Takagi on June 26, 1933, at the visiting room next door to Nakajima's office. The ¥10,000 was given by Nagano in mid-November as an additional gift. These were bribes, stated Hirata. Moreover, Nakajima asked Mitsuchi to cash in the 200 shares. This was done, and ¥30,400 was returned. During Nakajima's preliminary court examination, Mitsuchi was called as a witness; he denied accepting Nakajima's 200 shares, denied giving the ¥30,400, and denied receiving a 300-share gift. Because he refused to confirm confessions made by Nakajima and others, Mitsuchi was charged with perjury, concluded Hirata (he was not charged with bribery for accepting 300 shares).[3]

After Hirata finished, Nagawa Kanichi (Kuroda's lawyer and a Seiyūkai politician) pointed out to Judge Fujii the ambiguousness of the "facts" in the indictment and requested that Hirata enlighten the court on various points, because general statements about stocks being purchased and given away were inadequate. For example, the so-called fact that Nagasaki received 1,300 Teijin shares on about June 19, 1933, from Kobayashi: Why did Kobayashi give Nagasaki these shares? Whose name as owner was on these shares? Who has the 1,300 seized shares that were used for bribery? How did Nagasaki get these shares? What was the exact date? What was the date on which Nagasaki passed on the shares to Takagi? Did Takagi personally receive them? In presenting the shares to Takagi, did Nagasaki say that they were from himself and Nagano? How many people owned the 1,300 shares given to Takagi? Who sold the 1,300 shares, and by whom were they purchased? Was the transaction done in cash or by check? If the sale involved cash, where did the money originate? If it was done using a check, on which bank was the check drawn? These questions, stressed Nagawa, reflected the vague language and incomplete information in the prosecution's Final Written Decision of a Preliminary Examination (*Yoshin*). Continuing, Nagawa asked if Nagasaki and Nagano each gave ¥5,000 to Okazaki and Koshifuji. Was that money a gift? Or was it money gotten from the Bank of Taiwan group (Shimada, Takagi, and Yanagida) and passed on? The *Yoshin* stated that 300 shares were cashed in for ¥42,000, and ¥14,000 of this sum was given to Ōno, Aida, and Shidomoto as gifts. What happened to the balance of ¥28,000? Moreover, the *Yoshin* claimed that Okazaki and Koshifuji had the idea of giving money to Finance Ministry and Bank of Japan officials, and that each of them contributed ¥5,000 to this gift. Was it really their idea? Next, Nagawa asked procurators about the various conspiracies cited in the *Yoshin*: Kuroda knew about one between Shimada and Takagi; Nakajima knew about one by Shimada, Takagi, Nagano, and Nagasaki; and so on. What were these conspiracies all about? Procurators charged that Mitsuchi was asked by Nakajima to cash in 200 shares and that they were sold for ¥152 per share: a total of ¥30,400 given to Nakajima by Mitsuchi. When and where, asked Nagawa, did Mitsuchi cash in these shares? Was the form of payment cash or a check? Furthermore, said Nagawa, Procurator Hirata's opening statement was unclear on the charges against all of the defendants; for example, which ones were charged as bribers or bribees or both? Nagawa next challenged the prosecution to explain the use of specific words in the misfeasance charge. Procurator Hirata promised to do so. Concerning the bribery charge, Hirata added that the *Yoshin* was correct, and it would be proven during the trial. Dissatisfied, Nagawa again pointed to the vague nature of the prosecution's facts. According to the Code of Criminal Procedure, prosecution documents should be based on concrete facts. Putting suspects on trial based on such vague "facts," he said, was wrong. In conclusion, Nagawa predicted that unclear "facts" would be a troublesome problem for the court.[4] Lawyer Nagawa's argument was prophetic, because the specter of vague facts haunted the courtroom for two and one-half years.

Judge Fujii, however, anxious to move forward, brushed aside these factual concerns by declaring that the bench recognized the *Yoshin*. Nevertheless, he added, the court would carry out a thorough examination of the case.[5]

Matsumoto Shigetoshi (Shimada's lawyer), a distinguished scholar, claimed that the indictment was invalid: which laws had the procurators used to examine the accused? Furthermore, he noted that there was suspicion that the interrogations had been performed illegally.[6]

Judge Fujii then asked each defendant to respond to each charge. Shimada, who replied first, repudiated his confession as forced and denied knowing about the 1,300 shares of stock given to various people. Other defendants also denied criminal acts and repudiated confessions. Nakajima, however, did admit receiving ¥10,000 but claimed that the money had no connection with the current case. Nagano and Kobayashi verified this claim. Mitsuchi, outspoken as usual, denounced the procurators and preliminary judges; it was wrong to try him for perjury. The first hearing adjourned at 11:40 A.M.; the next was scheduled for June 25.[7]

Examination of Defendants

On June 25, Judge Fujii focused on the procurators' primary target, Takagi. At this session and for the next nearly two dozen, Fujii inquired about Takagi's personal affairs, his career, how bank business was conducted, the bank's relationship with the defunct Suzuki Company, its relationship with the Teijin Company, the government loan to the Bank of Taiwan, how the bank came to possess 225,233 Teijin Company shares, the estimated value per share in June 1933 (¥120.25), who had authority to sell the 100,000 shares, how many people applied to purchase Teijin shares, the role played in the sale by Nakajima, the series of telegrams exchanged between Takagi and Shimada (who was in Taiwan), why the bank finally agreed to sell 100,000 shares to the syndicate Kawai represented (a large repayment was due to the bank of Japan in September 1933), and so on.[8]

Judge Fujii also asked who had authority to dispose of the stock shares. Takagi replied: "As a practical problem, this can be done easily, though legislatively speaking, the Bank must apply to the Finance Minister through the official comptroller." "Is the Finance Minister in a position to stop sales or order any change in the terms of sales?" asked Fujii. Takagi replied, "Yes."[9] Interestingly, on this point about the authority to permit the stock sale, a contradiction appears. Finance Minister Takahashi and Ōkubo Teiji told the Sixty-Fifth Diet that the Bank of Taiwan, after approval by the Bank of Taiwan Commission, had the authority (see Chapter 3). Ōkubo said that the bank need not obtain permission but that an official in the ministry watched over Bank of Taiwan transactions to be certain that they were handled properly. This official, however, had no veto power over a transaction. In sum, the bank had authority, but on an important transaction directors were expected to consult with the Finance Ministry. The Bank of Japan, which held the share certificates, had to be consulted as well. Although legally subordinated to the Finance Ministry, the Bank of Japan enjoyed some autonomy. Government officials, who were the players in these bureaucratic games, would have known about the written and unwritten rules.

At the judge's urging, Takagi outlined the fluctuations of Teijin share prices, noting that in early 1932 old shares were about ¥90 per share but gradually rose to about ¥158 by December. They fell, however, by late January 1933 (¥107) because of unsettled international conditions. Later, there was another recovery to about ¥131 in early May. Owing to the rise of the yen in value and to conditions in Manchuria (seized by Japan in late 1931), Takagi's view of the market was gloomy, with the threat of a tax increase looming on the horizon. For these reasons, Takagi decided to sell some of the shares (also, the Bank of Japan was pressing for payment of loans). Next Fujii asked about Takagi's dealings with Kawai. Takagi claimed to have driven a hard bargain after prolonged negotiation:[10] "As regards the first 100,000 shares Mr. Kawai insisted on the ruling price of ¥117. Explaining the projected increase of capital, the publication of which was certain to influence the market, I asked Mr. Kawai for an increase in his offer. . . . As regards the remaining 100,000 shares, I turned down

Mr. Kawai's proposal to buy at ¥122, inclusive of dividend, with a month's option."[11] Reading aloud from one of Takagi's telegrams to Shimada, Fujii inquired why Nakajima was to distribute the shares among the insurance companies. Takagi replied that Kawai asked that he be mentioned. The judge then asked about the role played by Nakajima in recommending Teijin Company directors (Takagi heard about that after the contracts were signed) and the relationship of bank management with Hatoyama Ichirō and Shōriki Matsutarō (Takagi knew little about the involvement of either person). Takagi admitted that he had heard that Hatoyama used a political friend to obtain an interview with Shimada. Was Vice-Minister Kuroda involved in this sale? Before the negotiations with Kawai, Takagi replied, Kuroda several times had inquired about the Teijin shares. As negotiations with Kawai progressed, Takagi said, he reported to Kuroda. Fujii asked if he had heard that he and Shimada would be dismissed if the negotiation failed. Replying that he had not heard, Takagi added that they would have taken no notice anyway.[12]

Takagi disputed the preliminary court finding "that ¥125 was the ruling price, and that the publication of the capital increase scheme would have caused the quotation to jump. . . . If this argument is to be accepted, the quotation ought to have jumped to ¥150 on May 31st or June 1st, but actually it rose only to ¥131."[13] Takagi continued by pointing out that "the ruling price of ¥122 had already discounted the capital increase scheme." Moreover, looking at "the fact that the average yield point at that time was five per cent in the case of national bonds and 5.5 per cent in the case of Kanegafuchi Spinning shares," the price of ¥125, equivalent to 6 percent, was quite reasonable.[14] Why was Kawai's offer accepted? Takagi again mentioned the fear that the stocks' value would decline and reminded the court that the Bank of Japan was pressing for repayment. Also, he added, the bank management was correct in selling to the cotton yarn dealers and insurance companies, because no one else was capable of paying the enormous sum of ¥12,400,000.[15]

In the midst of examing Takagi, Judge Fujii questioned Shimada about the ¥125 share price. Shimada replied: "In view of the persistent demand of the Bank of Japan for the repayment of loans and for other reasons already explained . . . [we were] anxious to bring the negotiations with . . . [Kawai] to a successful termination." Shimada added that, contrary to the incorrect statements in the *Yoshin*, the directors did not receive any offers from Fujita and Kaneko.[16] Pursuing this line of inquiry, the judge asked Takagi to explain why the Kawai group was considered the best candidate for a sale. Kawai's syndicate was the most suitable buyer, replied Takagi, "because the Bank needed cash payments. It is quite rare for such a huge number of shares to be sold for cash."[17]

Takagi, throughout the hearings, moved from outbursts of anger to floods of tears (illness soon removed him from the courtroom for one year). On June 27, for example, he criticized Procurator Biwada's interrogation tactics; he was calmed by a stern warning from Judge Fujii.[18] At a later hearing, as he insisted that the sale price was correct and that the bank did not lose ¥1,600,000, Takagi, in tears, complained that it was wrong to prosecute him because of a rise in share prices.[19] Reading from the *Yoshin*, Fujii pointed out that three business world witnesses agreed that a capital increase, by a leading firm like Teijin, was bound to cause a sharp rise in the price of shares, to between ¥140 and ¥150 each. It was impossible to predict such a rise at the time, Takagi insisted. Next, Takagi challenged similar statements by stockbrokers who were expert witnesses at the preliminary examination. Takagi asked why, if these brokers really thought that the shares would jump as high as ¥158, they did not purchase them. Would it not have been better to wait for a higher price? asked Fujii. Takagi refused to accept that argument.[20]

On July 30, Takagi reiterated that false statements were given to the procurators and the preliminary judges: he did not receive a 1,300-share bribe from Nagasaki. To explain these lies, on which the prosecution's legal case rested, Takagi cited his terror of Procurator Kuroda, whom he termed a "fascist." During examinations, recalled Takagi, "he often burst into cries of indignation at the social conditions then prevailing. His favorite phrases were—What are the political parties doing? Aren't they in collusion with the plutocrats? What use is the Banchōkai? . . . The Department of Finance is corrupt. Wasn't it the Finance Ministry which tried to hush up the Meiji Sugar Company's tax dodging case when the Procuratorial authorities wanted to impose a heavy fine on the Company Management?" "I began to be terror stricken when I faced him," said Takagi. "As if I was mesmerized, I would give the answers he wanted."[21]

Judge Fujii noted that according to the *Yoshin* Takagi converted 300 of the 1,300 shares received from Nagasaki into cash (¥140 per share). Then, Takagi, Shimada, and Yanagida discussed what to do with the money: Shimada got ¥12,000; Takagi got ¥15,000; Yanagida got ¥5,000; Koshifuji got ¥5,000; and Okazaki got ¥5,000. Each of them contributed to a pool of money to reward Ōno (¥7,000), Aida (¥5,000), and Shidomoto (¥2,000). Moreover, Takagi, Shimada, and Yanagida decided to give money to Bank of Japan directors Nagaike Chōji and Shijō Takahide. Takagi insisted that this information was false. When he was interrogated in Osaka, he said, the procurators forced him to admit to receiving 300 shares, but after he arrived in Tokyo, the number grew to 1,000. Later it became 1,300. Under pressure by Procurator Kuroda, Takagi agreed to pile lie upon lie.²² By this point, desperate to escape the seemingly endless interrogations, Takagi had become a willing accomplice in the fabrication of a confession. It was clear, testified Takagi, that Kuroda and his colleagues were determined to implicate Finance Ministry and Bank of Japan officials, with specific people in mind as targets. Unless Takagi helped them he could expect endless interrogation sessions.²³ At one point Kuroda said: "You must have given to Ōno and Aida. If you agree, then the Finance Ministry part of it is completed."²⁴ As for the Bank of Japan officials, procurators kept returning to that subject. Indeed, procurators were so eager to connect bank officials to this transaction, recalled Takagi, they helped him calculate the amount of bribe money given to Okazaki and Koshifuji, in order to produce an extra ¥8,000 to give to Nagaike and Shijō. Always striving for a perfect confession, Kuroda even explained to Takagi how the money for Ōno, Aida, and Shidomoto was carried (in paper bags), where it was taken, and so forth. Procurator Biwada, concluded Takagi, must recall how difficult it was to fabricate this confession.²⁵

At one hearing Takagi was confronted by the 1,300 shares seized at the office of the Asahi Oil Company (thirteen certificates, each valued at ¥100). Picking up the only folded share certificate, Fujii noted that it was the one Takagi confessed to giving to Ōkubo, which was delivered by Okazaki. Takagi replied that he first saw that specific share at the preliminary examination. Why did you not correct the record at that time? By that point, replied Takagi, he was trying to gain the goodwill of the procurators.²⁶

Takagi described being handcuffed: "For three days and nights I was handcuffed as I underwent examination by the procurators. With my hands manacled to a big band, I couldn't even wash my face properly. I shall never forget that experience."²⁷ Lawyers interrupted to press Fujii to display cuffs and other things used to torture suspects. Fujii consented. Then the judge quizzed Takagi about bribes sent by Kawai. Takagi replied: "The procurator told me that any bribes received from Mr. Kawai would not constitute a crime. Furthermore, as he would not be satisfied unless I replied I had received something, I made that false confession."²⁸ Fujii next read from the *Yoshin*. Afterward Takagi replied: "It is only natural that the Presiding Judge should wonder why I tried to persuade Mr. Shimada to confirm my confession, thereby digging my own grave deeper. But you must appreciate my suspense and mental agony. To-day I have no hope in life. I am ready to die if I can prove my innocence."²⁹

On August 10, Takagi stated that as he piled lie upon lie during the interrogations, he kept thinking that the open trial would clarify everything. Then Takagi reminded the court that the prosecution's evidence was based on the *Jiji shinpō* articles. Suspects, he said, were manipulated by procurators and became victims of "judicial fascism" (*shihō fassho*). The humiliation at the hands of Biwada together with the forced confession were things he would never forget, concluded Takagi.[30]

As Takagi's testimony was ending, Mitsuchi Chūzō's *Yūshū tsurezure gusa* (Essays done during prison idleness) appeared. Readers were told that the author, who was imprisoned seven weeks, spent this vacation time reading and thinking. After pronouncing his innocence of any crime, Mitsuchi asked what it was that makes some men strong and other men weak. Friends in the legal field had told him that among criminal suspects there were quite a few who confessed to made-up stories at the preliminary court. Such people not only criminalized themselves, opined Mitsuchi, but also stained innocent people. Especially shocking were instances of self-confessions by highly educated people who held public positions. Why did such people, who were supposed to be role models for others, confess? Some observers pointed to physical and psychological stress. Mitsuchi agreed with this view, up to a point, but it drew too simple a picture. In the Teijin case, he noted, some suspects, who were not tortured, gave false statements; others firmly denied criminal charges. Why was there such a dramatic difference? In fact, concluded Mitsuchi, a person's character held the key to whether a suspect falsely confessed or stood firm against pressure. Mitsuchi next discussed his meetings with Takagi and Nakajima during the investigation. Authorities began to pressure him, he wrote, because he would not agree to their version of events.[31] "But as a Japanese man at the sacred court I could not possibly tell these lies."[32] In addition to the Teijin affair, Mitsuchi's essays covered a wide range of subjects: for example, "The Position of Men and Women," "Books Written by Bismarck," "The Moral Code and Yourself," "The Difference between the Poor and the Rich," "Stiff Government Officials," and "Fifty Years of Life."[33]

After a twelve-day adjournment, the trial resumed on August 22, with Shimada in the judicial spotlight. During this session and the one on August 24, Shimada explained why the bank possessed Teijin shares. Shimada emphasized that they were sold for a reasonable price. Indeed, in 1931 the bank even considered selling them for no more than ¥100. Quizzed by Judge Fujii about Takagi's appointment as president of the Teijin Company, Shimada admitted that the bank pressured the company's board of directors. The purpose of putting Takagi and others in charge, however, was to improve the company's management, said Shimada. Following Shimada's testimony, handcuffs and other so-called torture implements were displayed by the court.[34]

At the August 27 hearing, Shimada denied the misfeasance charge. "Because the Bank of Formosa [Taiwan] possessed the bulk of the Teijin shares . . . the Presiding Judge appears to be under the impression that the Bank Management knows everything in regard to the rayon industry. He is expecting too much. As a matter of fact, I had only a general idea as to the rayon outlook."[35] At the following session (August 29), Fujii reminded Shimada that he had had a pessimistic view of rayon's future, adding that the business journal *Diamond* was very optimistic. Shimada replied: "When the Bank sold 10,000 shares to Mr. Tamura at ¥150 each, I was rather surprised at the price. . . . Shortly afterwards, however, the quotation collapsed to ¥120. Even such an expert as Mr. Tamura, who is fully acquainted with the rayon business, can make a mistake like this. Economic matters may be explained afterwards, but it is not easy to make a forecast correctly."[36]

Visitors and journalists at the August 31 session were shocked by Shimada's repeated attacks on Biwada and Hirata, whom he called traitors. The words he used were "perfidious subjects and rebellious sons" (*ranshin zokushi*). Procurators Biwada and Hirata demanded a withdrawal of the statement, and Judge Fujii told Shimada to comply. "At whatever sacrifice, I will not withdraw my statement. . . . When I was first arrested I kept silence, for I did not know the reason for my arrest. Procurator Hori [not involved in the trial] . . . then abused me as 'traitor,' striking the table and stamping on the floor."[37] Fujii called a recess until noon. After some discussion and a repeated warning from the judge, Shimada withdrew the offensive statement.[38] And so the hearings moved into September, with Shimada firmly denying misfeasance and outside pressure to sell to a particular person. At one court session, Shimada attempted to set the record straight on his appointment as bank president. "Many people seem to be under the impression that as I had been appointed president of the Bank through the recommendation of Mr. Mitsuchi . . . one of the accused, and the late Mr. Inoue, former Finance Minister, I had to act according to their wishes. However, this is quite unfounded. I was never influenced by outsiders during my term in office." As for the decision to sell to Kawai's syndicate, Shimada noted that Kawai was first interviewed in March 1933, when the value of each share had fallen to ¥103. The bank, he told Kawai, was unwilling to sell at such a low price. "When approached by Mr. Kawai again . . . however, I told Messrs. Yanagida and Takagi . . . that the Bank might sell 100,000 shares at a unit price higher than ¥120."[39]

On September 19 the trial's somber mood took on an air of comedy. This occurred when a question was raised about a report that Fujita Kenichi, angry over being left out of the stock sale, threatened a lawsuit against the Bank of Taiwan directors. Fujita, a former member of the House of Peers and a former head of the Tokyo Chamber of Commerce, after involvement in several notorious scandals, was identified publicly with corrupt business practices. Indeed, in the Gōdō Woolen Cloth Company case, the Supreme Court decision upholding his three-month prison sentence for misfeasance, with a stay of execution for three years, was issued just nine days after this comedy interlude.[40] Takagi and other defendants denied that Fujita's threats had influenced the stock sale. Judge Fujii, wanting to hear more, called on Nagano. Fujita, said Nagano, needed to be placated. "When I interviewed Mr. Fujita at the Industrial Club, together with Mr. Shoriki, of the *Yomiuri*, he strongly complained of the contract to his exclusion. He was so excited that he burst into tears and screamed. Moreover, as I was told by Mr. Shoriki later that when he met Fujita the previous day, Fujita, stretching himself at full length on the linoleum floor, demanded some solatium. I persuaded my friends to give the money to him."[41] Fujita was given ¥50,000. After relating this story, Nagano told the court that an angry Fujita was behind the so-called Teijin scandal. Turning to Shimada, Fujii asked why he had confessed. Mainly, he replied, because Procurator Hori had threatened to shut down the Bank of Taiwan by seizing all of the bank's books. Faced with this threat, Shimada said whatever appeared to please Hori. Procurator Kuroda was criticized by Shimada as well for his bitter denunciation of businessmen and politicians as corrupt.[42]

During the sessions of September 26 and 28, Shimada maintained his innocence: "My statements at the Procurator's Office, as well as in the preliminary examination, were entirely false. . . . I was forced by Procurator Kuroda to make false statements in order to make them agree with those of Takagi." Why, asked Judge Fujii, did you make such statements and immediately, after release on bail, hand a petition to the court repudiating statements made during the preliminary examination? "As I wanted to be released as quickly as possible, I gave such answers as would please the preliminary judge."[43] During the next to last session (September 26), several witnesses corroborated Shimada's denial of bribing Nakajima on June 26, 1933. Shimada stated that he had visited Nakajima's office only once, on June 29, not on the earlier date. At the June 29 meeting, new directors were chosen for the Teijin Company. Fortunately, for Shimada, two employees at the office swore that the visit was on June 29; the desk calender in

Nakajima's office also contained that date. Furthermore, a policeman at the official residence plus several other people swore that the visit was on that date.[44]

Shimada's lawyer, Matsumoto Shigetoshi, asked the court to drop the charge against his client, because the preliminary court decision was based on an illegal examination. Procurator Hirata objected. Fujii reserved a reply. Shimada again denied colluding with other bank officers to sell Teijin stocks too cheaply. He was not, therefore, responsible for a bank loss of ¥1,600,000.[45]

Former bank director Yanagida stood before Judge Fujii on October 3. Mainly, he confirmed previous testimony. Why, asked Fujii, did the share value rise so steeply? Yanagida felt that the Manchurian Incident (September 1931) was the direct cause. Like Takagi and Shimada, Yanagida argued that the outlook for the rayon business was bad, and thus the bank's profit on the stock sale was reasonable.[46] At his last appearance, Fujii inquired about the 1,300 shares. Everything in the record about the 1,300 shares is a lie, insisted Yanagida. The false statements were made to escape the procurators' bad treatment. Handcuffed and subjected to great pressure by procurators, he had lied. Furthermore, at the preliminary examination, he went along with the judges' view on the division of the 300 shares.[47]

At a later hearing, lawyer Matsumoto made another appeal for Shimada's release. The procurator's actions "were an infringement of personal rights recognized under the Imperial Constitution. Although the Procurator pleads that no force was employed in the examination, the detention of the accused in handcuffs was clear proof of coercion." Moreover, said Matsumoto, "the method used by the Procuratorial authorities was in contravention of the Code of Criminal Procedure."[48] Although at times the argument between Matsumoto and Hirata was heated, it ended with a victory for the prosecution.[49]

During the following weeks it was the turn of first Koshifuji and then Okazaki to defend their amended pleas, explaining why they signed confessions that were repudiated. On January 23, 1936, Okazaki, who remained in the dock, was still refuting a bribery charge.[50] By early February, Judge Fujii was conducting a "supplementary examination" of the five Bank of Taiwan officials. Nagano appeared as well. As before, all denied the charges.[51] At one session, Nagano said: "I cannot believe that I was handcuffed by the prison authorities in the fear that I might commit suicide. I am still convinced that it was a sort of torture."[52] Nagano, in tears, was calmed by the judge.[53]

At the eighty-fourth hearing on February 18, 1936, Nagano was still standing before Judge Fujii. A newspaper article noted that the predicted trial length of eighteen months was probably too optimistic; judicial authorities blamed the delay on defendants' retraction of confessions. Furthermore, noted the article, the really prominent accused were not yet examined.[54] Doubtless, public interest in this long, tedious trial was flagging by late February. Then, on February 26, an army coup in Tokyo, which nearly overthrew the Okada Cabinet, rocked the political world. Editors and journalists, not surprisingly, concentrated on this sensational story. News about events in Judge Fujii's courtroom moved to newspapers' back pages.[55]

During March, April, and May, Judge Fujii continued to raise questions about the stock sale. No doubt newspaper readers wondered why so many months were spent on every conceivable aspect of economic conditions and the workings of the stock market. Judge Fujii, in a postwar interview, answered this question: "We did not know much about the stock market and share prices."[56] Therefore, if newspaper readers thought that Fujii's circular method of questioning was designed merely to entrap defendants in a web of contradictions, they were mistaken; the bench was also learning about the financial world. A newspaper article, describing the 116th hearing (May 14, 1936), illustrates this learning process. Kawai, who lectured on economics at Tokyo Imperial University, grew indignant as Fujii asked about alleged stock deal irregularities. Kawai corrected the judge, saying that in fact he was merely a broker and was involved only in the sale. When the judges returned, after a brief recess, Kawai handed Fujii his book on economics plus other documents, saying that they contained details about the operation of the financial world. It was difficult, Kawai added, even for experts to predict stock prices.[57]

As the trial neared the one-year mark, with no appearance of prominent defendants, public interest hit a low point. Just at this time, however, a procuratorial irregularity and a division in the ranks of justice officials surfaced. This problem, which grew to epic proportions over the following months, not only opened a wedge for exploitation by lawyers but must have gladdened the hearts of newspaper editors. The problem surfaced in early June, when Procurator Biwada stated that he had obtained permission from Preliminary Judge Morozumi Seiei before showing a letter written by one defendant to another defendant (suspects were isolated during the preliminary examination phase; permission was required for any communication).[58] At the next hearing, however, Biwada confessed: "To my embarrassment, the preliminary judge now declares that he never gave the permission. . . . I swear that I obtained his permission." Caught by surprise, Judge Fujii adjourned court for several minutes. On reopening, Fujii asked if Biwada was suggesting that Morozumi lied. "I do not mean to say that the Preliminary Judge had gone back on his word. There is no evidence to prove it, but my conviction is that I received his permission."[59] Judge Fujii managed to shelf this problem, but only for two days, because at the June 6 hearing lawyers, who knew about messages exchanged between suspects during the initial interrogation and the preliminary examination phases, which they viewed as part of a process to force confessions, were eager to put this issue before the court and the press. Biwada again denied any criticism of Preliminary Judge Morozumi. "I never said that the judge has gone back on his word." One lawyer replied: "Your explanation is mysterious. You claim you received the permission of the Judge before you consented to the accused exchanging letters. But the Judge holds that he does not remember having given such permission. If you insist on your stand, then the Judge's statement must be questioned."[60]

Although this was not the first public airing of the passage of "advice notes" (*kankokusho*) from one suspect to another, it was the first time in this trial that a public split had appeared in judicial ranks. Lawyers, knowing that these "notes" were used to push and pull suspects toward a confession, were eager to challenge them. Indeed, Nagawa (Kuroda's lawyer) asked Justice Minister Ohara at a Budget Committee meeting in February 1935 if Preliminary Judge Morozumi had given permission for their use. Permission had been given for procurators to act as go-betweens and to carry these notes back and forth, confirmed Ohara.[61]

Nonaka Moritaka, a political journalist who observed this trial and published several books about it, wrote that correspondence between suspects and with outsiders became a very contentious legal point. Not only did this issue produce sharp questions in the Diet, but it disrupted the trial. The central point was whether or not the procurators had Morozumi's permission. Moreover, noted Nonaka, written material was not the only issue at hand; visiting rights also came under scrutiny. Nine of these "advice notes" were exchanged (Nonaka lists only eight, because one was lost by the prosecution) and sixteen visits: a total of twenty-five contacts during the so-called isolation period. For example, on May 3, 1934, Takagi addressed a note to Okazaki, which was carried by Procurator Yagi Hikouchi; later Yagi showed it to Shimada. At about the same time, Shimada sent a note to Okazaki (Yagi acted as go-between). This continued throughout May, with Yagi showing Mrs. Ōkubo a note from her husband about May 24. It appears that these "notes" played a key role in obtaining confessions. For example, the lost note from Takagi to Yanagida, which Takagi wrote on the back of a name card, stated that since he had told the procurator about the gift from Nagasaki, Yanagida should feel free to talk about it. According to Unno Shinkichi (Okazaki's lawyer), both Yanagida and Okazaki (who was also shown the name card) were so shocked by this message that they began to help procurators prepare confessions. Asked by Unno if he knew about the name card note, Biwada agreed that Yagi took the note to Yanagida. As for face-to-face meetings, the first appears to be on April 27: Takagi met with his wife (Procurator Kuroda was present). The sixteenth was on about October 17 between Nagano and Kobayashi (Procurator Hori was present; it is unclear if this was Hori Takatsugu or Hori Masamichi). As in the case of the "notes," at issue was the matter of the preliminary judge's permission.[62]

Once this crucial issue of correspondence and conferences surfaced in open court, lawyers kept reminding Judge Fujii that the only way to settle the matter was to call Preliminary Judge Morozumi. Not surprisingly, procurators objected.[63] Although the prosecution won the first battle on this issue, it was a short-term victory, because Judge Fujii, dogged by lawyers, called Morozumi before the court in May 1937. This important decision is discussed on page 138.

Public interest was rekindled with the examination of Vice-Minister Kuroda on October 13. As one newspaper put it: "This was the 164th hearing, a record in Japanese Court history. . . . Mr. Kuroda was the first accused of accepting bribes to be examined. Besides Mr. Kuroda there were present the two important figures, viz., Mr. Mitsuchi, former Minister of Railways, and Baron Nakashima, former Minister of Commerce and Industry." Before the examination, noted the paper, attorney Nagawa asked the bench "to give special consideration to the written petition sent by Mr. Kuroda . . . to Chief-Procurator Iwamura . . . [since] this is generally rumoured to have been responsible directly for the downfall of the Saito Cabinet."[64] Kuroda was asked by Fujii to explain his relationship with Nakajima, Mitsuchi, Shimada, Takagi, and other defendants. Next Kuroda discussed the 1927 financial panic, the Teijin shares held by the Bank of Japan, Japan's withdrawal from the League of Nations (1933), the rayon industry, and so on. Regarding the Bank of Taiwan's policy for selling Teijin shares, Kuroda pleaded no knowledge.[65] Like other defendants, Kuroda repudiated his confession in a pretrial document submitted to the Justice Ministry, and, like the other defendants, he repudiated his confession on the trial's opening day. On October 20, 1936, he again denied that he had received any Teijin shares.[66]

Long-circulating rumors that Kuroda's "petition" had caused the fall of the Saitō Cabinet were correct. Political reporter Nonaka noted that, while Takagi's confession merely "shook" the cabinet, the petition "crushed" it. Even after the arrests on April 5 in Osaka and Tokyo, followed by the arrest of Vice-Minister Kuroda on May 19, the premier and the cabinet held firm, waiting for proof to appear. On June 25, 1934, Saitō heard from Justice Minister Koyama about the contents of Kuroda's petition. For Saitō, the most shocking information was about money received by Takahashi Koresaka (Finance Minister Takahashi's son) from Kuroda. Moreover, procurators planned to interrogate Koresaka, said Koyama. Therefore, after a discussion with Finance Minister Takahashi and Home Minister Yamamoto, Saitō decided to resign.[67]

Readers will recall that Justice Minister Ohara, in an attempt to calm a protest over infringement of personal rights, submitted documents to the lower house. Among these documents was a "thank you note" (*reijō*) written by Kuroda, dated June 22, 1934. This note was, in fact, merely the first part of the petition. Kuroda addressed Chief Procurator Iwamura as "excellency," begging his pardon for the trouble he had caused: "Procurator Kuroda tells me that your excellency is very concerned about me. I am overwhelmed by your concern. Of course, from the beginning of the interrogation it has been my duty to tell the truth without causing trouble for everyone."[68] Finally, on October 22, 1936, the petition was revealed fully, because it was incorporated in the formal report from the procurators to the preliminary judge, who in turn included it in the *Yoshin*. Judge Fujii pointed out at the October 22 hearing that this document was a "petition" (*tangansho*), not a proper written report; it appears that he was both puzzled and irritated at its inclusion in the *Yoshin*.[69] Following the thank you note section, Kuroda wrote that he had brought this sad predicament upon himself. "Therefore, I am not hiding facts or maneuvering to get a lighter sentence. There is nothing I want more than to smoothly and quickly clarify the facts and to receive a sympathetic trial. It is over a month since interrogations began, but as yet I have not been able to clarify everything. I am frustrated, because I do not remember everything, especially the names of people with whom I entrusted money and what they did with it." He continued by saying that he relied on procurators' sympathy "in order to clarify the truth." Kuroda's memory problem "has caused them lots of trouble, so much so that it may appear that I am hiding the truth." After reassuring Iwamura that he was eager to discover the truth, Kuroda wrote: "I have violated the law. . . . Furthermore, at this point, I do not even have a clear memory of doing it." Kuroda explained that perhaps his inability to sleep properly was the reason he had difficulty recalling things. "Your excellency," he concluded, "I am openly telling you everything and appealing for your mercy."[70] The balance of this document details how he received money from Nagasaki and what he did with it (this is discussed earlier).[71]

Judge Fujii asked about the origin of this strange document. Kuroda said: "I was ordered to write a petition by Procurator Kuroda. It appears as if I requested to write it, but I never even thought about it. I never did request to do it. Procurator Kuroda urged me strongly to write a petition." Kuroda noted that the preliminary judge never once asked about it. Moreover, he said, after Kuroda dropped out of the case, other procurators never mentioned it. "While in jail I began to wonder, what was the purpose of doing it?" Kuroda said that he was told by Procurator Kuroda and others that he must write a detailed statement about what happened to the money. The procurators, however, were unhappy with his first draft. Vice-Minister Kuroda then requested a visit with Chief Procurator Iwamura; Procurator Kuroda replied that a meeting could be arranged, but only after he had petitioned Iwamura. Since Procurator Kuroda insisted the letter be in petition form, the vice-minister returned to jail and wrote it. According to the vice-minister, although he wrote most of the petition in pen himself, it was dictated by Procurator Kuroda, who supplied details about who received money. On seeing the vice-minister's draft, Procurator Kuroda had said that not enough respect was shown; he suggested that "excellency" (*kakka*) be added. The vice-minister started to rewrite the draft, but Kuroda stopped him, saying that official paper could not be used. Do it after you return to your cell, he said, using regular writing paper. The vice-minister was concerned that others would read it, so prison authorities were ordered to seal it. Vice-Minister Kuroda rewrote the petition, gave it to a guard, and saw Chief Procurator Iwamura on July 7, 1934.[72]

Since this petition was so important for the prosecution, inquired attorney Nagawa, why was there no record of Finance Minister Takahashi's son's interrogation about the ¥30,000 loan? Because the vice-minister's statement changed, replied Biwada. This strange answer reflected another of the loose ends in the prosecution's case; perhaps Procurator Kuroda's death contributed to this omission. Judge Fujii, too, thought it a strange omission. Therefore, he called Takahashi Koresaka and another person during the witness phase of the trial (see below).[73]

At the October 27 hearing, the petition remained the focus of attention. "The petition" insisted Kuroda, "was not submitted by me voluntarily but at the insistence of the procurator in charge."[74] Kuroda pointed out that a voluntary written petition would have gone to Justice Minister Koyama or

Procurator General Hayashi, whom he knew.[75] Pressed by Fujii about the petition, Kuroda replied: "I only wrote it because they told me I would be released immediately."[76] At that time, he said, I trusted what procurators told me. Moreover, he believed that if he did not write the petition, he would never be released. Therefore, he wrote it, planning to clarify everything later. At one point, said the vice-minister, he heard that Takahashi Koresaka had been questioned on July 7, but later he heard the opposite. Naturally, he informed his lawyer about this strange development.[77] In fact, Kuroda was mistaken, because Takahashi gave a deposition to Procurator Nagao Takeo (see below).

At the October 27 hearing, Nagawa, who was one of the most aggressive lawyers, demanded that procurators prove that shares were cashed in. Furthermore, he concentrated on exposing the origin of Kuroda's "petition." Nagawa pointed out that, after Kuroda and Ōkubo confessed, procurators had sent a report to Justice Minister Koyama. Koyama replied that confessions were not enough. He asked these questions: Where did the shares come from? Do the suspects have the shares? If they possess the shares, where are they? If they cashed them in, how much money did they receive per share and what happened to the money? Koyama warned procurators that confessions alone were inadequate proof and urged procurators to conduct a deeper investigation. Asked to comment on this, Biwada said he knew nothing about it. Were there any facts proving the crime of bribery before Kuroda's petition or Ōkubo's statement? Biwada was unable to comment immediately. Nagawa pressed harder. If you view trial documents, there is no proof until June 22—in brief, no proof until Bank of Taiwan and Finance Ministry officials confessed. Is this correct? Biwada repeated that he was unable to comment. Sarcastically, Nagawa suggested that Biwada, whose sole duty for nearly three years was the Teijin scandal case, was strangely ill-informed. It appears, said Nagawa, that in June 1934 the investigation became bogged down, because procurators concentrated on suspects receiving bribes. This investigative imbalance even caused problems for the preliminary courts, stated Nagawa. I am unaware of that, replied Biwada. Did you have any kind of evidence between June 22 and 29? I can't give that answer here, said Biwada. Nagawa replied for him, by saying that it was clear from the documents that the prosecution did not have confirming evidence before June 29.[78]

Unable to pry open Biwada, Nagawa asked Kuroda to describe his first interrogation. Procurators Biwada and Kuroda met me on May 19 at the Justice Officials' Association Building, said Kuroda. Procurator Kuroda said: "Oh, you are Mr. Kuroda. I am Kuroda. This is Procurator Biwada.

I have wanted to meet you for a long time."[79] Although the vice-minister was puzzled by this remark, he well recalled Kuroda from the Meitō Incident tax scandal. From the face-to-face meeting, he had the feeling that Procurator Kuroda held a personal grudge. As they talked, Procurator Kuroda told him that it would be best to pretend he had spent all that money.[80] "Since you are going into politics, you already have been spending money on politics, haven't you? You took that money to Finance Minister Takahashi. Probably, you will never admit that, even if you are dying." Biwada and other procurators, said Kuroda, insisted that he admit this. "They pressured me a great deal to agree that if I didn't take the money to Takahashi, then I took it to Koresaka [Takahashi's eldest son] or to Korefuku [his second eldest son]."[81] As procurators pounded away on this point, they discovered that Kuroda had helped the eldest son get a company directorship. Procurator Kuroda then suggested that he must have handed the money over to Yasuda Hikotarō, who passed it on to the eldest son, recalled Kuroda. After that was decided, said Kuroda, the procurators helped me move numbers to make sure figures were in balance. Finally, said Kuroda, it was decided that Yasuda got ¥30,000; that is how it appeared in the "petition." Nagawa interrupted, reminding everyone that the petition was a key document. Indeed, Nagawa stressed, it was so important it should have been submitted as evidence, but procurators held it back until ordered by the court. Stung by Nagawa's sharp attack, Biwada replied: The petition was not presented, because procurators regarded it more like private correspondence; besides that, they considered its impact on the vice-minister's reputation, so it was withheld. Nagawa scoffed at this reply, saying that, since Kuroda was already a defendant, how could his reputation be further damaged? Moreover, said the lawyer, was there not another reason? Biwada denied any other motive. Nagawa continued to attack Biwada, pointing out that it was this "petition" that had caused Saitō to resign. Koyama's report to Saitō, however, which should have been based on a proper interrogation record and physical evidence, was flawed badly. In fact, it was based on Kuroda's petition, which even procurators did not consider accurate. Moreover, there was no physical evidence. Without doubt, stressed Nagawa, it was this badly flawed prosecutors' report presented to Koyama that had destroyed the cabinet. Nagawa was positive about this fact, because Saitō had told him so.[82]

The 171st hearing, on October 29, marked the end of Kuroda's examination. Like others before him, Kuroda apologized: "I am extremely sorry that because my replies to the procuratorial authorities at the very beginning were misleading, I have caused considerable inconvenience to the

court and the other parties concerned. . . . I repeat that I am quite innocent. My arrest was indeed unfortunate."[83]

At this point, the trial's sedate pace accelerated, with the bench managing to complete examinations of Ōkubo Teiji (director of the Banking
Bureau), Nakajima, and Mitsuchi before the New Year holiday. Ōkubo,
who followed Kuroda, also denied, again, all charges. Ōkubo was pressured
to admit guilt, said lawyer Hozumi Shigetō. The key to enlisting Ōkubo's
cooperation was simply to tell him that Okazaki, his tubercular brother-
in-law, was spitting up blood. Sign this statement, they said, and we will
hospitalize him. By signing it, Ōkubo was confirming Okazaki's story.
Biwada was involved in obtaining this confession.[84]

On December 5, Baron Nakajima stood in the dock. Of particular
interest to the court was former minister Nakajima's role in the stock sale.
Judge Fujii asked about his connection with the Banchōkai, his relationship with Mitsuchi, and his role in the transfer of Teijin stock. The baron
said that in his official capacity he played no role in the supervision of stock
exchanges. As for the listing of shares on an exchange, that was in the hands
of the Commercial Affairs Bureau. Even here, however, companies were
only required to file a report after the stock was listed. Thus, Nakajima was
making a key point: His permission was not required for any part of the
Teijin stock transaction. Asked about the ¥10,000, he emphasized that it
was a political contribution.[85]

Court sessions on December 10 and 12 focused on the alleged two hundred shares received by Nakajima and converted to cash by Mitsuchi.
Nakajima again denied his *Yoshin* statement. Judge Fujii asked why he had
confessed receiving shares from Takagi and turning them into cash. Why
did he also give details about how the money was used? "When I recall
those days," replied the baron, "it makes me want to hide in a hole." One
reason for the lies, said Nakajima, was his hectic official life; he simply
could not recall all the details about it. Moreover, other defendants, at the
interrogations and preliminary examinations, insisted certain things happened on certain dates. "I never imagined that some of the defendants who
handled the public shares transaction would lie to the authorities about me.
Therefore, I accepted most of what they said, and their claims appear in
my statement."[86] Before his interrogation, Nakajima pointed out, procurators questioned Nagasaki, Takagi, Nagano, and Kobayashi. As for his
statement, he could not recall the procurator in charge reading it to him.
Therefore, the contents came as a surprise when he first heard it in court.[87]
Doubtless, Judge Fujii was getting the message that procurators, having
prepared confessions, made Nakajima's mesh with the others.

Nakajima had "voluntary" talks with Biwada until his arrest on July 21. Fujii asked about these sessions. On July 5, replied the baron, Biwada had informed him that Nagano was very worried about his health. Nagano was willing to sacrifice himself for you, reported Biwada, even if resulted in a long prison term. Indeed, said Biwada, Nagano knelt as he begged me to prevent this case from harming you. This report, said Nakajima, moved him deeply.[88]

At the next interrogation, procurators pretended that they knew everything about the stock transfer, including 200 shares he had received, recalled the baron. For example, they claimed Takagi visited his official residence. Thus, said Nakajima, he was faced by Takagi and Nagano's agreement that he got 200 shares. The procurators, recalled Nakajima, stressed that the matter would be settled if he simply agreed with the other confessions.[89] If he cooperated, he told Fujii, they promised "not to prosecute him formally" (*mitometa nara kiso no tetsuzuki mo torazu*) or to hold him physically.[90] Hearing this testimony, the courtroom audience must have marveled at the gullibility of this big businessman/minister. Next Nakajima recounted the July 6 conversation with Akiyama (his lawyer) at his residence. Chief Procurator Iwamura, Akiyama said, would neither hold nor prosecute Nakajima if he admitted receiving the shares. On July 21, Biwada switched to tougher tactics, as he browbeat Nakajima into admitting that shares were received. Nakajima told Judge Fujii that he had decided to lie in order to make this problem disappear. Nakajima confirmed that the 200 shares were handed to Mitsuchi, who converted them to cash at the same time that he cashed in his own 300 shares. What Nakajima did not realize was that this statement supported Takagi's perjury that he gave the 300 shares to Mitsuchi. Besides repudiating his *Yoshin* testimony before Fujii, Nakajima mada a public apology to Mitsuchi.[91]

On December 17, Judge Fujii pressed Nakajima for details about the ¥10,000 given by Nagano. The money came from Nagano, Shibusawa Masao, Takanashi Hiroshi, Nagasaki Eizō, and Kobayashi Ataru, replied Nakajima. Although they called this money a "*seibo*" (end of year gift), said Nakajima, it was in fact given to pay for expenses as a state minister. Some people see that as a "return gift" (*sharei*, i.e., a bribe), said Nakajima, but it was not given as such. "This money was for my necessary public expenses [*kōyōhi*, i.e., political expenses]."[92]

To illustrate this point, Nakajima talked about the Kasuikai (Kasui was the baron's haiku pen name) political support group. Together with supporters, Nakajima had organized this group after entering the cabinet. Nakajima viewed the Kasuikai, whose members heard reports and discussed current affairs, as an unofficial group whose advice aided him in official duties. Members were Parliamentary Vice-Minister Iwakiri Shigeo, Parliamentary Councilor Matsumura Kōzō, Gotō Kunihiko (a director of the Keisei Railway Company and a Banchōkai member), Zen Keinosuke (a director of the Industrial Club), Nagano, Kawai, and several others. After a bit, the meetings stopped. A second Kasuikai, however, was created on October 13, 1933. Nakajima said that Nagano, Nagasaki, Kobayashi, Shibusawa, Shimizu Iku, and Takanashi Hiroshi attended. Toward the end of October, recalled Nakajima, Nagano told him that the members planned a political support group. Therefore, Nagano suggested invitations to members and their wives for a party at his residence to launch this group. This gala occasion was on November 2, 1933. About two weeks later, Nagano informed the minister that members of the second Kasuikai wanted to give an "*oseibo*." Nakajima thanked him; a few days later Nagano arrived with ¥10,000 in an envelope, which was left with the minister's secretary (Sawada), recalled Nakajima. Unfortunately, he added, the procurators looked at it as a bribe for help with the Teijin Company stock transaction (under interrogation Nagano said the money was a quid pro quo). Nine thousand yen out of this sum was placed by Secretary Sawada in a special bank account used for the baron's political affairs. One thousand was given, at Nagano's suggestion, to lower house member Koike Shirō.[93]

Asked by Fujii if he had recommended Nagano and Kawai for Teijin Company directorships, Nakajima said yes. He noted, however, that both had well-established business reputations, and other people would have recommended them. Thus, said Nakajima, there was no reason for them to express their appreciation. As for the Teijin sale, Nakajima insisted that he did nothing to promote the sale or to increase the price of shares.[94] Was the baron hard-pressed for money at that time? asked Fujii. Not too pressed, replied Nakajima, but, he added, after becoming a state minister, he was obligated to give donations and to do other things to help people.[95]

Weary court clerks, police guards, defendants, procurators, and judges must have thought the trial had reached its climax on December 19, with the appearance of former minister Mitsuchi, the last defendant to be examined. In fact, these hearings continued for another year. Mitsuchi, as always, firmly denied receiving 300 shares, denied cashing in 200 shares for Nakajima, and roundly condemned the charge of perjury.[96] Replying to Judge Fujii about the stock deal, Mitsuchi said: "I knew nothing about the transaction previously. Nor was I interested in it." He admitted, however, that in early June 1933, at the premier's official residence, Nakajima asked him to recommend Nagano for a Teijin Company directorship. Fujii asked about the 300 shares the *Yoshin* stated that he received. "What a thing to say," replied Mitsuchi. "It's rubbish." But, said the judge, Nakajima and Takagi admitted this fact. "Is your statement really correct?" Mitsuchi replied: "I swear my statement is correct." Reflecting on the preliminary examination, Mitsuchi recalled: "Takagi was quite emaciated, and he looked like another man. Moreover, as I was warned by the Preliminary Judge not to say anything that might excite him, I talked with him very quietly. But as Takagi talked a lot of nonsense, as though it was the truth, I could not check my temper, and I remember having shouted 'Do you mean to trap me?'" Mitsuchi continued: "I was firmly under the impression that Takagi . . . would not tell any lies. . . . It turned out to be quite the opposite, however, and as I thought that any further debate would be useless, I retired, considerably provoked." Takagi, again crying in court, called out: "I'm sorry for Mr. Mitsuchi."[97]

On December 22, Mitsuchi, prompted by Judge Fujii, analyzed the Teijin Incident. When the *Jiji shinpō* articles appeared, Mitsuchi regarded them as just another "comedy" (*chaban kyōgen*). Noticing that procurators were investigating, he thought it was merely a formality because of the Diet uproar. Then, Bank of Taiwan officials and people in the buyers group were arrested. Still, Mitsuchi saw this as merely the work of inexperienced procurators untutored in the workings of the financial world; it would soon be clarified, he thought. Soon, however, Finance Ministry officials were arrested. "I thought something evil was going on among the *Jiji* people and also behind the scene among the procurators. Perhaps some procurators were cooperating with a plot (*inbō*) because of the Meitō Incident. Since I am well informed about the Finance Ministry, I have always believed that Mr. Kuroda and the others would never be involved in such a dirty thing as bribery. I still think that today."[98] A bit later, newspapers began to print that Mitsuchi was under suspicion. "However, I had nothing to do with the Teijin shares transaction (*Teijin kabu no baibai ni wa issai kanshite inai*). Therefore, as these articles appeared, I thought they they must have been written by plotters (*inbōka*)." Soon Mitsuchi was asked to appear "voluntarily." On August 21, 1934, he met Chief Procurator Iwamura and Baron Nakajima. "There, for the first time, I learned something about the incident." Mitsuchi recalled that Nakajima had requested the meeting for two reasons: to ask a favor and to warn him (what to expect from the procurators). Nakajima told Mitsuchi that, except for establishing the share connection between the two of them, the investigation was over.[99]

According to Mitsuchi, Nakajima said that he had confessed that he had received two hundred shares and Mitsuchi had received three hundred, but this point needed clarification. Nakajima assured Mitsuchi that he need not worry about being charged with bribery, because the stock transfer in no way touched his ministerial duties. "Please recognize this fact," pleaded the baron. "If you do not recognize this fact, I will be accused of perjury, and there is a possibility I'll go to prison. Based on my experience of over a month in jail, I won't be able to tolerate the pain any longer." Nakajima urged Mitsuchi to think about the painful experience of other suspects as well. "If you admit transferring the shares to cash and receiving the three hundred, it will help everyone."[100]

Mitsuchi told the court that Nakajima had added that he would give a detailed explanation later. Iwamura heard everything. Mitsuchi asked Nakajima if he had admitted getting the shares. "When I heard him say yes, I thought that he must have lost his mind. I looked him in the eyes and I said that I would not do such a thing, even if my head would be cut off." Before leaving, Mitsuchi told Nakajima to "please stop talking nonsense." At home, when he recounted this amazing experience, everyone laughed, recalled Mitsuchi. The next day Mitsuchi was ordered before Preliminary Judge Morozumi as a witness. "I said that I knew nothing."[101]

Next Mitsuchi gave the bench a lecture on procuratorial misconduct based on experience plus conversations with lawyer and former justice minister Hara Yoshimichi (Mitsuchi was education minister in the same cabinet: Tanaka Giichi, 1927–1929). In some cases procurators do not judge facts properly, he said, and end up with a fabricated incident. Unfortunately, innocent people who are prosecuted suffer physical and psychological damage; because of pain they admit to anything, which hurts others as well. Thus, when Mitsuchi heard Takagi's and Nakajima's statements read by the preliminary judge, he realized what had happened.[102] "Takagi is a wonderful person," said Mitsuchi. "The sweet words of being released must have swayed him. Others, after seeing Takagi's statement, admitted to being involved." After hearing Nakajima's statement, said Mitsuchi, "I told the court that the statement was entirely fabricated" (*sono kyōjutsu wa zenbu tsurigoto de arimasu*).[103]

Recalling his next appearance as a witness (August 28), Mitsuchi said that Takagi, as they sat face-to-face, began to cry. Preliminary Judge Morozumi encouraged Takagi to talk, and Takagi repeated the lies in the statement. It was obvious that he feared the procurator, said Mitsuchi, and wanted to escape as soon as possible. "I asked him how he could tell such lies with a straight face."[104] At his August 29 appearance, Mitsuchi said he again faced a begging Nakajima (Judge Morozumi was present). As before, Mitsuchi refused to join the defendant's effort to please procurators.[105]

After explaining that he was indicted for perjury on September 13, released on October 31, and then again called on November 24, Mitsuchi lectured the court. The Teijin Incident, he stressed, was based solely on forced confessions. Procurators used human weaknesses to fabricate an incident, which caused a political change. "If this sort of thing is permitted, the destiny of cabinets will the maneuvered by a couple of low-ranking procurators. . . . To abuse the power of justice is a more fearful thing than a pistol, bayonet, or bomb. This Teijin Incident introduced to the world a suspicious-looking low-hanging cloud of justice fascism (*shihō fassho*). Whether this was caused by stupidity or whether it was a malicious plot, whoever brought this case to this point should take responsibility before the nation by committing suicide."[106]

Even today, said Mitsuchi, since he did not know why he was on trial, he was extremely angry at people who made false charges. All of them, said Mitsuchi, came to apologize after his release from jail. The more he heard from defendants, however, said Mitsuchi, the less his anger was directed at defendants and the more it turned toward the procurators. Nevertheless, these respectable people who lied should have conducted themselves properly.[107] Imagine Mitsuchi turning to look at fellow defendants: "Why couldn't they take a more resolute attitude and act like Japanese men?"[108]

Mitsuchi said that, as he sat in the courtroom, hearing the contradictions and seeing the confusion, it became obvious that the entire Teijin Incident was fabricated. Before he became involved in this incident, he had never realized that justice authorities would do such a terrible thing.[109] Unwilling to depend solely on newspaper reports, the defense team published, on January 16, 1937, a shorthand record of Mitsuchi's December 19 and 22 court testimony.[110]

Testimony of Witnesses

Newspapers picked up the thread of the Teijin trial after the New Year holiday. At a hearing on February 4, 1937, Fujii decided that seventy-one prominent people would be called to help the court evaluate evidence. That many less prominent people would be heard as well is reflected in the total number of 101 witnesses (242 appeared during the preliminary examination). Besides hearing from housemaids, doctors, dentists, Nakajima's chauffeur, financial experts, government officials, and others, the court planned to visit the Bank of Taiwan's Tokyo office, the Finance Ministry, Nakajima's official office, and other places.[111]

Fujita Kenichi was the first witness (February 16). His appearance, no doubt, produced both frowns and smiles, not only because of his recent conviction for misfeasance, but because of a notorious earlier scandal in which he purchased an imperial decoration. Fujita discussed efforts to buy Teijin Company shares. Besides seeking advice from Baron Gō, Fujita stated, he had tried to approach Prime Minister Inukai through Diet member Hatoyama. Fujita had hoped political pressure on Bank of Japan and Finance Ministry officials would result in pressure on Bank of Taiwan officials to approve a sale. Fujita added that Privy Councilor Itō Miyoji was also approached. These activities, however, were interrupted by the murder of Inukai. Next Fujita discussed Nagano's role in this effort to buy stocks. In the end, he recalled, they had disagreed over how the stock deal should be handled.[112]

Shōriki Matsutarō of *Yomiuri Newspaper* appeared on February 18. Asked about his involvement, Shōriki claimed that Fujita had asked for help. After Fujita withdrew, Shōriki remained, working with others. For his aid, he received ¥95,000. What was his relationship with Baron Gō? asked the judge. Shōriki admitted that the baron had supported him for the newspaper presidency. What was he promised by Fujita? If the deal succeeded, Fujita promised to build a new office building for the newspaper or give one million yen in gifts, replied Shōriki. What did he do for Fujita? In his reply, Shōriki mentioned the name of Vice-Minister Kuroda; unexpectedly, the vice-minister interrupted the testimony, denying that they had met. Although he visited Education Minister Hatoyama's office in November or December of 1932, said Kuroda, Shōriki was not present. Shōriki replied that he recalled meeting Kuroda at Hatoyama's office.[113]

As the trial proceeded, infringement of personal rights was debated in the House of Representatives. For example, Justice Minister Shiono Suehiko was interpellated at a Budget Committee meeting of February 24. Tachikawa Taira (Seiyūkai) stated that one cause of the High Treason Incident (1910–1911) was officials' infringement of personal rights. Look at recent cases, he said, and in the background you will find official misconduct, including torture. Recently, the Teijin trial is a notorious example, noted Tachikawa. Shiono should, opined Tachikawa, clarify the disagreement over who ordered Ōkubo handcuffed. Was it the jailer or was it Procurator Biwada? Shiono replied that he did not know. Lawyer Nagawa (Seiyūkai) pushed Shiono to investigate this serious matter. Can the dignity of the law be maintained, he asked, if Procurator Biwada remains on duty at the trial? Shiono replied that Judge Fujii would make that decision.[114]

"Waiting for Confessions" was an editorial headline on February 24, 1937. "Police and procuratorial methods are under scrutiny again," began the column, "but it is doubtful whether the interpellations in the Diet will have any lasting effect." Makino Ryōzō (Seiyūkai) "did not confine his accusations to the police but went on to attack the general method of handling criminal cases. The procuratorial authorities, he pointed out, are not only in the habit of detaining suspects for an unduly long period, but are occasionally known to re-examine the prisoner after he has gone before the preliminary judge. This, of course, is against all the rules of procedure." The editorial noted that it was a matter of common knowledge that procurators abused their powers. "The Teijin scandal . . . is providing an outstanding example. All the accused . . . are men of substance. After arrest they were kept in police cells, without being allowed to see their lawyers. . . . Finally they were released on bail after having signed statements which amounted to confessions. In Court all the accused . . . [explained] that only by signing confessions could they secure a respite in an examination which threatened to break their health." The editorial commented on Justice Minister Shiono's excuse for procurators' conduct: the lack of enough procurators to handle an increased workload. "This explanation sounds suspiciously glib, but it is perfectly true that there are not enough procurators. The number of juridical officials is about the same as at the beginning of the Meiji era, but three times the number of suspects are examined." Lawmakers should insist on the appointment of additional procurators, "if only for the sake of depriving the Ministry of Justice of the excuse that the abuses of authority complained of, and the protracted examinations which are against the provisions of the criminal code, are due to harassed officials trying to keep up with too big a burden of work."[115]

On March 11, Judge Fujii announced the appointment of three expert witnesses (the head of the Tokyo Stock Exchange, the managing director of the Osaka Stock Exchange, and a university professor) who were to submit written reports on the Teijin Company stock transfer. At this same hearing, Muraji Kyūjirō, an Osaka broker chosen by Nagano as a liaison with cotton yarn merchants, explained his role in the Teijin stock sale.[116]

On-site inspections followed. The judges, accompanied by Biwada, visited the Fukoku Chōhei Insurance Company and the Tokyo office of the Bank of Taiwan on March 19. The following day the Finance Ministry and the home of Ōkubo were investigated. The twenty-fourth found them at the Osaka Prefectural Office inspecting basement police cells. Takagi and Okazaki together with their lawyers were there as well.[117]

Judge Fujii attempted, on April 15, to clear up the controversial ¥30,000 loan to Takahashi Koresaka (eldest son of the deceased finance minister). Besides Takahashi, Madam Mitsuhashi Tei, who managed a *machiai* (a drinking and eating place) bearing her name, appeared. Asked about his relationship with Vice-Minister Kuroda, Takahashi replied that they had attended high school together but that after graduation they did not meet for over ten years. In more recent years, while they occasionally met at official functions, they did not socialize. When Kuroda became president of Greater Tokyo Railway Company (Kuroda got permission from the minister to accept this position), Takahashi was invited to become a company auditor. Asked about Yasuda Hikotarō, Takahashi recalled meeting him after becoming an auditor. He was, however, unaware of the relationship between Kuroda and Yasuda. When he met Procurator Nagao Takeo (part of the Teijin case team) at the Broadcasting Club, Takahashi learned that Yasuda had died (mid-August 1933). Judge Fujii then shifted the discussion to Kuroda's petition. Kuroda stated that you told Yasuda that you needed ¥30,000, that Yasuda got the money from Kuroda, and that it was passed on to you. Did you ask Yasuda for money?[118] Takahashi replied: "Absolutely not! I never borrowed money from anyone in my lifetime. Especially, from Mr. Yasuda, whom I hardly knew."[119] Takahashi then said that Kuroda, after release from detention, paid him a visit to explain how he was forced to write a confession. Judge Fujii asked if Procurator Nagao was alone when Takahashi met him. Yes, replied Takahashi. Did Nagao or anyone else write down your conversation? No, but the procurator made a few notes in pencil. Since Takahashi was not carrying a seal, he applied a thumb print. Did Takahashi go to the Mitsuhashi with Kuroda? They went, he replied. This information was given to Nagao. What about Kuroda's petition? Did your father mention it? Takahashi said he knew nothing about it until the trial. In sum, Takahashi's testimony spotlighted the fact that the procuratorial team had Takahashi's deposition in which he denied receiving a ¥30,000 loan from Kuroda. This crucial information, however, was not included in the investigative record. Since judges depended on procurators and preliminary judges to compile an accurate factual record, this glaring omission must have further undermined Judge Fujii's confidence in the *Yoshin*'s reliability. When Madam Mitsuhashi appeared, she acknowledged knowing Takahashi and Kuroda but said that Kuroda was a more frequent patron. The judge asked if Kuroda had entrusted her with anything for safekeeping. She replied no. Pushed by Fujii to explain, she said that in about June 1934 Procurators Kuroda and Nagao asked to see some of the *machiai*'s books at their office.

After inspecting the books, they asked if the vice-minister had left something with her. She replied that she was holding nothing. Then, in mid-July Procurator Nagao told her that the vice-minister was positive that he had left something with her. After that, she told Fujii, they inquired about this mysterious something many times. Finally, on a trip to the procurator's office, she wrote in a statement that she was entrusted with nothing. Actually, she added, she could not write, so the *maichiai* shoeman, who accompanied her, wrote. Fujii then told her she was supposed to be holding a white envelope for Kuroda. She replied that something must have gone wrong with Kuroda's head (earlier she said this to the procurators).[120]

This white envelope contained, according to the petition, a receipt for the money loaned to Takahashi. Kuroda told Judge Fujii that Procurator Kuroda had told him to include this in the petition. Also, he was to write that he had instructed Madam Mitsuhashi to tell no one she had it, not even to admit having it to police or judges.[121]

Lawyers renewed pressure on Judge Fujii to call Preliminary Judge Morozumi as a witness. Imamura Rikisaburō had pointed out months earlier that whether or not Morozumi gave procurators permission to circulate notes among suspects and to permit suspects to visit each other was of crucial importance. If procurators would admit not having permission, the judge need not be heard, said Imamura; if they insisted they had permission, Morozumi must be heard.[122] Indeed, said the lawyer, "this is the most important matter in judging the Teijin Incident."[123] By May 18, 1937, Fujii was convinced. He noted that although Biwada claimed that Morozumi permitted both the exchange of notes and the visits, the procurator could not recall the date or how permission was received. Moreover, since Morozumi remained steadfast in denying that permission was given, Fujii announced that Morozumi would be called.[124]

Morozumi, standing in the dock on May 22 at the 233d hearing, was the first preliminary judge in Japanese judicial history to appear as a witness. "On about July 22nd, 1934, when you were in charge of the present case, did you receive a request from the procurator in charge to consent to an exchange of notes between the two accused, that is to say the handing of a letter written by Baron Nakashima to Nagano urging the latter to confirm his statement to the procurator that he had the 200 Teijin shares . . . realized by him?" Morozumi replied: "As the question is very important, I would rather submit my answer in writing." Fujii then asked: "Is it true that when the procurator confirmed the matter later you denied having given such approvals?" Morozumi said: "That too, I would like to answer in writing."[125] After more attempts to obtain a "yes" or "no," Judge Fujii dismissed

Morozumi. The preliminary judge, however, did promise a reply at the next hearing. Journalists reported that Judge Fujii was annoyed by Morozumi's evasions. They noted, moreover, that this legal point was important, because an exchange of notes and visits between suspects was strictly forbidden.[126] Lawyer Imamura wrote that "everyone was shocked" by Morozumi's reply.[127] So shocked, indeed, that the Imperial Bar Association submitted a resolution to Justice Minister Shiono and Procurator General Motoji Shinkuma complaining about Morozumi's refusal to give evidence. This attitude, said the grievance resolution, not only set a bad legal precedent but invited public scorn. When reporters asked about his attitude, Morozumi refused comment.[128]

Morozumi reappeared on June 8. Asked by Fujii about the exchange of notes, Morozumi pointed out that a year earlier he had submitted a report to Judge Kitō Toyotaka, president of the Tokyo Criminal Court, detailing the entire case. "Since the last hearing, I have studied the question carefully and have now come to the conclusion that I am not qualified to give evidence, and therefore am unable to answer the first question. I am sorry to disappoint you, but I cannot help it." Pressed further about Biwada's approaching him to confirm that permission was given, Morozumi replied that it was not Biwada but Hirata who asked. "In the latter part of June [1936] I visited Ichigaya Prison in connection with the Shimpeitai [God's Soldiers] affair, when Hirata asked me whether Procurator Biwada's statement that he had obtained my consent to the exchange of the note between the accused, was true or not." What did you say? asked Fujii. Morozumi replied: "Sorry, I cannot mention that here." If you told Hirata, responded Fujii, why will you not tell me? "Because I am not qualified to do so as a witness; I cannot touch upon the contents of the case. You can obtain full information in the report which I have submitted to President Kito of the Criminal Court."[129] Fujii also asked Morozumi if he knew about Justice Minister Ohara's reply to lawyer Nagawa in the Diet (Ohara said that Morozumi gave permission for suspects to meet). Morozumi claimed that it came to his attention at the May 22, 1937, court appearance.[130] One press report on the exchange between Fujii and Morozumi opined that it represented "one of the most serious legal questions in the Court history. . . . Holding that the attitude taken by the witness is against the provisions of the Criminal Procedure Law, Counsel for the accused urges the Court to take drastic action against him. The attitude of Presiding Judge Fujii is being watched with considerable interest."[131]

The following day Fujii requested, from Judge Kitō Toyotaka, Morozumi's report. On June 10, armed with this report (dated June 5,

1936), Judge Fujii read out the answer for which the packed visitors gallery was waiting: "In reply to a question put by you today, that is whether or not I gave permission to the procurator or procurators for the exchange of a note between the accused in the course of the preliminary examination of the Teijin case, I stated to you that I did not. As the question is important, I hereby report in writing that I never gave permission regarding the exchange of notes between the accused."[132] In one section of this report, Morozumi described meeting Procurator Kuroda "one day near the dining room of the Court, when Procurator Kuroda asked him if he could show a memorandum written by one of the accused to another in the course of the examination, to which he replied in the negative." Notwithstanding this answer, the justice minister replied to lawyer Nagawa, saying that permission for the exchange of notes was given by Morozumi. In the report to Kitō, Morozumi said that this was irritating, but, "convinced that a juridical official should not touch upon political affairs, he did not take any action." Yet Biwada told the court time and again that he had secured the preliminary judge's permission. Morozumi also wrote that "on about May 20 this year he was approached by Procurator Biwada and Procurator Hirata and was shown by them some notes. As they stated that he had given permission for the exchange of these notes, he says he made it quite clear to them that he had not done anything of the kind."[133] Hearing Morozumi's report, lawyer Imamura asked the procurators if they wished to change their statements. Both insisted that Morozumi had forgotten that he gave permission.[134]

A frustrated Fujii called on Morozumi to appear at the June 10 hearing, but a newpaper announced that Morozumi was bedridden with influenza. Nevertheless, people, eager to witness this historic event, waited outside the court building from early morning. After the courtroom opened, the visitors gallery overflowed. Morozumi, disregarding a doctor's advice, staggered into the courtroom. A chair was provided. Judge Fujii, after reading Morozumi's report, asked for confirmation that the report was his. Morozumi nodded. A thirty-five-minute question and reply session followed. Morozumi's replies, however, amounted to no more than statements that everything was correct in the report.[135] Thus, Morozumi refused to budge from his written statement to Judge Kitō: he did not give procurators permission for suspects to exchange notes or to visit.

As Judges Fujii and Morozumi engaged in a verbal tug-of-war, the June (out in May) issue of the widely read magazine *Chūō kōron* carried "Gōmon" (Torture) by Suzuki Yoshio (Takagi's attorney). It was necessary, wrote Suzuki, for criminal justice system authorities to employ scientific investigative methods. Unfortunately, however, old methods of forcing self-confessions continued. Offering the Teijin case as an example, Suzuki outlined the court's visit to Osaka, where Takagi was mistreated. Aside from the terrible living conditions, noted Suzuki, Takagi suffered only minor physical abuse, but his mental anguish was extreme. Nevertheless, opined Suzuki, there were ongoing cases of physical torture, of which the Kanagawa incident was an outstanding example.[136]

Next, Suzuki pointed out that it was recognized widely that self-confessions were an unreliable foundation for a criminal case. This was understood by everyone in the criminal justice field, from the lowest policeman to the highest judge. Nevertheless, self-confessions remained authorities' preferred proof. We should discard this obsolete viewpoint, said Suzuki, because self-confession often turned into the weakest part of an evidential chain. In fact, insisted Suzuki, authorities, by merely following the law, could complete criminal cases. Unfortunately, however, despite repeated requests by lawyers for authorities to follow the law, violations continued. Therefore, one conclusion, wrote Suzuki, was that laws are flawed and require modification. First among Suzuki's proposed reforms was the abolition of the preliminary court system. Another possible reform would give procurators the power to force witnesses to appear. On this point, however, he added that any change must be considered carefully. As for torture, which was an open secret, Suzuki argued that it could be prevented by raising public ethical standards and making changes in the legal structure.[137]

In the midst of the Morozumi drama, Judge Fujii received written reports on the proper price of Teijin stock shares from the head of the Tokyo Stock Exchange and other experts. The reports, which were leaked to the press, agreed that the sale price of ¥125 (minus one yen for Kawai's commission) was reasonable.[138]

Judge Fujii also received written comments from defense lawyers. On May 24, for example, Arima and Gujō (Ōno's and Aida's attorneys), requested clarification of the prosecution's indictments. Exactly what were the illegal acts committed? they asked. From the lawyers' perspective, the procurators' indictments and the *Yoshin* rested solely on the frail reeds of self-confessions, which suspects repudiated. Moreover, the government's weak case suffered a further setback, noted the lawyers, as the procurators failed, during the open trial, to present factual evidence to support criminal charges. This lack of evidence, wrote the lawyers, had become obvious as Judge Fujii meticulously examined suspects and witnesses.[139] If procurators maintained the flawed indictments, stated the lawyers, it was up to the bench to press for clarification on a number of points: If shares were transferred, how was this accomplished? What happened to the money? What was the motive in giving and receiving bribes?[140] This was not the first time that Arima and Gujō pointed out to the bench the weak factual base of the state's case. Indeed, on June 18, 1935, they had submitted a document that made similar points: no motive for the crime, no record of where the stocks supposedly used for bribery came from, no physical evidence showing the conversion of stocks to cash.[141] After two years of a steady defense drumbeat about the lack of evidence and after watching procurators slip and slide as they scrambled to reconstruct their case in the face of repudiated confessions, Judge Fujii was more inclined to see merit in Arima's and Gujō's request.

An editorial, "Reforming the Law," appeared on June 13. "The Teijin scandal trial appears to have developed into a test case on judicial procedure. There have been many points of special interest about this trial, and the question whether or not the judge in charge of the preliminary examination is qualified to be called as witness is not, perhaps, the most important of them. But the Court and the legal professional appear to be doing their best to make it so, which in many ways is to be regretted." After discussing the twists and turns of Morozumi's three court appearances, the editorial noted: "What is undisputed is that there was an exchange of notes between the accused, and their contents have been accepted as evidence. . . . If there is to be any complaint at all it ought rightly to concern the amazing possibilities there are for delay in the trial of criminal and civil cases. That is the real lesson of the present legal dispute. The drag which attends the examination has been commented on often enough. But the Teijin trial appears to possess the stamina necessary to set new records." If the defendants' charges of infringement of personal rights are true, concluded the editor, then the procurators' methods "are indistinguishable from the third degree."[142]

Following Preliminary Judge Morozumi's appearances, a public, no doubt weary of the seamingly endless hearings, was distracted by events in China. During the night of July 7, Chinese and Japanese troops skirmished at the Marco Polo Bridge near Peking. Although a local cease-fire was concluded by the eleventh, the Konoe Fumimaro Cabinet (June 1937–January 1939) announced mobilization plans and requested public support; the Nanking government responded in kind. On July 25–26 more fighting broke out between Japanese and Chinese soldiers. Then, on July 28, several hundred Japanese troops and civilians were killed in Tungchow. Japanese newspapers carried sensationalized accounts as the conflict spread to Shanghai.[143]

Although war stories dominated the news during July and August, the Teijin Incident was featured in the widely circulated *Chūō kōron* monthly. Wada Hidekichi's "My Views on the Teijin Incident" (Watakushi no mita Teijin jiken) was published in July (August issue), and Kawai Yoshinari's "Teijin mondai shinkyō ittan" (My partial opinion on the Teijin problem) appeared in August (September issue). This public exchange between a coauthor of the sensational *Jiji shinpō* 1934 series on the Banchōkai and one of the defendants must have caught public attention.

Wada stated that the Teijin affair should have been discussed as an economic and social problem, but, unfortunately, it had developed into a complex, difficult to comprehend legal case. Some people, wrote Wada, said that Mutō Sanji launched the "Banchōkai o abaku" series to increase the *Jiji shinpō's* circulation. This viewpoint, however, was incorrect, because Mutō had a long history as a social reformer. For example, during the financial crisis of 1927, Mutō fought the Wakatsuki Cabinet's plan to use tax money to bail out failed banks. Moreover, he was famous for denouncing collusion between politicians and businessmen who misused public funds. Thus, it was clear that Mutō was concerned deeply about maintaining political and business morality before the Teijin stock deal.[144]

Rumors circulating about various financial deals by members of the Banchōkai caught Mutō's attention, wrote Wada. Since Mutō felt strongly that these stocks were owned by the public (i.e., tax money was used to save the Bank of Taiwan), Teijin shares should have been sold at the highest possible price by the Bank of Taiwan. Mutō decided, after an investigation, that a corrupt deal had reduced the stock price, so he exposed the corruption. This decision brought not only external criticism but dissent within the paper's staff. Wada noted, however, that Mutō's self-confidence was very strong.[145]

At the time of the Teijin stock transaction, wrote Wada, the people who arranged the deal were advised by reputable, prominent lawyers. Thus, there was nothing illegal about the sale. However, people involved in the deal were guilty, opined Wada, of "bad morality" (*dotokuaku*) and "social evil" (*shakaiaku*). Therefore, although the stock sale may have been legal, it was unethical.[146] "I am interested in this case," said Wada, "because it is a problem of social morals. I believe that Mr. Mutō picked up this incident as a moral problem. Looking at the trial, since I am not a legal specialist, I cannot say whether the defendants broke laws, but the defendants, from the viewpoint of social common sense, acted in a dark manner and should be criticized."[147] Wada pointed out that the purchasers knew about the special nature of Teijin stocks—that they represented tax payers' investment.[148] Although Wada did not provide details about the proper price for Teijin stocks, it is clear that he considered the sale price too low.

Wada criticized Nakajima and Mitsuchi for their participation in the stock transaction. In light of their high positions, he wrote, their involvement was wrong morally. Even if they received no money, their involvement invited public suspicion that awards had been given.[149]

As for the problem of violations of defendants' personal rights, Wada stated that he did not know if the accusations were true. "But I can say," he continued, "that people who are at the leadership level of our nation confessed to committing crimes. . . . Even if there was torture, all those gentlemen confessed to lies. In a moral sense, this is worse than bribery. I do not know if these officials were involved in bribery or not, but these people present a frozen moral sense (*dōgiteki fukanshō*), because of their involvement in this deal. So it is natural to suspect them."[150]

Throughout this article, Wada, who must have noticed the declining fortunes of the procurators at court, sought to indict the defendants for an even more serious crime: unethical conduct and a lack of moral common sense.

Kawai's sharp rebuke appeared the following month. "Mr. Wada! A man must look at himself in the mirror. You must learn about yourself. Do you really think you are qualified to publish your opinion? Yes, how righteous Mr. Mutō's opinion was, as he walked over us in those articles. . . . The articles about the Banchōkai were based mostly on fictitious stories. They were the worst articles in our nation's newspaper history. . . . These bad lies caused public misunderstanding, caused justice authorities to act, and caused the Teijin problem of today."[151] It was Wada, noted Kawai, who had coauthored the *Jiji* series that led to the indictments and trial.[152] After a review of the Teijin affair, Kawai accused Wada of self-righteousness and hypocrisy, noting that in the *Jiji* articles and in the novel *Rayon* (*Jinken*), Wada expressed certainty that the defendants violated laws. Currently, noted Kawai, Wada was saying that, while defendants might not be guilty of Penal Code violations, they were guilty of moral lapses.[153] "I don't like your sneaky attitude, as you keep changing your comments to go along with public opinion. Since you did the Banchōkai articles and the novel, why do you not take responsibility for what you wrote?"[154]

Prosecution Summary

The prosecution's summary was presented on August 6, 7, 9, 10, and 11. Facing the procurators was not only a psychological ordeal for defendants but a physical ordeal as well, because no fans were working to relieve the intense heat. According to defendant Kawai, sweat ran down the procurators' faces. One newspaper reported that the courtroom was like a furnace. Nevertheless, the visitors gallery was packed.[155]

Procurator Hirata began by insisting that the evidence was rock solid and no fabrications had been inserted into the case. Moreover, political considerations played no part in the indictments. Since all the accused pleaded not guilty, said Hirata, the presentation of facts would be lengthy. Procurators became involved in the case, he recalled, when they received three accusations of wrongdoing, and, as they were checking on these complaints, the Teijin stock sale was discussed in the Diet. Procurators responded by redoubling efforts to discover what was behind the wrongdoing allegations. Then, in mid-April, Takagi confessed to accepting shares from Nagasaki. Next Koshifuji confessed accepting these shares, and Yanagida and Okazaki confirmed the exchange of these "gifts." "These simultaneous confessions," said Hirata, "are clear evidence of the illegal transaction." Hirata noted that it was not unusual for criminals to cover their tracks, "but never has there been a case so cleverly camouflaged. As soon as the case became a political and social issue, all men interested assembled in tea houses in Tsukiji, Akasaka, Nihonbashi, and other places, and made all the necessary arrangements as to replies to be given to the police. Several legal experts were engaged by them to supervise the effacing of evidence and otherwise advise them in their attempts to cheat the Law." Suspects' statements (except for four who denied everything), pointed out Hirata, were changed constantly. "It is up to the Court to decide to what extent their statements are reliable . . . but it must be remembered that their contention that they gave wrong statements simply for the purpose of obtaining an early release does not hold good. This is evident from the manner in which their statements were altered." Allegations of torture are entirely groundless, he emphasized. "It is not unusual for the accused to deny the facts . . . but it is almost unprecedented that all the accused have hurled criticism and abuse at the procurators in charge throughout the hearings. . . . Admittedly handcuffs were applied to one or two prisoners, but this was necessitated by the apprehension that they would commit suicide."[156]

Beginning with the misfeasance charge, on August 7, Biwada argued that the stock transfer had lost the Bank of Taiwan ¥1,600,000 in anticipated profit. The procurator presented a detailed account of the stock deal, from Fujita Kenichi's attempt in early 1932 until the 1933 sale. The roles played by government officials, politicians, and businessmen were explained. Biwada reminded the court of Hirata's presentation, directing attention to Shimada and Takagi. It is quite clear, he said, based on court documents, that the defendants could expect a rise in the price of Teijin shares at the time.[157] Pointing to various expert estimates, Biwada argued that a proper price per share was ¥140. Therefore, Shimada, Takagi, Yanagida, Koshifuji, and others were guilty of the crimes charged.[158]

Intense heat reduced numbers in the visitors gallery on August 9, as Procurator Biwada continued refuting statements by defendants that they did not accept bribes. Biwada pointed to conversations between Shimada, Takagi, and Vice-Minister Kuroda in May 1933. It was clear, said Biwada, "that Kuroda's previous approval had been given regarding the transfer of the 100,000 shares in question." As for Nakajima, it was based on his advice that various executives of insurance companies agreed to purchase Teijin shares. Moreover, it is evident that the 1,300 shares were taken from the safe at the Fukoku Chōhei Insurance Company. Despite defendants' denials that they had touched the shares between June 19 and August 15, said Biwada, it is obvious that the thirteen 100-share certificates were given by Kobayashi, manager of the Fukoku Chōhei Insurance Company, to Nagano, who sent them to Takagi. Biwada next summarized the distribution of the shares and the money from cashed-in shares. "These presents were made largely at the suggestion of Nagano, who played the most important role in the transfer talk."[159]

On August 10, Biwada outlined bribery charges against Finance Ministry officials. Nakajima received special attention as well. On June 26, 1933, stated Biwada, Shimada and Takagi visited the baron's official residence; as they departed, they placed on a waiting room desk two 100-share certificates and a power of attorney document enclosed in an envelope. When procurators asked about the "gift," Nakajima said he had planned to return it but changed his mind. He maintained this story until the trial began, when he said that he had lied to obtain a release from jail.[160]

The 241st hearing, at which Hirata spoke, was on August 11. First, he repeated material about the Bank of Taiwan obtaining Teijin Company shares. Since the bank owed the government a large sum of money, "it should have exercised the utmost care in the disposal of these shares." Biwada charged Takagi, who was "the principal accused," and others with misfeasance for not doing their duty. Turning to Nagano, Kawai, Nagasaki, and Kobayashi, the procurator pointed out that "although it is quite plain that any losses to the Bank of Formosa, a semi-official bank, are losses by the State, they acted in such a manner as to cause losses to the Bank. They prevailed upon leading politicians, businessmen, and Government officials either to find suitable buyers or to give assistance in the transfer talks. There are no extenuating circumstances in their offenses." Moving to the 1,300 shares given as "gifts," Hirata expressed regret that state officials never before stained by criminal charges were involved. Baron Nakajima, he said, "deserves special consideration, because he was long in the business world and did not possess much official experience." However regrettable it was to charge Mitsuchi with perjury, said Hirata, the crime "is clear from a study of two facts, viz. the presentation of 300 Teijin shares by Takagi to Mitsuchi and the realization by Mitsuchi of the 200 shares entrusted by Nakashima." It is "an indisputable fact," said Hirata, that Takagi visited Nakajima on June 27, 1933, and handed him the shares. During face-to-face confrontations with Takagi, noted Hirata, "Mitsuchi bitterly abused Takagi, but to the last, the latter did not change his statement. This alone bears witness to the fact." As for Nakajima's statement about Mitsuchi's role in cashing in shares, Hirata said that it was not possible for "such an amiable man as Nakashima" to make a fully false statement. Procurator Hirata demanded the following sentences: Mitsuchi, perjury, six months; Nakajima, accepting a bribe, one year; Kuroda, accepting a bribe, two years; Ōkubo, accepting a bribe, ten months; Ōno, accepting a bribe, eight months; Aida, accepting a bribe, eight months; Shidomoto, accepting a bribe, six months; Shimada, misfeasance and bribery, two years; Takagi, misfeasance and bribery, two years; Nagano, misfeasance and bribery, two years; Yanagida, misfeasance and bribery, one year; Nagasaki, misfeasance and bribery, ten months; Koshifuji, misfeasance and bribery, six months; Okazaki, misfeasance and bribery, six months; Kobayashi, misfeasance and bribery, six months; Kawai, misfeasance, fourteen months.[161]

Defense Summary

Lawyers, after enduring five hot days of Biwada and Hirata, were eager to respond. Imamura, the leading defense lawyer, spoke first (August 12–16). The seventy-one-year-old attorney, a veteran of numerous courtroom battles with procurators, pulled no punches in a sharp indictment of prosecution tactics. Unless intense heat curtailed attendance, the visitors gallery must have been packed.

Procurators, stated Imamura, began on the wrong foot, because they imagined themselves as avenging angels destined to purify society. Their improper attitude not only set the tone for the investigation, but also produced many errors. Compounding this attitude problem was the fact that procurators were eager to chastise Finance Ministry officials. When rumors circulated about Hatoyama Ichirō receiving ¥50,000, procurators assumed involvement by Finance Ministry personnel and Mitsuchi. Later they added Nakajima to the list. Selfishly motivated outsiders egged on the procurators by making written complaints about illegal activities. Thus, a mixture of self-righteous procurators, anger over the Meitō affair, outside complaints, and politics combined to produce the arrests and indictments. There were, however, cautionary signposts on the road to indictments that should have caused procurators to reconsider evidence. For example, at one point a Bank of Japan report stated that ¥124 per share was a proper price for Teijin stock sold by the Bank of Taiwan. Procuratorial preconceptions, however, blinded them to this report. Moreover, they ignored finance officials' replies as legislators quizzed them about the stock deal.[162]

The case began, said Imamura, with statements to procurators by Nakai Matsutarō (March 13, 1934), Kaneko Naokichi (March 19), and Fujita Kenichi (March 27). On April 4, Procurator Kuroda requested permission to start an investigation of Shimada, Takagi, and four others for misfeasance and embezzlement. What kind of evidence did procurators have against these people? They had the statements listed above, three bills of indictment (see Chapter 3), *Jiji shinpō* articles (reprinted in pamphlet form), and a printed version of Seki Naohiko's Diet speech. Given the background of Kaneko and Fujita (who failed to negotiate a Teijin stock deal and who were angry), procurators should not have trusted their information. As for the three bills of indictment, it is obvious that two (Nakai's and Katō's) were written by the same person, since they both contain the same errors. Someone behind a black curtain, thought Imamura, was manipulating them. If procurators could not see this, said Imamura, they were not well trained; if they knew that these bills of indictment were suspect, requesting a legal deposition was a rash act. What about the *Jiji* pamphlet? These newspaper articles, while flawed, came closest to being proof, noted Imamura. They accused Bank of Taiwan officials of lowering the share price from ¥195 to ¥125, giving the buyers a profit of ¥70 per share. Thus, the bank failed in its obligation to make the maximum profit. Moreover, go-betweens made ¥632,500. Furthermore, although the shares were handed over to the buyers in early June, they were backdated to the end of May. Nevertheless, concluded Imamura, taken together the statements, bills of indictment, and pamphlet were weak evidence. In fact, Procurator Kuroda, in making the April 4 interrogation request, relied primarily on the three bills of indictment. Imamura, however, viewed this action by Kuroda as a violation of law and an abuse of office. Before taking action, Procurator Kuroda should have questioned the people who wrote the bills of indictment. He should neither have accepted Seki's Diet comments as accurate nor accepted as fact the numbers cited by the *Jiji*. Also, he should have talked with the suspects before the Osaka-Tokyo arrests.[163] "From the beginning to the end," noted Imamura, "the procurators infringed upon the spirit of the Criminal Procedure Code."[164] Procurators abused their office after the indictment as well. Imamura suspected, in fact, that the procurators' goal was outside the scope of criminal procedure. Procurators responsible were Kuroda and Biwada, whom Imamura cited for two main abuses: the exchange of notes between suspects and Vice-Minister Kuroda's so-called petition.[165] Another abuse was the use of handcuffs, which prompted an outcry in the Diet and brought negative press comments. Authorities claimed that cuffs were used to keep suspects from committing suicide, but Imamura rejected this excuse, saying that in a long legal career he saw them used only once: in the case of Nanba Daisuke, who tried to kill the crown prince regent in December 1923. In the Teijin case, in contrast, they were used on six of the sixteen defendants: Nagano, Takagi, Nagasaki, Kobayashi, Koshifuji (leather cuffs), and Ōkubo (steel). A document given to the Diet by the Justice Ministry, noted Imamura, proves that Biwada ordered their use.[166]

Imamura viewed the telegram exchange between Takagi and Shimada as central to the case. The first telegram was sent on May 9, 1933, and the seventeenth (last) was sent on June 17.[167] "If you read them correctly, it is obvious that the suspects did not deal purposely with these shares in a manner that justified a charge of misfeasance. Unfortunately, however, these telegrams were read by prosecution authorities who were already harboring prejudice. Thus, they read them incorrectly."[168] In fact, noted Imamura, it is very clear that Takagi worked hard to get the maximum price per share. Indeed, the market price at sale time was ¥121.70; Takagi got, excluding the commission, ¥124. Therefore, he made a profit for the bank of ¥230,000. Nevertheless, the indictment charged that he sacrificed bank profit. Besides getting a reasonable price for the shares, concluded Imamura, Takagi handled the stock transfer in a proper manner.[169]

The key item in the bribery charge was the 1,300 shares seized at the Asahi Oil Company (Nagasaki was president; the 1,300 were, according to procurators, part of the following 5,000). These shares were a "fact," said Iwamura, as were the 5,000 purchased by Nagano, Kawai, and others. The 1,300 shares distributed as bribes, however, were an "imaginary number" (*kakū no sūji*).[170] As of August 14, 1933, the 5,000 shares were still in the safe at the Fukoku Chōhei Insurance Company, held as collateral for a loan taken out by Sekihara Kenji (Kawai's secretary). On August 15 Sekihara redeemed 1,300 of these shares. Ironically, noted Imamura, the prosecution did not find even one share in the possession of supposedly bribed defendants. This fact alone should have dissuaded procurators from charging bribery. During the trial, lawyers forced procurators to admit that the 1,300 shares supposedly used for bribery were the same 1,300 found at the oil company. Moreover, the numbers on these thirteen certificates (each certificate was worth 100 shares) were sequential. Furthermore, the 5,000 shares owned by Nagano, Kawai, and others were part of 30,000 shares (out of the total of 100,000) purchased in the Teijin stock deal (the Fukoku Chōhei Insurance Company was part of the buyers' syndicate). The 30,000 were delivered to the insurance company on June 19, 1933, at about 12:30 P.M. For the next three hours, two clerks inspected the shares. In the *Yoshin*, Nagasaki says that he met insurance company manager Kobayashi, and together they went to the company to pick up 1,300 shares. In fact, stated Imamura, Nagasaki and Kobayashi did not meet that day (a witness saw Nagasaki elsewhere, plus the two share inspectors were there during the afternoon). Therefore, not one share left the company that day. Imamura reenforced this point with details about the amount of paperwork required to transfer shares from one person to another; no such transfer documents were found implicating Nagasaki or Kobayashi. For example, just the matter of moving 1,300 shares from the group's 5,000 would require letters of attorney (i.e., to move each 100-share certificate from Sekihara's name to the new owner). Moreover, investigators, who went through the insurance company's two safes, found all documents were in order. Thus, the procurator's 1,300 shares bribe was a myth, concluded Imamura, because the transfer never took place.[171] This lack of a paper trail as the shares supposedly passed from one person to another as well as when the bribees supposedly cashed them in played a key role in the judges' decision.

After Imamura's thorough exposure of flaws in the prosecution's case, other lawyers reenforced the main point of his argument: indictments were based on false confessions. Defense summations, which continued until October 5, illustrated that facts supporting these confessions were often inaccurate or imaginary and that the procurators had not proven the bribery or misfeasance charges. The following defense presentations are illustrative.

Baron Hozumi Shigetō, who belonged to a distinguished legalist family and who was inducted into the Imperial Academy a month earlier, addressed the court on August 20. Again, the visitors gallery must have been packed because of Hozumi's reputation and his well-known friendship with

Ōkubo Teiji. Hozumi, who did not participate in the trial as a regular defense lawyer, appeared as a special defender. Hozmui first focused on Ōkubo's quick confession (he was arrested on May 21 and confessed on May 23, 1934). One reason for this, said Hozumi, was Ōkubo's unpreparedness for such an experience; another factor was the shattering impact of the word "imperial sanction" (*chokusai*) used by the procurators. Since Ōkubo held a "personally appointed" (*chokunin*) rank (i.e., personally appointed by the emperor; officials who held grades within this rank were the highest civil servants), justice authorities needed special permission to arrest him. Procurators showed Ōkubo the paper from the palace authorizing his arrest, said Hozumi, and used it as a weapon to pressure a confession. Ōkubo, humiliated and shocked, ceased all resistance. In fact, noted Hozumi, procurators were engaged in a theatrical performance (for the press, public, and defendants) when they used the term "*chokusai*" in legal documents to apprehend Ōkubo and Kuroda. Indeed, "*chokusai*" was not a legal term; the proper legal tem was "report to the emperor" (*sōmon*), noted Hozumi. On May 23, Biwada added another heavy stone to the weight pressing on Ōkubo when he showed him a note from Okazaki (his brother-in-law was ill with tuberculosis and spitting up blood). Procurators urged Ōkubo to cooperate so Okazaki could be hospitalized. This note, said Hozumi, had a tremendous psychological impact.[172]

Next Hozumi focused on confessions more generally. It was a basic fact in the criminal justice field to mistrust self-confessions, especially a self-confession with no corroborating evidence. All the defendants, noted the lawyer, repudiated their statements. Hozumi emphasized this point by invoking the name of Hiranuma Kiichirō, the famous procurator general and former justice minister. In a speech given on May 18, 1914, Hiranuma had pointed out that, unless a procurator was careful, his sense of fairness could be dulled. Therefore, procurators should take a middle path, check each matter several times, and avoid prejudice. If these steps were not followed, a procurator would hear only what he wanted to hear and truth would prove elusive. Furthermore, Hiranuma had said that peoples' rights should be respected, with care taken not to damage reputations. Hozumi noted that Hiranuma had said that during the interrogation period a suspect must be presumed innocent until proven guilty.[173] "I do not believe that there is a statute of limitation on Hiranuma's speech, so twenty-four years later it should still be the procurators' creed. Do you procurators know about this speech? Can you really say that you are not violating part of this?"[174]

The weakest point in the charge against Ōkubo, continued Hozumi, was the conversion of shares to cash. It was not explained clearly where the money came from and how it was used. According to the procurators' statement it was a bribery case if cash or goods were given or received. Where the money came from or what a suspect did with it, they argued, had nothing to do with establishing the crime of bribery. However, said Hozumi, if procurators do not know the details about the receipt of money, then one should be suspicious of the "fact" that money was given. Nevertheless, procurators claim to have no doubt about the "fact" that bribery took place.[175] Pursuing this theme, Hozumi cited a newspaper interview of Procurator Hirata. Hirata said: "Unfortunately, the fact of converting the shares to cash is not clear."[176] When I read this, said Hozumi, I had a strange feeling; when the procurators presented their summation, Biwada repeated these same words three times. If, as they kept saying, where money came from and what it was used for was not important, why did they also keep saying that it is "unfortunate?"[177]

The matter of violating personal rights had appeared repeatedly in this case, noted Hozumi, but he hoped these charges were not true. "Perhaps hard-working police and procurators were overzealous. This sort of thing should not happen."[178] Hozumi concluded with a reminder of Judge Fujii's request for procurators and lawyers to cooperate in finding the truth.[179]

In early September, defense lawyers submitted a joint statement to the Tokyo Criminal District Court. This document, drafted by lawyers Arima Chūzaburō and Gujō Korekazu, was based on Mitsuchi's court testimony and Baron Hozumi's remarks. It began by citing the procurators' emphatic denial of either a political plot behind the investigation or a fabrication of evidence. Nonetheless, the lawyers viewed the procurators as untrustworthy. A critique of the indictments followed. Grounds for a bribery charge appeared on April 14, 1934, when procurators claimed Takagi had confessed to receiving 100 shares. Procurators, however, said not one word about why Takagi made this statement. Nevertheless, the lawyers noted, procurators ordered police to check Takagi's home for share certificates. This was peculiar, since the crime of misfeasance involved the sale of 100,000 shares. Therefore, the investigation should have concentrated on the price of these shares. Moreover, the prosecution stated that, during this phase of the case, it was not necessary to establish where the money for the cashed-in shares originated or what was done with the money. All that was required, according to the prosecution, was that Takagi admit that he took the shares. Why would Takagi confess getting the alleged shares unless he was pressured by interrogators? Obviously, procurators heard a story that buyers gave out shares. Procurators, said the lawyers, kept insisting that he had received shares. If this fact is kept in mind, Takagi's confession to bribery becomes more understandable. Thus, from the start, procurators presupposed that gift shares were passing from the buyers' group to Bank of Taiwan officials and prominent government figures. The preliminary court record, noted the lawyers, reflected procurators dominating the proceedings and guiding the examination in the direction of discovering who received shares. Moreover, at the preliminary court examination, procurators refused to accept evidence favoring the defendants. Their refusal to consider favorable evidence continued during the trial. Furthermore, said the lawyers, the motive presented by procurators for giving the 1,300 shares was weak. Finally, no evidence was presented to confirm the transfer of 1,300 shares or to show what was done with the money from cashed-in shares.[180]

Suzuki Yoshio (Takagi's lawyer), who addressed the court on September 1, 3, and 5, criticized the prosecution in particular and the justice system in general. Like Hozumi, he emphasized the danger of basing indictments on self-confessions. It was wrong, he said, for defendants to lie, but procurators who pushed them to confess bore a heavier responsibility for twisting the truth. At first procurators focused on the 1,300 shares seized at the Asahi Oil Company, but at the preliminary examination they refocused their argument on a single folded stock certificate (worth 100 shares). If you talk about bribery money, said Suzuki, you must prove the existence of the money; to indict for bribery based only on a self-confession was a violation of the Code of Criminal Procedure. He then pointed out a pattern of courts in other cases relying too much on confessions. Turning to the Teijin case, Suzuki identified the *Jiji shinpō* articles as an "answer book" for procurators. Unfortunately, readers, including procurators, readily believed reports in this reputable paper. Recently, said Suzuki, I reread a pamphlet containing these *Jiji* articles and discovered many gross factual errors. Indeed, this case would have taken an entirely different turn if the slandered members of the Banchōkai had sued the newspaper! Procurators reacted to these sensational articles by arresting people and seizing documents. During interrogations, noted Suzuki, Procurator Kuroda condemned the worlds of business and politics and talked of a top to bottom reform. According to the procurators' closing summary, they did not think originally that a bribery indictment was appropriate; they claimed that bribery first appeared during Takagi's interrogation. We lawyers, said Suzuki, do not believe them. During mid-March 1934, a rumor circulated, stimulated by the *Jiji* articles (this was before the open criminal investigation), that the biggest bribery case in modern Japanese history would soon appear. Suzuki added that he had heard this rumor from a journalist who covered procurators at the Tokyo District Court.[181]

Arima and Gujō (Ōno's and Aida's lawyers) appear next in the illustrative presentation. Mercilessly, they spotlighted flaws in the state's indictments, especially the lack of physical evidence and factual mistakes. For example, the procurators' contention that 1,300 shares were used as bribes: According to Kobayashi's *Yoshin* statement, he took them from the insurance company safe and gave them to Nagasaki. Kobayashi, however, had repudiated this statement at the trial's opening session. Procurators, faced with this repudiation and a defense argument that Kobayashi could not have taken the shares from the safe, adopted a new argument in their summary: Kobayashi took the shares before they were put in the safe. But, again, they presented no proof. On top of this imaginary event, procurators also said that Kobayashi returned the 1,300 shares to the insurance company safe.[182] "Procurators say nothing, however, about how and when the shares got back into the safe. Did the 1,300 shares somehow take themselves back into the safe? This is a very puzzling phenomenon!"[183]

Unable to furnish details about the transfer of stocks to cash, procurators tried to camouflage this weakness with a cover of excuses: suspects colluded to destroy evidence, procurators were unable to investigate fully the financial details about each suspect, procurators hesitated to disturb financial institutions. About the suspects' so-called plot, said the defense team, the procurators had provided no details. Moreover, since the suspects were jailed, how could they have colluded? Furthermore, procurators were unable to illustrate how suspects transferred stocks and money.[184] "Thus, since the procurators found themselves facing a wall, they came up with a new argument: it is very difficult to investigate details about the suspects' plotting."[185] In fact, noted the defense, the prosecution had no physical evidence and had based the entire case on self-confessions.[186] As for the weak excuse that they hesitated to disturb financial institutions, the court should note, emphasized the defense, that Nagano's financial vita was investigated in exhaustive detail. Nevertheless, procurators found no concrete evidence illustrating the conversion of 1,300 shares into ¥180,000.[187]

The defense concluded by pointing out that procurators, during the summation, had attempted to explain why the state's case lacked factual evidence. "Instead of evidence, which they did not have, they again presented excuses explaining why they could not present concrete evidence, or they presented imaginary stories in place of evidence."[188]

Inui Masahiko (Nagasaki's lawyer) appeared on September 30, at the 263d session. During the previous examinations, he noted, "it has become very clear that the truth of this case is simply that no criminal facts exist."[189] Indeed, defense lawyers, from various points of view, demolished the factual basis of the prosecution's case. What is misfeasance? A careful reading of Penal Code Article 247 illustrates that for a crime to occur a person must fail deliberately to do his duty, which in turn results in damage to a business. Inui then discussed the predictability of damage and the difficult problem of predicting a future business situation (e.g., the price of shares). The telegrams exchanged between Takagi and Shimada, he continued, if read properly, illustrate their effort to maximize the bank's profit. Unfortunately, procurators read them incorrectly.[190]

Since other attorneys showed that the 1,300 stock shares were not used for bribes, Inui passed over this subject quickly and instead focused on self-confessions. The court was then presented with a worldwide history of the use and misuse of confessions.[191] He noted, in conclusion, that in this case there was no evidence other than confessions, which were given under duress. Therefore, these self-confessions were untrustworthy.[192] "If you look at only the self-confessions of Takagi and Nagasaki in connection with the 1,300 shares," he pointed out, "you must accept Nagasaki's confession as accurate in order to accept Takagi's."[193] However, he emphasized, these confessions do not become proper proof simply because they match; suspects were pressured strongly to write them. Thus "these self-confessions have no power to prove anything, a fact already demonstrated in the courtroom by other lawyers and defendants."[194]

Shortly after the epic courtroom battle ceased (the last hearing was held on October 5), the public read that Procurator Biwada was ill and planned to resign. According to newspapers, the circulation of a slanderous story about his private life had prompted this decision. It was said that Biwada had accepted a loan of ¥1,500 from a lawyer who was involved in an earlier case. According to the Osaka *Mainichi*, an official investigation found the criticism unwarranted, but Biwada was so shocked by the publicity that he had suffered a nervous breakdown.[195] In fact, the Teijin investigation and trial did inflict a heavy toll on the procuratorial ranks. Kuroda died, some said of overwork, before the trial. Assisting Biwada at any time during the trial were six procurators, two of whom died during the hearings (Kubota Masanori and Mochihara Koremitsu). Hirata Susumu, an assistant to the head procurator of the Toyko bureau, also played a role in the trial.[196] If Hirata is included, the total number of procurators is nine, out of which three died. A dangerous occupation indeed!

Verdict

Early on the morning of December 16, Presiding Judge Fujii Goichirō visited Meiji jingū. While the judge composed his thoughts at the silent shrine grounds, a crowd gathered outside the court building. The standing defendants, dressed in Western-style formal wear, faced the bench, with a platoon of lawyers behind them. At 9:00 A.M. the judges entered the courtroom. Fujii announced that, since it would take about seven hours to read the decision, defendants should be seated. As Fujii pronounced the not guilty verdict, journalists dispatched messengers to inform editors. Soon special editions were on the streets.[197]

Fujii first examined the charge that Shimada, Takagi, and others had caused a heavy financial loss for the Bank of Taiwan. The court found, said Fujii, that the sale price of ¥124 plus a one-yen commission was a reasonable price, given financial conditions. The prosecution contention that a potential profit was lost when the sale occurred, because the planned increase in the Teijin Company's capital was ignored, was mistaken. This fact was obvious, since the capital increase was widely rumored and the stock market would have considered this fact. Moreover, every expert witness, stressed Fujii, had agreed that it was nearly impossible to predict stock share price movements. Therefore, the prosecution's contention that a delay in the sale until after the official announcement of the capital increase would have profited the bank was not a certain fact. Moreover, the Bank of Japan was pressuring the Bank of Taiwan to repay loans. After reading for three hours, Fujii called a recess.[198]

In the afternoon, attention focused on the bribery and perjury charges. Evidence was insufficient to prove that 1,300 shares were taken from the Fukoku Chōhei Insurance Company and cashed in at the times cited by the prosecution, Fujii said. Each charge of bribery was examined and rejected. For example, although procurators alleged that Baron Nakajima received 200 shares at his official residence on June 26, 1933, from Takagi and Shimada, facts discovered during the hearings proved that it was impossible for the three to have met. Even a meeting between Shimada and Nakajima would have been impossible. Therefore, Nakajima's preliminary court statement must be considered false. As for the ¥10,000 alleged as a bribe by the prosecution, Fujii said that the court, after a careful review, saw it merely as a political fund contribution. Moving on to Mitsuchi's perjury charge, Fujii noted that he could not have cashed in the 200 shares Nakajima did not receive; nor was there any proof that he got 300 shares from Takagi.[199]

The state's case, which lacked physical evidence, rested on a pillar of twelve intertwined confessions obtained by procurators and preliminary judges. This pillar collapsed when Judge Fujii said: "It is clear that the suspects' statements were untrue."[200] Judge Fujii concluded this verdict with a hard slap in the prosecution's face: he criticized their evidence by likening it to "an attempt to scoop up the reflection of the moon from the water."[201] The court, as most people understood, was referring to a famous painting depicting a monkey on a tree limb trying to scoop up the moon's reflection from the water.[202] A journalist reported that Nakajima and Mitsuchi smiled and bowed to the bench; Procurator Hirata looked upset.[203] Following adjournment, journalists questioned the judges. Fujii stated that the verdict had to be not guilty, because "no criminal facts existed" (*hanzai no jijitsu ga sonzai shinai*). "In particular," Fujii cautioned reporters, "I hope that you do not make a mistake on this point."[204] Judge Fujii's press conference remarks put an indelible mark on what became known as the "no facts trial." The monkey analogy, too, left a deep scratch on the public mind.

"Thoughts on the Teijin Trial" appeared a day after the verdict. "It is not easy, two and a half years after the opening of the public trial, to recover the atmosphere of the original sensation of the Teijin scandal. . . . This Teijin scandal at one time promised—and to a certain extent has lived up to its promise—to be the most memorable [scandal] of them all. Indeed it has taken the more compelling drama of events on the Asiatic mainland [Nanking fell on December 13, 1937] to obliterate the sensation aroused in June 1935 when it became clear that charges were going to be brought against leading figures in the Saito Cabinet." The editorial recalled that the press had viewed the prominent defendants guilty, because the justice minister requested imperial permission to indict them. The most important aspect of this case, however, was "that the Court believed the oral testimony of the defendants as against their signed confessions." The editorial continued: "The Court's refusal to believe the evidence of the preliminary examination . . . has finally proved the distinctive feature." There were a few earlier cases in which judges doubted a preliminary examination record, wrote the editor, "but never before with the decision and publicity which has been the case in the Teijin trial." The editorial continued with comments on harsh jail conditions, procurators who refused to accept evidence favorable to defendants, the use of handcuffs, and the need for a detailed official report on these things. The paper pointed out that Judge Fujii did not "refer even indirectly to the defendants' charge of harsh treatment during detention. . . . It was not the Court's duty to ask why these false confessions were made and signed, but it is a question which must be asked and answered if public confidence in the Courts is not to be shaken."[205]

Commenting on the acquittal, the Osaka *Asahi* said that the case had "haunted the public." The first impression was that the defendants must be guilty, but as the trial proceeded, "the public began to suspect that there was something wrong with the working of the procuratorial machine." The general impression was, stated the paper, "that some judicial officials approached the case with the idea—not a proper one—of eradicating, by the application of the law, certain deplorable tendencies in society. It was due to this belief that the judiciary was at one time charged with Fascism." The Teijin case became notorious for charges of personal rights violations, and the accused won much public sympathy, noted the paper. How many poor defendants, asked the paper, have been mistakenly judged guilty? It was time, the *Asahi* concluded, to reform the prosecution in order to better protect personal rights.[206]

Newspapers speculated on whether or not procurators would appeal (they had one week from the verdict). Most papers opted for the view that procurators would retreat before Fujii's strong verdict. Some, however, felt that an appeal would be forthcoming, if only to save face. The public got an answer on December 23, when procurators said they would not appeal.[207]

The memoir of Matsuzaka Hiromasa (head of the Criminal Affairs Bureau) open a window on the decision by justice officials. The not guilty verdict shocked procurators, who were eager to retry the case. Justice Minister Shiono ordered Matsuzaka to review the case in order to understand the not guilty verdict. Therefore, on December 18, Matsuzaka met with Hirata to go over the trial record. The next day together with Shiono they discussed the case, seeking material to support a guilty verdict. Hirata, who worked full-time on this project from December 19 to 22, was saddled with a handicap, because he was not part of the original procuratorial team and Biwada was retired. It became obvious, to Matsuzaka, that reshaping the evidence for a proper appeal would be difficult. The problem was solved on the twenty-second: Shiono told Matsuzaka that he had decided not to appeal. Shiono reasoned, after a review of the case, that it could not be won and that a second defeat would compound the damage to the procuracy. That same day Matsuzaka visited Tokunaga Eikichi, chief procurator of the Tokyo District Court, who fumed over the verdict; Matsuzaka tried to calm him. Finally, on December 23, Shiono held a meeting with Procurator General Motoji Shinkuma, Tokunaga, and

Yoshimasu Kiyoshi (chief procurator, Tokyo Appeals Court). Yoshimasu noted that all the procurators considered the defendants guilty and urged an appeal; there should be no concern over winning or losing. Motoji saw weak parts in the indictment but felt problems could be overcome by removing doubtful items. Neither was confident, however, of winning an appeal. The strongest push for an appeal came from Tokunaga, who was angry over the wording of the verdict (perhaps he was thinking about procurators being compared to a monkey!). Shiono repeated his earlier comment to Matsuzaka: they would not appeal, because a victory was doubtful; another loss would increase damage.[208] To the public, however, justice officials offered an expanded explanation. Justice Minister Shiono said that procurators remained unshaken in viewing the defendants as guilty. It was, however, a very puzzling case, so it was unlikely that the higher court would reverse the decision. Furthermore, it would not be wise to extend an already too long case during a time of national emergency.[209]

Justice Minister Shiono's postwar memoir notes that he did not know the details of the Teijin case, but a four-day review of documents had convinced him that the arrest and indictments were proper. Nevertheless, his "sixth sense" told him that the charges were a mixture of truth and imagination. As he weighed what to do, he considered the damage done to the procuracy and the expanding China war. It would be best, therefore, to put this difficult case behind them.[210] Thus Shiono's account agreed with Matsuzaka's: justice officials thought that defendants committed crimes. Former justice minister Ohara Naoshi wrote in his postwar memoirs that, while the Teijin case called for reflection by justice officials, because of mistakes make by procurators, he thought that the court verdict was incorrect. Unfortunately, the judges were overinfluenced by the defendants' published and oral accounts. The case should have been appealed.[211] The editor of Ohara's memoir (Kaji Kōichi), who as a reporter covered the Teijin trial, pointed out that procurators knew little about the stock market and consequently made errors. There was enough evidence, however, to illustrate that money was given. Nakajima, he noted, confessed even before his arrest. It was unbelievable, wrote Kaji, that a wordly-wise person like Nakajima would confess unless he was guilty. Furthermore, procurators should have concentrated on the misfeasance charge. Kaji concluded that the actions of both defendants and procurators blurred the truth.[212]

Chief Judge Fujii and Associate Judge Ishida made postwar comments on this famous trial. In one interview, asked about errors made, Fujii replied that "there was no harmony among the procurators . . . who were not prepared fully." Preliminary judges added to the confusion by not conducting investigations in a proper manner. In some cases, the evidence of suspects meeting each other at certain times and places obviously was wrong, because it was proven that they were elsewhere. In sum, "the investigation was done improperly." For example, recalled Fujii, the preliminary court record stated that suspects met at a restaurant on a certain date to conspire to obstruct justice. One of the suspects, however, was at that time in Hiroshima, where he was the go-between at a wedding. Thus, said Fujii, inadequate investigation was behind all prosecution difficulties. Moreover, the sale of stock, a crucial item, was poorly understood by procurators. They were unable, therefore, to make a good misfeasance case against defendants. And procurators should have studied the rayon industry carefully, but instead they relied on hearsay from stock dealers. A poor understanding of the industry became painfully obvious during the trial. The prosecution case contained "various elementary errors," concluded Fujii. The judges were unanimous, recalled Fujii, in rejecting the prosecution argument; there simply was no evidence to convict anyone. The informal verdict was reached as the overworked judges, who had been staying at the court several nights each week, were on a working "vacation" in Izu. One day, as the four walked and talked about the case, they agreed that there was no evidence for conviction. The next step was to explain their reaction to the prosecution's evidence in a formal document. Asked about the famous statement about the moon and the monkey, Fujii replied that it had been written by Judge Ishida Kazuto. As the judges reviewed a draft of the judgment, there was a discussion about how the procurators would react, but they decided to keep it, said Fujii.[213]

In another interview, Fujii modestly said that the verdict was written by three associates (this included Kishi Seiichi, a supplementary judge): Fujii's contribution was merely adding a few words (e.g., "there were no facts at all; there was not enough evidence"). Asked if the verdict shocked the prosecution, he replied that the verdict was written with great care; the bench was prepared for a challenge from any quarter. The questioner noted that December 16 (the judgment was issued on that date) was a time when government offices were closing for the holiday. So why did the judges not wait until after New Year celebrations? The judges felt that the defendants had suffered enough and wanted to cheer them up, replied Fujii. " How did you reach the shocking no facts verdict?" By investigating the case from every possible angle and calling in lots of experts, he replied. "The court," Fujii confessed, "did not know much about the stock market and share prices." Based on the many hearings, however, the judges concluded that defendants were not guilty of misfeasance. "Did not the prosecution also use experts?"

They used some during the preliminary examination period, replied Fujii, but not enough of them. The interviewer questioned Fujii about the famous monkey and moon phrase, but either Fujii's memory played tricks or he was misinformed, because he said that Judge Ishida first heard it from a kendo instructor in high school. In a short postwar piece done for *Nihon no keizai*, Judge Ishida cleared up this point, noting that he heard the phrase in high school but from a philosophy teacher. Ishida viewed the trial as his most important case, recalling that he had put a lot of effort into writing the verdict. The judges, as they discussed the case, decided that they must make a strong comment on "how worthless the prosecution's statements were about the price of shares and the reasons they gave" for the claim of misfeasance. As he thought about the procurators' poor arguments, the moon in the water analogy came to mind. "Even until today," said Ishida, "I am confident that the crime of misfeasance did not occur. Also, in connection with corruption [i.e., bribery] not only was there no evidence to support the prosecution's charge, but, indeed, I became convinced that no facts existed."[214]

"Second Thoughts on the Teijin Trial" appeared on December 30. "It was cheering to read the press's comments on the Teijin scandal trial. It is the trial, apparently, which is now considered scandalous, or rather not the trial but the judicial proceedings before the public hearings." The press, noted the editorial, was asking if in other cases personal rights were denied. "It is not only possible, but certain," wrote the editor. Hopefully, the Justice Ministry, prodded by the Diet, will make a full investigation of infringement of person rights. "One obvious step . . . is an increase in the number of judicial officials, particularly procurators. . . . As for the charges of infringements of personal rights these could surely be . . . practically eliminated, by stricter adherence to the regulation which provides that no prisoner can be detained in a police station longer than a period of ten days, at the expiration of which each and every accused ought to have full access to his own legal representative." Pondering newspaper comments that certain justice officials wanted to use the Teijin investigation to reform society, the editor considered it a "rash" conclusion. This idea "wraps up an old charge that the judiciary has had Fascist leanings, and it is suggested that it was a desire to discredit politics and politicians that was the motive of the arrests. It is a rash conclusion in more ways than one, and certainly has less evidence to support it than was originally brought against the Teijin accused."[215] The editor noted that "in accusing the procurators it is only fair to remember that at the time, nobody questioned the probability of the defendants' guilt. . . . It would be better by far if the press confined itself to a campaign for legal reforms."[216]

Conclusion

From the lifting of the press ban in December 1934 until the trial's end in December 1937, charges of trampling on defendants' personal rights (i.e., violations of defendants' procedural rights based on law) were aired in the Diet, newspapers, magazines, and the courtroom. Despite the prominence of the issue, however, Judge Fujii never mentioned these charges of personal rights violations as he read the seven-hour verdict.

The postwar attorney-scholar Morinaga Eizaburō obtained a copy of a document titled *Teijin mondai jiken jūrin shū* (A collection of personal rights violations in connection with the Teijin problem). Morinaga suspected that this 128-page mimeographed document had been compiled by either defense lawyers or Diet members.[217] Since some lawyers were Diet members, the document was probably used by both groups.

The following examples from this document illustrate the pressures applied to squeeze confessions from suspects. In one interrogation room, two bamboo fencing swords were displayed on a wall behind the procurator, who threatened, as some future time, to use them on an uncooperative suspect. This same procurator (no name is given) threatened a suspect with an ashtray, threw a folded-up knife at a suspect, screamed at a suspect, and grabbed a suspect by the chin, violently forcing his head backward. Another procurator slammed an ashtray on a desktop, screamed at a suspect, and, as he grabbed his lapels, pushed him into a corner. A third procurator screamed into a suspect's ears until they rang. Extremely tight leather handcuffs, which caused swollen fingers, were use to punish recalcitrant suspects. Bedbug-infested cells were employed as well to force suspects' cooperation. Stinking, hot, cramped waiting rooms, where suspects might wait a day, were part of this softening process, which was designed to gain suspects' cooperation in producing confessions. Urging suspects to write notes to each other and showing a suspect a memo written by another suspect were methods employed by procurators. Suspects were told by procurators that the interrogations were performed in the name of the emperor; anyone who resisted confessing was viewed as antiemperor. Once suspects were categorized as such, said procurators, they would be treated as leftist radicals (i.e., they would be treated more harshly). Finally, the ultimate threat perhaps, suspects were told that, unless they confessed, they would be held indefinitely.[218]

Compared to the brutal methods sometimes used on communist suspects and on some regular criminal suspects during this era, Teijin suspects were not "tortured."[219] As Morinaga aptly pointed out, however, the Teijin "suspects were high-class people, who were unable to tolerate this level of torture."[220] Procurators and police understood this point. It was not necessary to hit them with bamboo swords or leather belts, or to beat their bare thighs with iron rods, or to suspend them from a ceiling beam with the rope tied to hands bound behind them. Indeed, for high-class people like Takagi and Kuroda, isolation, a dirty jail cell, and persistent questioning were enough to force a confession. Nevertheless, given their elite background, some Teijin suspects must have felt that what they suffered was "torture." Moreover, procurators did cross the boundary between legal and illegal interrogation acts.

Since there was much discussion of personal rights violations in the media and in the courtroom, Fujii and his colleagues knew about procurators' interrogation methods. Why, then, did the court not comment? First, recall what the court did say: "It is clear that the suspects' statements were untrue." In effect, the judges said that the procurators' case was a tissue of lies. Procurators were thus spotlighted as either manufacturers of an elaborate network of lies, or as incompetent, or both. A further public insult was the monkey-moon comparison. Perhaps the judges felt that this much public humiliation was adequate. Or perhaps they decided that bringing the personal rights violations into the verdict would force humiliated, infuriated procurators to appeal the decision. Or perhaps the judges agreed with the newspaper editor who pointed out that it was not the court's responsibility to inquire how the false confessions were made and why they were signed. From the editor's perspective, it was the duty of others within the Justice Ministry to investigate the charges of personal rights violations.

CHAPTER 6
Aftermath

EVEN AS THE PUBLIC CHUCKLED over the monkey-moon analogy, Imamura Rikisaburō's courtroom defense summary was being set in metal type. *Teijin Incident Summation* (*Teijin jiken benron*) was privately issued on January 1, 1938. This book, which presented the public with details about the sensational Teijin trial, must have annoyed already angry procurators.

In several places Imamura cited examples of illegal actions by procurators in this and other cases (e.g., leaking information from Tokyo procurators to the press, pressuring a suspect in a high-profile political case to change dates in his statement in order to implicate another person, telling suspects that it was the duty of procurators to purify society corrupted by businessmen and politicians).[1] It was not surprising that Imamura, who had suffered at the hands of arrogant procurators for decades, had a dim view of them. In a lecture given at Minseitō headquarters several months before the book was published, Imamura argued that procurators were increasingly dominating courtrooms, pushing judges aside. This tendency for procurators to move into the center of political cases began, he thought, with the High Treason Case (1910–1911) and was developed fully by the time of the Teijin Incident. Starting about 1929, said Imamura, Tokyo procurators began trying to destroy cabinets by using their power of selective prosecution. The Teijin affair, which destroyed the Saitō Cabinet, was the fruition of this trend. This problem could be solved, he concluded, by restoring power to judges and by urging all court officers and the police to obey laws and accept moral responsibilities.[2]

Imamura's scathing criticism of the procuracy was echoed a month later by political journalist Nonaka Morita in *Teijin o sabaku* (Judgment on Teijin), which was published by the distinguished Heibonsha and reprinted repeatedly during following months. Nonaka, who covered the entire trial for the *Asahi Newspaper*, criticized Justice Minister Shiono for issuing inconsistent posttrial statements to the press and the Diet (see below). Authorities should, he wrote, investigate the Teijin Incident to show the public who bore responsibility for it.[3]

Nonaka's book was introduced by former Saitō Cabinet communications minister Minami Hiroshi and Hisatomi Tatsuo, chief of the Tokyo *Nichinichi*'s political section. Minami wrote: "I hope that this book will elevate public opinion enough to ensure that a similar unfortunate incident will never occur and that public opinion will spur a great reform in the system of justice. I believe that the purpose of Mr. Nonaka's book is to further the above aim."[4] Hisatomi pointed out the pressing need to reform the criminal justice system. Nonaka's account, he thought, would focus public attention on righteousness and personal rights.[5]

The irrepressible, outspoken former defendant Mitsuchi Chūzō expressed his views in "Teijin jiken o kaeri mite" (A review of the Teijin Incident), in the February 1938 (out in January) *Chūō kōron*. Prominently displayed on the article's first page was "The Teijin Incident was the most disgraceful case in our national judicial history. There is no comparable case in which judicial officials have lost so much prestige."[6] Identifying no official by name, Mitsuchi recounted a tale of young, inexperienced procurators making stupid mistakes. Blame for the Teijin case, however, fell on senior justice officials who should have realized what was happening.[7]

One factor behind the prosecution's court debacle was procurators' determination to obtain admissions of guilt. Here, Mitsuchi thought, egotistical procurators were unable to admit that the arrests were a mistake. Mixed with this attitude was a certainty that to drop the charges would harm the legal system and lessen the prestige of the procuratorial corps. Fortunately, wrote Mitsuchi, Justice Minister Shiono, who had nothing to do with the case in the beginning and thus bore no responsibility for the outcome, prevented procurators from making the final mistake of appealing the verdict. Next, Mitsuchi speculated on Shiono's public statement (see below), which some people thought was made to save face for the procurators. If this was true, it was more harmful poison issuing from the Justice Ministry.[8]

Recently, noted Mitsuchi, the Justice Ministry had been promoting the notion of respect for law, with a special week designated for that purpose. Instead of giving public lectures on this subject, justice officials should have private conversations about respecting law. In recent years, continued Mitsuchi, more and more reports had circulated about violations of personal rights. To make this point, he mentioned several notorious examples of such violations. Unfortunately, he wrote, once a person becomes a criminal suspect, he is labeled guilty by authorities and by newspapers.

Although the Criminal Procedure Code spells out protections for suspects, and the Penal Code cites punishments for authorities who ignore regulations, violations had continued. In the Teijin case, Mitsuchi opined, prosecution authorities operated in this illegal manner; suspects were treated improperly and subjected to physical pain in order to induce self-confessions. Was this not an abuse of the law by officials sworn to uphold it? The arrest and treatment of Takagi and Okazaki were presented by Mitsuchi as prime examples of official misconduct. The illegal exchange of messages and meetings of suspects was also discussed.[9]

Until recently, wrote Mitsuchi, he thought that law-abiding people had nothing to fear from authorities, because laws protected them. The Teijin case, however, in which good citizens were pressured to give untruthful self-confessions, had altered this viewpoint. Procurators forced these statements in violation of Criminal Procedure Code regulations. Although the code permitted holding suspects if circumstances were unusual (e.g., if it looked like they might run away or destroy evidence), Mitsuchi pointed out that, once he gave sworn testimony before a preliminary judge, there was no need to hold him. Thus, said Mitsuchi, he and others were held by procurators in order to obtain the all-important confession. During the Teijin case interrogations, procurators told some suspects that they would be kept in jail for a year or even two if they refused to confess. In sum, wrote Mitsuchi, it was clear that procurators considered self-confessions as the only worthwhile evidence.[10]

Before his arrest, wrote Mitsuchi, he had wondered about preliminary examinations, but he had no idea that personal rights were so badly violated.[11] "Based on my own experience in the Teijin case, I believe that the preliminary examination is manipulated by procurators."[12] In order to prevent abuses, he concluded, we "must diminish the procurators' improper power" (*kenji no motsu futō no seiryoku o gensatsu seneba naranu*).[13]

Readers of this hard-hitting article probably felt that the author was, as usual, being very frank. A comparison with Mitsuchi's December 1936 court testimony, however, illustrates that the former minister was more circumspect in early 1938. Why? Perhaps the not guilty verdict mellowed Mitsuchi's outlook, perhaps he considered the deepening war with China, or perhaps he feared rightist reprisal. At any rate, his trial testimony includes scathing remarks about the Teijin affair originating from a political plot in which procurators had participated, whereas the article cites youth, inexperience, and lack of supervision by senior officials. Although it was rumored that Justice Minister Shiono was involved in the 1934 plot, Mitsuchi credits him with stopping the procurators' appeal. He does, however, take exception to Shiono's comment after the trial if the minister's remarks were designed to protect mistaken procurators. Nevertheless, in general these comments show great restraint. Perhaps Mitsuchi reasoned, as he assumed his restored place in the power elite, that it was time to mend a few fences. Despite Mitsuchi's subdued tone, his comments were sharp enough to worry *Chūō kōron* editors, who three times employed self-censorship in the article's sections on self-confession. The technique they used was called "*fuseji*" (literally, "conceal a letter"). This form of self-censorship, long used by authors and editors, simply substituted *x*'s or some other meaningless mark for words that might trigger a publication ban.[14] Comments on procurators threatening suspects and Mitsuchi's asking Procurator General Hayashi Raisaburō (his position at the beginning of the Teijin affair; later he was justice minister) what he thought about procurators' rough treatment of suspects in this fabricated case attracted several editorial *x*'s. The third place *x*'s were used also deals with procurators forcing self-confessions.[15]

The February *Chūō kōron* also contained a copy of lawyer Hozumi Shigetō's eloquent courtroom defense of Ōkubo Teiji. Introducing this document, Hozumi expressed his "deepest respect for Judge Fujii's and the other judges' clear and courageous judgement." He also cited Justice Minister Shiono, Procurator General Motoji, and prosecution authorities for wisely and properly handling the situation.[16]

The February 1938 issue of *Kaizō*, in an article on the Teijin scandal, described a chance meeting in December between Judge Fujii and an admirer. Fujii, who was at the Meiji Shrine, was approached by an old man. After shaking Fujii's hand, the old man, with tears in his eyes, spoke to the gathering crowd. "This gentleman is Mr. Fujii, chief judge on the Teikoku Rayon scandal case. My name is Noda, and I used to be a branch manager of the Bank of Japan. I owe neither grudge nor favour to any of the defendants in the case, but I am now offering thanks as a private man to Mr. Fujii for having acquitted all of them, and thus having maintained the prestige of judicial authority."[17] By printing this story, *Kaizō* reenforced public notions about equitable justice. Some readers no doubt viewed Judge Fujii as a modern version of Ōoka Eichizen-no-kami, while others perhaps marveled that courts could maintain fair, objective justice during a time of national emergency.

Seventy-Third Diet

The termination of the "no facts" trial did not silence Diet critics who attacked procurators for violations of personal rights. Comments were sharpened after Justice Minister Shiono promoted Iwamura Michiyo (head procurator at the Tokyo District Court from early April 1934) to vice-minister.[18] This promotion, one can suspect, was Shiono's method of showing support for procurators; critics, no doubt, read an additional meaning into this promotion: Shiono's determination to make no major changes in ministry policy. By this point, Shiono was serving a second of three consecutive tours as justice minister (now in the Konoe Fumimaro Cabinet, June 1937–January 1939).

Although the Seventy-Third Diet faced an expanding China war, which forced rethinking of the proposed five-year industrial plan (early 1937), legislators found time to grill officials. What was the government doing to correct abuses of personal rights? Who would take responsibility for the false prosecution of the Teijin case defendants? What was Justice Minister Shiono's true position on the Teijin trial verdict? Some legislators were dissatisfied with the minister's press statement, in which the national emergency, lack of sufficient proof to overturn the verdict, the puzzling nature of the case, and the length of the investigation and trial were the reasons given for accepting the verdict. Shiono, however, did not limit himself to these comments but also added that "the conviction of the procurators still remains unshaken." Compounding this less than tactful comment, the minister opined that, because of the indictment and the trial, "the accused would learn a lesson and behave in future."[19]

On January 24, 1938, Hamano Tetsutarō (Minseitō) raised the issue of indiscriminate prosecution, citing the Teijin affair together with a notorious arson case in Kanagawa Prefecture. In the latter incident, he noted, 180 people were prosecuted, but 90 were released after the preliminary court examination. Even those released, however, suffered under jail conditions for eighteen months. Moreover, the example of the Teijin trial made him doubt the soundness of the Justice Ministry's policies. Since the Teijin defendants were acquitted, argued Hamano, officials involved should be held responsible. Hamano also criticized Shiono's decision to promote Iwamura (before his promotion Iwamura did offer to resign).[20] Andō Masazumi (Seiyūkai), after charging officials with violating personal rights, complained about a posttrial published statement by Shiono, who spoke "as though an appeal against the judgement had been waived despite the suspicions which still attached to the accused. The Minister also indiscreetly said that the accused would learn a lesson and behave better in future."[21]

At the Budget Committee session on January 31, Sunada Shigemasa (Seiyūkai) brought up the Kanagawa Prefecture arson investigation, the Teijin trial, and election law violation cases. Pointing out that people had been forced to make false confessions, he asked Shiono if the ministry planned to pay compensation to the innocent who served prison time. The justice minister replied that this matter would be investigated. Was there a special reason for Iwamura's offer to resign? asked Sunada. No special reason, replied Shiono, but the action indicated Iwamura's sense of moral responsibility. Next, Sunada pointed out that the court's judgment showed that Kuroda's petition was a fabrication. It was, he noted, Iwamura who had sent this mendacious petition to the justice minister. Sunada asked if Iwamura's conduct was permissible. Although he knew about the petition, replied Shiono, he did not know how Justice Minister Koyama had handled it. Sunada replied that a conversation with Premier Saitō's private secretary made it clear that this document had caused the cabinet's fall. Therefore, Iwamura should take responsibility for this matter. Switching to the treatment of Nakajima and Mitsuchi, Sunada asked about the legality of the meeting between the two former ministers. Nakajima requested the interview, noted Shiono, and, moreover, Iwamura told Nakajima beforehand not to discuss details about the case. Sunada responded that this sort of thing damaged the prosecution's prestige, since it was a serious matter to arrange for an interview between one of the accused and a witness. Shiono pointed out that, because the preliminary judge was informed previously, it did not affect the judges' view of the case. Which provision in the Criminal Procedure Code justifies such a proceeding? Shiono agreed that there was no provision. In conclusion, Sunada denounced the Teijin affair as a fiction created by procurators.[22] During this exchange, Shiono stated that "he has always held that the judgement pronounced by the . . . [court] was right. At the time, the procurators concerned were desirous of appealing against the judgement, but he caused them to give up their idea." Shiono emphasized that "he believes as firmly as ever that the facts were as shown in the judgement. He dismissed as unfounded the newspaper reports which represented him as expressing discontent with the judgement."[23] No doubt this firm public support for the judges' verdict took some heat off Shiono and the Justice Ministry, but privately Shiono did not accept all the "facts" in the judgment. In his memoirs he recalled that at the time he viewed the case as half truth and half imagination. Furthermore, he was certain that some of the defendants were guilty.[24]

Viscount Mimurodo Yukimitsu, in the House of Peers on February 2, expressed dissatisfaction with Shiono's replies in the House of Representatives. Those replies, he stated, were "irreconcilable with 'justice,' which the Konoe Cabinet jealously advocates. It is with good reason . . . ," he declared, "that the Imperial Bar Association passed a resolution at its general meeting on January 20th urging the judicial authorities to take responsibility for the outcome of the Teijin case." Shiono professed sorrow for defendants' prolonged detention. With regard to the bar association's resolution, he insisted that, "as the procurators . . . did what they were called upon to do in fulfilment of their official functions, they need not take responsibility for the result of the examination of the case."[25] A peculiar answer from the top law officer, indeed. This frank reply, however, exposed Shiono's true feelings about personal rights more than he may have intended.

Nine days after this exchange with the viscount, Shiono addressed a conference of high justice officials. Referring to the spate of acusations about personal rights violations, Shiono admitted that in some cases these acusations were valid. This admission coupled with the fact that suspects in sensational cases were acquitted resulted in public concern about procuratorial methods. This state of affairs must be corrected in order to maintain procuratorial prestige and public trust in the administration of justice. Shiono urged officials to make a strong effort.[26]

At a Budget Committee meeting (House of Peers) on February 20, Iwata Chūzō urged prosecution system reform. Many complaints illustrated that justice machinery was defective, he pointed out; cases like the Kanagawa Prefecture arson affair and the Teijin scandal showed that complaints were justified. Were the errors made in these two cases common? he asked. If justice officials regarded these two cases as exceptional, what caused them? Some people think, stated Iwata, that the basic cause was the fact that criminal search and prosecution officials had overreached themselves or that the position of judges was too weak compared with that of procurators. Shiono replied that errors by authorities were uncommon. In the Kanagawa case, for example, there were too many suspects for the overworked procurators, so they ordered policemen to help. Shiono pledged to prevent this sort of mistake. Iwata, dissatisfied with this excuse, pointed out that in other cases it was not overwork but misdeeds that had caused problems.[27] As an example, he cited Vice-Minister Kuroda's petition. Although the document forced the resignation of Premier Saitō, "it was not in any way helpful to the investigation of the case. In reply of an interpellation in the House of Representatives the other day, the Minister of Justice stated that he had made no inquiry as to how Mr. Koyama . . . dealt with Mr. Kuroda's petition, as the matter had no bearing on the guilt or otherwise of the accused." Nevertheless, said Iwate, making a suspect write a petition and submit it to the Justice Ministry was "a serious matter." Shiono evaded a direct reply. Next Iwata asked why Mitsuchi was charged with perjury. It appears, said Iwata, that it was punishment, because he would not certify what procurators had extracted from Nakajima. "Was it not because the procurator in charge did not credit Baron Nakashima's testimony that Mr. Mitsuchi was summoned as a witness and examined? How, then, could Mr. Mitsuchi reasonably have been charged with giving false testimony simply because he did not confirm what Baron Nakashima had stated?" The justice minister replied that while it was not advisable to bring a witness and a defendant face-to-face, it was not illegal. Furthermore, it was done with the preliminary judge's permission. Iwata expressed dissatisfaction with Shiono's reply, but the minister remained silent.[28]

Meanwhile, the two major parties prepared a joint resolution, urging reform of the prosecution system. In their resolution, which cited the Teijin case as one example, officials were charged with having little regard for personal rights, using illegal methods to gain confessions, and fabricating evidence.[29] Saitō Takao (Minseitō), who introduced a motion to pass the resolution on March 1, apologized for bringing up this matter during a national emergency, but, he said, it was too important to neglect. After tracing the development of the Teijin Incident, including the fabrication of the Kuroda petition, which caused a cabinet resignation, Saitō noted that no justice official had accepted responsibility, which was highly improper. True, said Saitō, Iwamura had offered to resign, but the justice minister had promoted him. The government must punish those responsible for the Teijin prosecution, said Saitō. Otherwise reform of the prosecution system will be impossible. If flaws in the prosecution system remain, Shiono should resign, concluded Saitō. The resolution passed with a large majority.[30]

Teijin Trial Echoes

Given the twists and turns of the long Teijin trial, lawsuits and demands for apologies probably surprised few newspaper readers. In a certified letter received by the Tokyo District Civil Court in early June 1937, Ōno and Aida threatened a lawsuit unless they were paid damages and given an apology by Shimada, Takagi, and three other defendants. These people, said the letter, had signed false confessions implicating Ōno and Aida, which had caused them to lose their Finance Ministry positions. They were initiating legal action, said the letter, because the law stipulated that action must be taken within three years. After the Teijin verdict, they requested that Judge Fujii review their suit. Shidomoto, too, filed a suit against Shimada and Takagi.[31]

Upon hearing Judge Fujii's verdict, the press discussed state indemnification for the four former defendants who did not confess (Mitsuchi, Ōno, Aida, and Shidomoto). "Of these men, Mr. Shidomoto intends to demand compensation in consideration of his livelihood, while the three others are apparently similarly inclined although they have no financial worries."[32] According to an early March 1938 article, Judge Fujii approved these requests for compensation, but the amount granted was not mentioned.[33]

Newspaper articles discussed the Criminal Compensation Law (*Keiji hoshō hō*) of January 1, 1932. The provisions of this law applied to defendants acquitted after a trial, people detained but not tried, and those who had a guilty verdict overturned. This narrowly written law excluded many victims of police brutality, false arrest, and false prosecution. For example, excluded from compensation were those who confessed to a crime even if the confession was overturned during a trial. Applicants were to apply for compensation, within sixty days of acquittal, at the trial court; maximum compensation was five yen per day of detention or imprisonment (based on the date of the arrest warrant).[34] Indeed, this law's fundamental character was exposed by Justice Minister Watanabe Chifuyu in Diet discussions before its passage: "Even though the state had no obligation to give compensation, it wished the law enacted to illustrate that the government rested on a foundation of benevolence. Giving compensation, he emphasized, would not mean that the state had any obligation to compensate people because of the state's illegal act."[35] Thus compensation was to be viewed not as a victim's inherent right, but rather as a favor extended by a paternalistic state.

Lawsuits threatened by Shidomoto and other Finance Ministry defendants were settled outside of court. Shidomoto demanded ¥13,200 in damages but withdrew the suit after reaching a private agreement with Shimada and Takagi. Shimada, Takagi, and Yanagida dealt with the other lawsuit by visiting the Finance Ministry on April 29, 1938, when they apologized for the damage done to officials and to the prestige of the ministry. In return for this public display of contrition, the lawsuit was withdrawn.[36]

Another Teijin trial echo, one that reverberates until today, is the term "fascism by the prosecution" (*kensatsu fassho*). Indeed, Ōuchi Tsutomu argues that "'fascism by the prosecution' was born" as Kuroda and other procurators pressured Teijin defendants to make false confessions.[37] Ōuchi's point is well taken, since this term became synonymous with the procurators' handling of Teijin suspects. Nevertheless, procurators had certainly been called "fascists" earlier, especially by communist and other leftist defendants charged with violations of the Peace Preservation Law (over four thousand leftists were indicted from 1928 through 1935).[38] The Teijin trial, however, marked indelibly on the public mind the image of procurators as fascists. Although the term "judicial fascism" (*shihō fassho*) was used as well during the investigation and trial, this term was eclipsed by "fascism by the prosecution." The decline in the use of "judicial fascism" is understandable, because many people saw the Teijin trial judges as heroes and the procurators as villains. Thus "fascism by the prosecution" more clearly fixed responsibility.

Hattori Takaaki, a Tokyo District Court judge, wrote in 1963: "The prewar procuracy enjoyed independence similar to that of the judiciary, at least as far as political or other outside pressure was concerned. This comparatively strong guarantee of independence is one of the most important reasons why the procuracy in prewar Japan had a reputation for impartiality and proved itself highly capable in dealing with numerous scandals in political circles—an ability which won it much support from the general public around 1930." Judge Hattori noted that "the strong procuracy later was criticized for *kensatsu fassho* (fascism by the procuracy), though it has never been made clear in any objective study whether *kensatsu fassho* really existed or, if it did, exactly what it was."[39] A footnote to Hattori's comment, citing the Supreme Public Procurators' Office, states: "*Kensatsu fassho* seems to be generally used to describe the monopoly of the power to prosecute held by the procurators which made it possible for them to exercise this power for political purposes; for example, if they so desired, they could deal with political evils in such a way that the overthrow of a cabinet might result, or at their discretion they could leave the matter as it was."[40]

Given the fact that Judge Hattori was a 1935 graduate of Tokyo Imperial University and that he was appointed to the bench in 1938, his puzzlement about the existence of *kensatsu fassho* and how to define it is strange. What Teijin trial defendants, defense lawyers, and Diet supporters had in mind when they used this term was the employment of illegal tactics by procurators who manufactured a criminal case that evolved into the Teijin trial. Some users of "*kensatsu fassho*" apply the term to the overthrow of the Saitō Cabinet as well. In this latter case, however, the matter of whether it existed or not is open for debate, but the narrower definition of illegal tactics in the investigative stage of the Teijin Incident is not open to debate, because judges certified the case as a "no facts" case. The "facts" that were created by procurators and then pushed through the preliminary court stage were generated by procurators in violation of articles in the

Criminal Procedure Code that were designed to protect personal rights. When Takagi stated in court, on July 30, 1935, that "Procurator Kuroda was like a Fascist," he had this illegal treatment in mind. When Iwata Chūzō criticized procurators as fascists (House of Peers, January 29, 1935), he had in mind both the violations of personal rights and the attack on the existing political order by Procurator Kuroda.[41] The Osaka *Asahi* commented on the Teijin trial after Judge Fujii's verdict: "Even though the trial left nothing to be desired, the public's suspicions will not be dispelled entirely. On the other hand, the impression is fairly wide that some judicial officials approached the case with the idea—not a proper one—of eradicating, by the application of the law, certain deplorable tendencies in society. It was due to this belief that the judiciary was at one time charged with Fascism."[42] In sum, Takagi, Iwata, and other contemporary critics used "fascism" as a pejorative term to brand illegal actions that violated personal rights. Some of these critics also used the term to condemn procurators for illegal actions against the Saitō Cabinet. It is more than a little surprising that Judge Hattori, who was in training to become a legal official in the mid-1930s, does not provide a better definition of *kensatsu fassho*. It must be noted that procurators and other authorities can act in a "fascist" (i.e., illegal) manner within a state structure that is not fascist (I do not accept "fascist" as a proper label for the Japanese state during the 1930s and early 1940s).

Damage to the procuracy in the "no facts" trial might have been ameliorated if Justice Minister Shiono and other high ministry officials had apologized for errors and displayed "sincerity" and "responsibility." Any well-educated person of the time knew that Confucius identified "sincerity" as the greatest virtue.[43] Many people would have used the term (i.e., *makoto*) in daily conversation. Following the procuracy debacle, on December 16, 1937, justice officials could have shown "sincerity" by taking "responsibility." It was customary for leaders to resign or in extreme cases to commit suicide if serious errors were made by people in organizations under their control.[44] This ingrained behavioral response, which was expected, indeed demanded, by some members of the public, was ignored by Justice Minister Shiono. Kuroda could not take responsibility. Biwada resigned because of illness. The logical person to take responsibility was Iwamura. It is puzzling, then, that Shiono refused to accept his resignation. The former head of Tokyo police, Fujinuma, insisted that Shiono "had no choice but to promote Iwamura instead of firing him, because Iwamura knew too much of the background" (i.e., Shiono's pressing Kuroda to prosecute, using information about Kuroda's ethical lapse in dealing with Meitō shares).⁴⁵ This view of Shiono blackmailing Kuroda, however, seems far-fetched in light of Kuroda's eagerness to settle a score with Finance Ministry officials and to make a grand statement against corruption in general.

Another source of the blackened image of procurators that emerged during this period was the prosecution of election law violations as part of the Election Purification Movement (inaugurated via imperial ordinance in May 1935).⁴⁶ In the late 1920s and early1930s, procurators, who were the cutting edge of the state's anticorruption sword, appear to have enjoyed great popularity as they indicted prominent politicians and businessmen for corruption. Economic hard times, no doubt, increased their public support. Overzealousness in pursuit of election law violators, however, produced a harsh response by politicians, who attacked procurators for personal rights violations. Unfortunately, for the procurators, these vitriolic attacks came as the Teijin trial was nearing a climax. Not unexpectedly, Diet attacks on police and procurators increased after the September 1935 prefectural and February 1936 general elections (the delay in politicians' response was due to official suppression of information). On February 16, 1937, in the House of Peers, Kokubo Kiichi (Kōyū Club) complained about reports of violations of personal rights. "In connection with the prefectural elections of 1935 and the general election of 1936 . . . many cases of the use of torture by the police were reported. Such cases occurred in Kanagawa, Kagoshima, Yamaguchi, Iwate and Okayama prefectures, and the forms of torture resorted to by the Kanagawa police were the most shocking. . . . This is a serious blot on Japanese constitutional government."⁴⁷ Six days later, Makino Ryōzō (Seiyūkai) grilled Justice Minister Shiono about procuratorial abuses of personal rights. "The nation is now concerned about the abuse of public authority by the procuratorial and police authorities. . . . The period of detention is very long. The Justice Ministry, admitting this, pleads that this is due to the insufficient number of procurators and judges. Even so, I think that the period is absurdly long. Nowadays most cases take 100 to 200 days. There is a tendency to prolong the period of detention when the suspects are those of public standing."⁴⁸ Justice Minister Shiono, already under siege over personal rights abuses in the Teijin trial (by this date the sixteen defendants had been examined, and Judge Fujii was preparing to call witnesses), appeared contrite, replying that officials would be warned to respect personal rights. Dissatisfied, Makino pointed out that procurators kept suspects under detention until they confessed. There was one case of a high railway official, he noted, who was held from the spring of 1936, because he would not confess to alleged corruption. Shiono admitted that procurators tended to hold suspects in order to obtain confessions.[49] Makino continued: "There is a fascist atmosphere in juridical circles, especially among procurators. Today public trials are influenced by the statements of prosecution and those prepared by preliminary judges, and it must be remembered that such statements are often made after torture and undue pressure has been brought against the accused."[50]

In early August 1937, the *Asahi* reviewed the accomplishments of the seventy-first extraordinary Diet session. Noting that only one government bill had been defeated (the Jury Revision Bill), the newspaper concluded, "Its fate was due not so much to opposition to the Bill itself . . . as to general discontent with the judiciary or rather the procuratorial organ in connection with charges of infringement of personal rights or torture in the examination of the accused in the mass incendiary case and election offences in Kanagawa prefecture." The Justice Ministry, opined the paper, "should take this fact to heart and take the necessary steps to remedy any drawbacks in the administration of justice."[51]

After the trial Baron Nakajima and former vice-minister Kuroda were reinstated as members of the House of Peers. Nakajima appears to have avoided politics after this brush with the law, but in the postwar era he was head of the Foreign Trade Association. Nagasaki, too, remained active in the postwar financial world. Kuroda fulfilled political ambitions by gaining a seat in the House of Councilors in the first postwar election. The distinguished politician Mitsuchi (first elected in 1908) was awarded the high imperial decoration held up by the criminal proceedings (it was to have been presented on April 29, 1935). On January 29, 1938, he received the Order of the Rising Sun, First Class.[52] Besides that honor, a ministership without portfolio was his in the first Konoe Cabinet, and in 1940 he was elevated to the Privy Council. Postwar Mitsuchi held two ministerships in the Shidehara Cabinet. Kawai and Nagano also held postwar cabinet seats; Nagano continued deal making as a political go-between and power broker (he had a close relationship with Prime Minister Yoshida Shigeru). Kobayashi, too, fared well, by becoming one of the four most powerful leaders in the postwar industrial-business community.[53] Bank of Taiwan officials (Shimada, Takagi, Yanagida, Okazaki, and Koshifuji) slipped from public view.

Finance Ministry officials extended a helping hand to former colleagues by reinstating Ōno and Aida. The latter became a department head, and the former was made trade commissioner to China, a post vacant for many years. It appeared that Ōno got a seat by the window to wait for the proper number of years to accumulate for retirement pay. That is not what happened, however, because luck and good colleagues moved him along to a vice-ministership when Ishiwata and Aoki became finance ministers (Hiranuma and Abe cabinets, 1939–1940). Although efforts were made by colleagues and powerful political-business figures like Ikeda Seihin, Ōkubo could not be reinserted into the Finance Ministry's hierarchy, because his former juniors were running the ministry. Eventually, he became president of the North China Development Joint-Stock Company (head office in Tokyo). As for Shidomoto, it appears that, sometime between the Teijin stock sale and his arrest in May 1934, he resigned from the ministry. This explains why no sources mention his return to the ministry.[54]

Trial officials, except for Procurator Biwada, appear to have suffered no personal damage from the Teijin case. Former chief procurator Iwamura, whose offer to resign was rejected by Justice Minister Shiono, became justice minister during the Tōjō Hideki Cabinet (October 1941–July 1944). Chief Preliminary Judge Morozumi received a registered letter from angry defense lawyers in which he was urged to resign as a token of accepting responsibility for mistakes. Ignoring this demand, he became chief judge at several district courts and retired from the Supreme Court in July 1944. Associate Judge Ishida, who wrote the memorable phrase about the monkey scooping the moon's reflection, rose to chief justice of the postwar Supreme Court. By March 1942, Judge Fujii was chief judge at the Tokyo Appeals Court. In a postwar interview, Fujii said that it was rumored after the trial that procurators rejected him, but there was no visible impact on his career. One special and one defense lawyer took high Justice Ministry positions: Hozumi Shigetō became a postwar Supreme Court justice, and Suzuki Yoshio was the justice minister in two postwar cabinets.[55]

Personal Rights

Although the sensational Teijin trial of prominent defendants, in an unprecedented manner, focused national attention on official abuses of personal rights, older newspaper readers were aware that illegal arrest, illegal detention, brutality, torture, and forced confessions were long-standing abuses. Indeed, these unpleasant facts about the criminal justice system were subjects for Diet debate and newspaper comment. For example when a hysterical "red scare" swept the nation, with thousands of suspects arrested under provisions of the 1925 Peace Preservation Law, personal rights of suspected "reds" together with those of their lawyers became a discussion topic. Conservative Diet members and the mainstream press, however, easily disregarded the personal rights of leftist radicals. In contrast, the Teijin affair, which involved members of the political and financial elites, generated widespread support for criminal suspects' personal rights.

Before the Teijin affair, upper-class criminal suspects were better insulated from police and procuratorial brutality than were suspects of lower social rank. A newspaper editorial on January 8, 1931, sums up this unequal system of justice: "There have not, it is true, been wanting cases where men of some distinction complained bitterly of their treatment at the hands of police and procurators; but as a rule, men of high position find that the wind is tempered to them." The criminal suspects "who suffer severely . . . are mostly fellows who are not regarded as being of any particular importance."[56] There were some politicians, professors, journalists, and lawyers who exposed personal rights violations throughout the pre-1945 era regardless of the class status of victims;[57] their weak calls for justice system reforms were magnified unexpectedly by the social rank of the Teijin trial defendants and their many prestigious supporters.

Justice officials, spurred into action by the Teijin trial procuratorial debacle, expressed concern for criminal suspects' rights. For example, Procurator General Motoji Shinkuma (from December 1936 until he was made head of the Supreme Court in February 1939) emphasized to justice officials, especially procurators, that the personal rights of suspects must be protected. These confidential in-house comments are more valuable for understanding the impact of the Teijin trial on the Justice Ministry than are public pronouncements, because Motoji could be very frank in a closed conference or in a confidential instruction to subordinates. In "A Policy for Enforcement of Prosecution Rights" (presented in a 1938 speech and then circulated in print), Motoji said that, to maintain the dignity of the procuratorial office and to keep the people's trust, procurators must follow the law, respect personal rights, avoid severe judgments, and follow a moderate course.[58] Although a similar message was put forth at an earlier conference,

> there is quite a bit of public criticism about the application of prosecution rights. I wish I could say that there is no fear of losing public trust in prosecution rights. . . . Exercising prosecution rights does not include impulsively accusing people. . . . Recently, however, in a regretful phenomenon, cases have resulted from improper application of investigation and arrest. We should strictly prohibit such a grievous phenomenon. There are people, however, who are overzealous in performing their duty, which results

in improper investigative procedure and invites noisy comment about abuse
of personal rights. Such a thing is against the spirit of the prosecution and
will cause a weakening of public trust. This is the point for which we must
be most on guard.[59]

After emphasizing the duty of justice officials, police, and procurators
to stay within the limits of the law, Motoji pointed out a need to revise laws
to permit justice police and procurators to hold expanded powers (i.e., to
do legally what some of them were doing illegally). Concluding, Motoji
stated that procurators must pay special attention to self-confessions.[60] "I
regret that recently there are more than a few actual cases that do not follow this point [i.e., proper procedure]."[61]

Also in 1938, Judge Kawakami Kan completed "About the So-Called
Infringement of Personal Rights," a confidential in-house document.
Kawakami investigated nonideological criminal cases from 1932, based
on reports from various procurator bureaus. After reviewing many cases
of official abuse, Kawakami concluded that police and procurator obsession with written confessions was tied in with most personal rights abuse
cases.[62] Although Kawakami focused on police, excoriating them for
numerous abuses of suspects, procurators, too, were accused of legal violations.[63] Indeed, the judge cited a comment by Justice Minister Shiono
Suehiko: "Well, a recent tendency you often see is among justice police,
of course, but also even the procurators are forcing confessions from suspects and defendants."[64] Kawakami concluded this careful, impressive
study by echoing Procurator General Motoji's call for expanded legal
powers to cope with changing times. Kawakami called for police and
procurators to have greater powers of arrest and legally expanded periods for detention. If these changes were made, he concluded, criminal
justice officials would not feel so hard pressed to complete interrogations; consequently, there would be fewer forced self-confessions.[65] In
sum, both Motoji and Kawakami advocated an expansion of legal limits
so that current illegal activities by police and procurators would become
legal actions. Although it is doubtful that this thought entered the minds
of Motoji and Kawakami, their solution brings up the issue of the difference between a state based on the "rule of law" and one based on "rule
by law." In theory, at least, a state based on the former would find it awk-
ward and difficult to abrogate parts of the public's "human rights," but a
state, like Japan, based on rule by law had only to change laws any time
it was convenient; the emperor gave those rights, and his men could
remove them.

Even before the Teijin trial, criticism of police, procurators, and preliminary court judges generated soul searching within the Justice Ministry. During 1934, for example, the ministry polled judges, procurators, lawyers, and law professors on their opinions about preliminary courts. Professor Ōno Seiichirō of Tokyo Imperial University was of the opinion that abolishment would be best, but with procurators given enhanced powers.[66] Ōno and like thinkers advocated this radical measure, because it was clear to informed people that the courts were obsolescent. Reflecting on Ōno's recommendation, a distinguished panel of postwar legal scholars noted that the preliminary system, as originally designed, served an important function: the judges, in secret sessions, carried out an independent investigation the results of which could be compared with police and procuratorial reports. By 1934, however, judges were more inclined to follow the investigative path created by procurators. The panel was uncertain why procuratorial domination became so obvious in the early 1930s, but one possible reason, they agreed, was simply that procurators did a thorough job of preparing cases in order to be certain that evidence was not ruled insufficient. As for judges, they probably adopted the viewpoint that procurators would not submit a case unless they were certain of a conviction.[67] As a result, judges were less inclined to depart from the paper pathway constructed by procurators. Then, by rubber-stamping procurators' investigative documents, judges certified them as correct factually, which further strengthened the prosecution's position during the open trial.[68]

There were outside pressures for reform of the criminal justice system as well. For instance, Makino Ryōzō (Seiyūkai) pushed a private bill through a Diet committee on March 15, 1935 (three months before the start of the Teijin trial), that aimed to shorten the permissible detention period for criminal suspects from two months to one month. A renewal could be issued with a written explanation for the extension. After the committee passed the bill, Justice Minister Ohara Naoshi said that "the reduction of the period of detention is a good thing as it accords with the spirit of the protection of personal rights, guaranteed by the Constitution." Ohara promised, if the proposed revision of the law was enacted, to "see that each renewal of the detention period is supported by good reasons."[69] Several weeks later the *Asahi* reported that the justice minister, reacting to loud protests in the recent Diet session, planned, at a forthcoming meeting of justice officials, to insist that reform plans be thoroughly implemented. Any officials who felt unable to carry out ordered reforms should retire, said Ohara.[70] At this judicial conference, which began on May 22,[71] Procurator General Mitsuyuki Jirō stated that suspects "must be treated as innocent before they are convicted." He also noted "the increase of cases where people bent on the promotion of selfish ends have filed plaints or laid accusations against others. In handling of such cases, the utmost care is needed. The fullest inquiry must be made into the objects, motives, and contents of the plaints, as well as the background of the accusers."[72]

Justice Minister Hayashi Raisaburō (Ohara's successor) reenforced this order for fair treatment of suspects and scrupulous obedience of regulations. In a conference of high justice officials in June 1936, he noted that "there have been cases where the accused have been detained too long. This calls for reform. . . . It is up to the officials in charge to use every care and circumspection and endeavour to remove evils." Given the nation's situation, he said, "it is very important to maintain the dignity of the national Constitution and the law. Even if the motives are unalloyed illegal methods must be sternly punished."[73] The justice minister, however, at a meeting of procurators on March 23 and 24, stated: "Corrupt practices by Government officials or by those of high social standing are glaring cases of contempt of the law, and their subversive effects on the public morals are incalculable. An effectual end must be put to such irregularities."[74] This comment was made in the midst of the first phase of the Teijin trial (the examination of the sixteen defendants: June 1935 to December 1936), well before the deficiencies in the procurators' case were publicly exposed. Besides having the Teijin defendants in mind, perhaps Hayashi was also targeting outspoken Diet members.

In late July 1936, it appears that critical legislators and inquiring journalists influenced justice officials. A newspaper article stated that a Judicial System Commission was investigating, as part of a reform program, the preliminary examination system, with the aim of preventing infringement of personal rights. Also under review was the indictment phase of investigations (i.e., procurators' tactics), which was another problem area.[75] The *Asahi*, in another article, noted that Procurator General Hayashi was lobbying for an increase in the numbers and salaries of judges and other officials. As an example of understaffing, Hayashi cited overworked procurators during the Teijin case investigation and trial. As for the shortage of judges, Hayashi pointed out that there were 140 fewer in 1936 than in 1891.[76]

Politicians made radical judicial reform proposals. At a meeting of Minseitō leaders on July 7, Noda Bunichirō suggested the abolition of the Justice Ministry, dividing its duties between the Supreme Court, the Procurator's Office, and the Legislative Bureau. Moreover, he said, the status of the president of the Supreme Court should be raised in order to increase judicial independence; procurators should be detached from courts, since their position should be below that of judges.[77] The following month the party's Legal Affairs Committee concluded that preliminary courts were unduly influenced by procuratorial examinations. Therefore, reform was required to protect judicial independence.[78] A newspaper editorial commented: "The old complaint has come up again concerning the position of the procurator. . . . It has often been denied that the procurator tries always to get a conviction; but in all cases reported he has every appearance of doing so. . . . The real trouble as pointed out at a Minseitō meeting . . . lies in the amount of prestige that the procurator commands." In fact, wrote the editor, procurators tended to dominate courts, which made doubtful the validity of many verdicts. Besides that problem, the editor noted that by the time a defendant could meet a lawyer, that defendant had already been interrogated by police, procurators, and preliminary judges. Thus, about all a lawyer could hope to do in open court was "appeal to the softheartedness of the judge" and pray for leniency.[79]

This matter of judicial reform came to a head on March 8, 1937, in a joint resolution introduced by the Minseitō and the Seiyūkai, which stated that in view of procuratorial missteps and other Justice Ministry problems, the government should appoint a study commission and introduce suggested reforms at the next Diet session. According to the press, Justice Minister Shiono opposed the resolution but failed to persuade party officials to withdraw it. Shiono pointed out that the personal rights debate in the Diet was disturbing the public mind and that, if the resolution was passed, it would further incite popular sentiment against police and justice officials. Party officials replied that, instead of making real reforms, the ministry merely asked for an increase in personnel. What was most important, they said, was for judicial authorities to endeavor sincerely to stop illegal acts.[80] The joint resolution passed the lower house in late March.

It took scathing criticism after the Teijin trial verdict to prod Shiono into establishing an investigative committee. Funds for this committee, according to an early March 1938 article, would be appropriated in the Supplementary Budget for the next fiscal year. Justice Minister Shiono's Judicial System Investigation Committee was established on July 13, 1938.[81] By the turn of the year, newspapers reported that the committee was considering the abolition of the preliminary court system and the expansion of procuratorial powers. The right of police to detain suspects would be decreased. The Imperial Bar Association and the Japan Bar Association protested this plan, because it would increase procurators' power. Instead, they argued for maintaining the preliminary court system, with safeguards added to protect criminal suspects from illegal police actions.[82]

"The Preliminary Court System," an editorial published on January 12, 1939, addressed this issue. "The need for some reform in the criminal law courts system has long been felt. It was given dramatic emphasis by the notorious Teijin Rayon trial when a number of distinguished prisoners retracted in open court the confessions they signed before and after examination by the preliminary court. They were acquitted, a verdict which automatically implied condemnation of the proceedings in the preliminary court." Because of this situation, wrote the editor, a thorough inquiry was expected and perhaps the filing of criminal charges against officials, but this did not happen. Instead, Justice Minister Shiono established the Judicial System Investigation Committee, which appeared "to have reached the conclusion that the simplest method of avoiding repetitions of the Teijin affair is to abolish the preliminary courts . . . whose only function is a continuation of the procuratorial examination." It appeared, said the editor, that the committee thought that abolition of the preliminary court would speed up the process of handling criminal suspects (i.e., reduce the amount of time they would be in detention). After noting objections by the two bar associations, the editorial supported the Justice Ministry's abolition plan, because it would expedite the processing of criminal suspects. Abolishing the preliminary court, however, would not ensure proper treatment of criminal suspects. "As for the abuses that are complained of, it is not revision of the system but revision of its practice that alone can end them."[83] Although judicial reform discussion continued, no substantial reform occurred during 1939. The Judicial System Investigation Committee, however, recommended the abolition of the preliminary trial system and the complete integration of the Taiwanese and Korean colonial legal systems with the homeland's.[84]

At the Budget Committee on February 14, 1940 (Yonai Mitsumasa Cabinet, January–July 1940), Nagawa Kanichi (Vice-Minister Kuroda's former lawyer) interpellated Justice Minister Kimura Naotatsu about procurators collecting money for a program to help former prisoners. After hearing Kimura defend this practice, Nagawa mentioned past cases of procuratorial authorities infringing on personal rights. "In the notorious Teijin case, he recalled, some procurators even tried to exploit it for the overthrow of the Cabinet then functioning. In the 73rd session of the Diet, the House of Representatives adopted a resolution unanimously, urging the reform of the machinery of prosecution, but very little has since been done by the Government in the direction urged."[85]

Nagawa's comment neatly sums up the judicial reform effort: lots of discussion but little change. This lack of reform can be attributed in part to conservative justice officials and lawyers used to the current system, but another obstacle to change was the deepening wartime crisis; more pressing national problems overshadowed the need for judicial reform.

The Teijin Incident left a permanent mark on society. Tokyo procurators, who enjoyed popular support for their anticorruption and anticommunist prosecutions during the late 1920s and early 1930s, suffered a humiliating defeat at the Teijin trial, which was indelibly labeled as the prime example of a fabricated "no facts" case, the most sensational violation of personal rights in interwar judicial history. During the trial, critics of the government's case branded procurators "fascists." Decades later, writers reflecting on the Teijin case use the same language. As Ōuchi Tsutomu puts it, "fascism by the prosecution was born at this time" (that is, the use of severe pressure to force false confessions gave rise to this term).[86] Former Justice Minister Hatano Akira (Nakasone Cabinet, 1982–1987) agrees that "fascism by the prosecution" originated during the Teijin trial.[87] Murobushi Tetsurō, who coined the term "structural corruption" (*kōzō oshoku*), notes that following the Teijin trial the term "prosecution fascism" became very popular, because people suspected that justice officials had used their investigative power to destroy the cabinet.[88] Thus, the trial witnessed a shift in public perception of the procuracy. Earlier public applause from the press turned to often severe reproach as details about the investigation and trial came to light. Moreover, exposure of roughshod tactics in other investigations (e.g., election offenses and the Kanagawa arson cases) further blackened procurators' public image.[89] Yet distinguished legal authority John Haley sees the Teijin case in a different light: "The 1935–37 Teijin case is recalled repeatedly as the exemplary prosecution."[90] He precedes this statement by a comment on the postwar procuracy's great concern with insulation from politics and strict impartiality. At the end of this section on Teijin, after noting that the defendants were acquitted, Haley concludes: "Nonetheless, the trials [*sic*] confirmed public views, buttressed by results of earlier prosecutions, of the intrinsic corruption of Japan's political and business elite and the role of the procuracy as an agency that, free from such fowling influence, was worthy of the public trust."[91] Leaving aside the public view of the political-business elite, the balance of Haley's statement flies in the face of evidence presented in these chapters. Surely, the severe battering procurators and preliminary judges received in the Diet, in newspapers, in magazines, and in books changed the viewpoints of many readers. Moreover, procurators' image was defamed by the bribery conviction, in the midst of the Teijin trial, of a former Osaka District Court procurator whose illegal acts occurred during his tenure. Furthermore, admissions that criminal justice system reforms were needed, followed by reform attempts, indicate that Justice Ministry officials sensed an erosion in public confidence.

In fact, it was judges who emerged from this sensational trial with prestige not only intact but enhanced. The public saw in the court's decision another example of strong-minded judges steering an independent course, which reinforced a deeply rooted ideal of a transcendental legal authority offering objective judgment. In the minds of some people, no doubt, Judge Fujii was viewed as personifying the equitable justice dispensed by Ōoka Echizen-no-kami. The matter of judicial independence must have crossed some minds as well because of the intense political storm raging outside Fujii's courtroom. Thus, the Teijin case, like the Ōtsu Incident trial decades earlier, presented the public with another example of judges resisting outside pressures. This outstanding example of a court rendering a balanced judgment, during an emergency period (war in China began nearly six months before the judgment) and in the face of increasingly severe rightist pressures, must have reinforced the public's confidence in judges and the justice they rendered.

Perhaps the Teijin trial should also be viewed as a watershed for lawyers whose prestige increased as that of the procurators decreased. Interestingly, in the aftermath of the Teijin trial, the Judicial System Commission recommended that the government obtain better procurators, judges, and other court officials.[92] In the House of Representatives, in early February 1939, Nakayama Fukuzō (Minseitō) urged Justice Minister Shiono to open the bench to qualified lawyers. Those who have practiced for over ten years, he said, would be suitable candidates.[93] The following June a newspaper noted that sixty lawyers would be appointed as judges and procurators. This was not the first time a lawyer had changed seats in a courtroom, noted the article, but it was unprecedented for so many simultaneous appointments.[94]

Finally, most scholars who write on the Teijin scandal and trial mention public perception of the affair's outcome. For example, Gordon Berger states: "Although the accused party leaders and businessmen were finally acquitted in 1937, the parties' public image greatly suffered during the three-year period of official inquiry and trial."[95] Matsuo Takayoshi writes: "Since the government failed to prosecute the Justice Ministry officials who brought the charges of malfeasance, the public was left with an impression of corruption in both the bureaucracy and financial circles."[96] John Haley opines that the public was left with a view "of the intrinsic corruption of Japan's political and business elite."[97] If these judgments are correct—and one wonders about the accuracy of such sweeping statements—then judges must have stood out as islands of probity in a sea of corruption. Not even the army could duplicate this spotless record, after three-star general Uemura Haruhiko was convicted of bribery in April 1937 (see Chapter 4).

CHAPTER 7

Postwar

CRITICISM OF THE CRIMINAL JUSTICE SYSTEM was reinforced after August 1945 by the views of foreign reformers. During the American-dominated occupation, the problems of abuses by police and procurators as well as flaws in the court system were revisited. Thus, criminal justice system reforms put in place during the early postwar era are a synergetic product produced by domestic and foreign reformers. No doubt many foreign reformers were unaware of the Teijin scandal, investigation, and trial, but many of them were aware of police misconduct and the lack of safeguards to protect human rights.[1]

Reforms

The basic American reform program that aimed to disarm and democratize was crafted in Washington, D.C.; General Douglas MacArthur, as Supreme Commander for the Allied Powers (or SCAP), was appointed to implement Washington's directives.[2] Planning for the postwar world began in late 1939, after the outbreak of European warfare, at the initiative of State Department officials. Following the attack on Pearl Harbor, these officials took the lead in researching how to treat a defeated Japan. By early 1943, officials had decided that America could play a predominant postwar role. This decision raised questions about a direct or indirect occupation, the use of native administrative personnel, and the extent of interference in domestic political life. Civil rights, one document stated, would become a focus of research and discussion if Washington decided to intrude into internal politics. Within the core group of Japan specialists who worked on the various position papers, a cautious approach was adopted, with a reluctance to suggest extensive political reform. Moreover, these key planners were aware of practical problems, like the limited number of people with appropriate training to administer the defeated nation.[3] "Therefore, if changes, even of a limited nature, were deemed desirable, then the victors would have to find another way to bring them about, some form of encouragement or inducement short of coercion. Their answer, essentially, was to postulate the existence of moderates and liberals who could be expected, in the aftermath of defeat and humiliation of the military, to assume the basic responsibility for reforms."[4] Hugh Borton, one of the key planners, "conceded that effective political reform was linked to changes in 'the Japanese mentality,'" a transformation that would take a long time.[5]

In early 1945, policy planning accelerated, with the heads of the State, War, and Navy departments creating a special committee to make policy recommendations for the president's approval. A Subcommittee on the Far East grew out of this new planning structure. Together with the larger committee, the subcommittee listed priorities for Japan: administration of justice was included.[6] On July 26, 1945, shortly before the war's end, the Allied powers issued the Potsdam Declaration, which, among other things, included postwar plans. Under point 6, Allied leaders promised to promote peace, security, and justice; point 10 declared that obstacles to democracy would be removed, and respect for basic human rights would be encouraged.[7] After the war, Washington policy planners issued a late August document (SWNCC 150/3) that made clear that the governing would be indirect, with MacArthur exercising authority via Japanese administrative machinery. Besides SWNCC 150/3, a more detailed directive was rushed to MacArthur, which ordered an extensive purge of police administrative personnel.[8] On October 4, Occupation headquarters issued what is usually called the Civil Liberties Directive (SCAPIN 93). Aimed at encouraging the growth of democratic tendencies, this directive removed laws and regulations restricting human rights, abolished various police units, released political prisoners, and ordered an end to mistreatment and physical punishment of criminal suspects and prisoners.[9]

After destroying the military machine, the most critical issue for General MacArthur was constitutional revision. Under the Shidehara Kijūrō Cabinet (formed in October) a Constitutional Problem Investigation Committee headed by State Minister Matsumoto Jōji (who replaced Nakajima in 1934) was established. Simultaneously, at MacArthur's General Headquarters, a Government Section was established. Its Public Administration Division, presided over by Colonel Charles Kades, had, among its duties, the making of recommendations on a new government structure. The judicial affairs officer of this unit, Lieutenant Colonel Milo Rowell, was ordered to watch Japanese efforts to produce a reformed constitution and to examine governmental practices.[10] Kades also suggested that Rowell make a list of governmental abuses of authority, which would be useful in reviewing Japanese constitutional drafts. An eleven-point list was submitted on December 6, 1945. Among listed items were excessive procuratorial influence over the courts, the lack of individual rights, and the need for an independent judiciary. Individual rights, Rowell felt, would be best protected by a guarantee in the constitution enforced by an independent judiciary.[11]

Meanwhile, the Matsumoto committee submitted to the Americans several constitutional drafts that maintained the basic elements of the 1889 constitution.[12] Why did the Matsumoto committee, in light of the American request for substantial reform, fail to make acceptable revisions? Hata Ikuhiko suggests that the Japanese, who did not anticipate "that the SCAP policy of 'demilitarization and democratization' would be pushed forward so thoroughly or quickly, tried to ride through the period with only lukewarm reforms." Matsumoto and others adopted this stance, because they "misjudged the climate within SCAP and in Washington by overestimating the influence on decision making of . . . the 'Japan Crowd' [i.e., officials and civilians who urged that Americans permit the Japanese to follow their own reform course]. SCAP officials, for their part, wished to rule only indirectly and therefore sought some signs of reformist zeal on the part of Japanese leaders."[13] Two developments, however, pushed SCAP into taking over constitutional revision: the unexpected publication in the *Mainichi Newspaper* of one of the conservative Matsumoto drafts and concern that the Far Eastern Commission, which would be operative in late February, would take over the drafting process and demand constitutional changes more radical than SCAP envisioned.[14] Therefore, frustrated Americans pushed the Japanese aside and took over the drafting of a new constitution.

On February 3, Colonel Kades' Public Administration Division was ordered to compile a model draft constitution, which was due on MacArthur's desk by the twelfth.[15] Kades established a three-person steering committee and divided the rest of his section into seven committees, one of which dealt with civil rights and another with the judiciary. Each of the seven groups was ordered to write an assigned part of the draft document; the steering committee oversaw this activity and made a final decision on the entire document. Five of the sixteen members of this team were lawyers in civilian life; the steering committee members (Kades, Rowell, and Commander Alfred Hussey) were among these five.[16] During this period of round-the-clock work, Kades, Rowell, and Hussey "became the chief drafters of the Government Section model. . . . They, individually and collectively, wrote many of the provisions of the draft and rewrote, revised, or vetoed most of the provisions drawn up by their colleagues."[17] According to an Occupation official, Rowell and Hussey, when they attended civil affairs training schools, "had been exposed to the despotic character of the Imperial Japanese regime, and in Government Section they had made studies of minimal constitutional changes that would be required to bring about 'a peacefully inclined and responsible government.' Hussey concentrated on changes needed in the executive branch, Rowell on those needed in the judicial branch."[18] Kades, in an article published decades later, notes that the group "did not draft the model constitution in one week from scratch. . . . Quite the contrary: Japanese sources were most useful. Used to good advantage were outlines of draft constitutions that had been published by the Progressive, Liberal, and Socialist Parties; and other draft revisions which had been prepared by private groups and individuals."[19]

Rowell, who had attended Harvard Law School but completed the degree at Stanford, got a crash course in Japanese constitutional law as he prepared the eleven-point list of abuses for Kades and a January 11 memorandum on the Constitutional Research Group headed by Morito Tatsuo, Baba Tsunego, and Takano Iwasaburō.[20] As one scholar notes, he was "educated by Japanese lawyers in regard to this problem [i.e., the relationship between procurators and judges] in the Meiji Constitution."[21] Indeed, the steering committee discussed "the curtailment of procurators' abuse of power and . . . agreed that procurators should be subject to the supreme court's rule-making power."[22] Although it is impossible to know how many lawyers who had suffered at the hands of procurators spoke with Rowell, Hussey, and Kades, their influence on the steering committee is clear. No doubt the Americans were predisposed to the idea of an independent judiciary, but detailed information they received from Japanese lawyers and other reformers about abuses in the criminal justice system also influenced them. One can only wonder if the foreign reformers heard comments about procuratorial abuses during the Teijin investigation and trial.

A special characteristic of the steering committee draft was its human rights provisions. Of the three members of the Civil Rights Subcommittee, two (Harry Wildes and Beate Sirota) lived in pre-1945 Japan and had firsthand experience with human rights under the Meiji Constitution. Wildes, who taught at Keio University during 1924–1925 and who authored several books on Japan, was especially knowledgeable about abuses in the

criminal justice system.[23] For example, among the topics covered in
"Enforcing the Law," a chapter in Wildes' *Japan in Crisis* (1934), were
police, torture, the Penal Code, forced confessions, and the courts.[24]

At a tense meeting between Japanese and American officials on
February 13, the Matsumoto draft constitution was rejected, and the
Government Section draft was presented. The Japanese were shocked
beyond measure.[25] After Japanese delegates reviewed the draft, General
Courtney Whitney, head of Government Section, pointed out that "the
Supreme Commander has been unyielding in his defense of your Emperor
against increasing pressure from the outside to render him subject to war
criminal investigation. . . . But . . . the Supreme Commander is not
omnipotent. He feels, however, that acceptance of the provisions of this
new Constitution would render the Emperor practically unassailable. He
feels that it would render much closer the day of freedom from control by
the Allied Powers." Whitney then explained that MacArthur would prefer
that the cabinet present this constitution to the public, but, if necessary,
MacArthur would do so. "General MacArthur feels that this is the last
opportunity for the conservative group, considered by many to be reac-
tionary, to remain in power. . . . I cannot emphasize too strongly that the
acceptance of the draft Constitution is your only hope of survival."[26] With
some minor modifications, the American draft was sent to the House of
Representatives in June 1946, then to the House of Peers, and back to the
lower house, where it was approved on October 7. The new constitution,
after formal promulgation by the emperor on November 3, became effective on May 3, 1947.[27]

The importance the steering committee attached to fundamental
human rights is illustrated by the fact that nearly one-third of the document's 103 articles are devoted to this subject. In contrast to the 1889 document, the new constitution "recognizes no formal abridgement on the
enjoyment of rights and freedoms."[28] Articles 31 through 38 are aimed at
correcting official abuses. For example, a judicial warrant is required for
an arrest unless a suspect is caught in a criminal act (33); criminal suspects
must be informed of the charge and given access to a lawyer (34); torture
and cruel punishments are prohibited (36); suspects have a right to a speedy
trial and the assistance of a lawyer (37); and confessions made during prolonged detention or under some form of compulsion are not recognized as
evidence (38).[29] The last section of Article 38 states: "No person shall be
convicted or punished in cases where the only proof against him is his own
confession."[30] Moreover, the committee's goal of a fully independent court
system is spelled out in detail in Articles 76 through 82.[31] The first article

reads in part: "The whole judicial power is vested in the Supreme Court and in such inferior courts as are established by law. . . . All judges shall be independent in the exercise of their conscience and shall be bound only by this Constitution and the laws."[32]

Kades' busy division also revised the criminal, civil, and procedural codes in order to make them mesh with the new constitutional framework. The primary figure in this endeavor was Alfred Oppler, who, with a support staff of Government Section lawyers, worked with Japanese legal specialists. Oppler, driven out of Germany by the Nazis, was a former associate justice of the Prussian Supreme Administrative Court. Sent by Washington to assist SCAP, he arrived shortly after Kades' group produced the model draft constitution. An expert on German civil law, he would have been a valuable addition to the model constitution team. Nevertheless, Oppler's impact on legal changes was dramatic. "Oppler will long be remembered," states one scholar, "for his revision of the Japanese codes of law along democratic lines. It was he who brought about the sweeping reforms . . . that breathed life into the new constitution. He saw to it that the best features of the Continental and Anglo-Saxon legal systems were adopted without imposing by fiat unsuitable American legal practices. . . . He stressed the rule of law and individual rights as opposed to the power of government." Unlike the insistent, combative approach adopted by the Constitutional Steering Committee, Oppler, in order to persuade Japanese legalists to "accept radical changes . . . divided his staff into standing committees in which all points were freely and fully discussed . . . until a meeting of minds was reached. This practice of democracy won for him the respect and gratitude of Japanese legalists."[33] Reflecting on legal reform activities, Oppler writes that he tried to correct "undesirable aspects of the police state" by increasing penalties for officials who abused criminal suspects or prisoners. "In light of the third-degree methods that prevailed among Japanese police and prison personnel, this was deemed imperative."[34] Moreover, attention was paid to the matter of arrest warrants, the time limit for holding suspects, a suspect's right to remain silent, and confessions.[35] "One must remember," Oppler noted, "that the procurator had often obtained a confession from the accused which he presented to the court before the trial, and also that the defense counsel in such cases advised the accused to stick to the confession and then merely plead . . . for clemency."[36] With this old pattern in mind, Oppler regarded the constitutional prohibition of a conviction based on self-confession as particularly important.[37] Reflecting on the reform era, Oppler writes that producing the amended Criminal Procedure Code, enacted on July 10, 1948, and effective from January 1, 1949, "was the most complicated and time-consuming legal reform. This was the consequence of the rich catalogue of safeguards in the new Constitution." These safeguards were required, because SCAP had "resolved to introduce fundamental rights."[38]

Richard Appleton, an attorney who joined General Headquarters later than Oppler, commented in 1949 on changes in the Criminal Procedure Code: "The foregoing provisions, reinforced by the new writ of habeas corpus, should go a long way towards changing the former lamentable situation in Japan, where it was true more often than not that prosecution was based upon confessions wrung from the accused by means of irresponsible detention and severe grilling lasting for months or even years, during the secret preliminary examination, which resembled a medieval inquisition. . . . The abuses of these secret preliminary examinations became notorious and tended to corrupt the entire judicial process."[39] Japanese and American reformers attempted to solve part of this problem by abolishing the preliminary court system in 1947.[40]

Police organization and practices were high on the list of planned reforms. This was to be expected, because of long-standing reports of police abuses. If personnel in Kades' group had questions about these tales of abuse, they had only to turn to colleague Harry Wildes, whose "The Japanese Police" was published in the *Journal of Criminal Law* in 1928. Wildes wrote: "When once the prisoner has been detained, every opportunity is given to police and procurators to obtain . . . [a confession]. By cross-examination and by bullying, the prisoner is told that continued contumacy in the face of his 'known guilt' can only serve the [*sic*] increase the punishment which will be visited. Torture and the third-degree . . . are employed, even to the point of murder."[41] In *Japan in Crisis* (1934), Wildes repeated this dark view of widespread illegal police practices.[42] SCAP attempted to break the traditional mold by abolishing political police units, purging police leadership, removing many traditional police duties, abolishing the Home Ministry, and decentralizing the police structure. Under the provisions of the Police Law (1947), municipalities with a population of more than five thousand were to support a local police unit. Rural areas were covered by a special force under the supervision of a National Public Safety Commission.[43] Moreover, efforts were made to reeducate police officers by inculcating democratic values and removing "the arrogant, overbearing attitude commonly manifested by the former police force."[44]

Americans who planned criminal justice system reforms were well aware of procuratorial abuses and of the need to protect judges from procurators' often overbearing influence. As a first reform step, they detached procurators from courts and placed them under Justice Ministry control. They also made an effort to insulate procurators from political influences.[45] Moreover, the reforms reduced procuratorial power. For example, the 1948 revision of the Criminal Procedure Code (Article 189) removed procurators' absolute monopoly to command criminal investigations. Nevertheless, the new code contained a built-in contradiction: Article 189 (2) gave justice police authority to investigate crimes; Article 191 (1) gave procurators an identical right. Not surprisingly, conflicts developed between procurators and police, as the former struggled to regain lost power and prestige.[46] It appears, however, that the conflict between Articles 189 and 191 was not regarded as such by the Japanese and American team that revised the code. Oppler wrote: "We Occupation lawyers would have welcomed a clear-cut division of responsibilities between the procuracy and the police, leaving the detection and investigation . . . to the police and the indictment to the procurator." Because of objections by procurators, however, the Americans compromised on this issue. The Japanese argued that the police were not only "often unable to handle complicated cases . . . but also . . . were exposed to local influences more than procurators, whether it be to bossism and intimidation, or to corruption. Here again the middle of the road was chosen: the Code confers on . . . [police] the primary responsibility to 'investigate the offender and the evidence,' but permits the procurator to investigate the crime himself."[47] Another member of the Occupation, writing in 1949, commented on the police-procurator relationship: "The new relationship becomes one of mutual cooperation and coordination instead of control, and its exact definition is being gradually evolved from actual experience rather than prescribed in advance."[48]

Some of the reforms were modified before the official end of SCAP's mandate (the Occupation ended in April 1952). For example, the drastic police decentralization that was unpopular among conservatives and small-town mayors, who lacked adequate finances to support local police, was modified in June 1951; an amendment to the Police Law permitted communities to merge police forces with the National Rural Police. Three years later an even more centralized police structure was approved by the Diet, after a bitter political battle.[49] Commenting on the modification of police reform, one scholar notes that the first reform "gave the prime minister somewhat greater influence over the system, and in 1954 the system itself was drastically reorganized. The National Public Safety Commission was placed under the jurisdiction of the prime minister; a national Police Agency . . . was created, with regional branches throughout the country;

local police administration was concentrated at the prefectural or equivalent [level] . . . the majority of police personnel were classified as local public servants, but the higher ranks . . . were designated national public
servants."[50] The push for change was not restricted to Japanese conservatives; the Americans set an example when they responded to the outbreak
of the Korean War (June 1950) by ordering the formation of a National
Police Reserve, which was supplied with U.S. equipment. From this
"police" force, a new "army" developed.[51]

Modification in the position of procurators occurred with the 1953
revision of the Criminal Procedure Code, which expanded the power of
prosecutors to direct the police.[52] Nevertheless, conflicts between police
and procurators continued. Eventually, procurators and police worked out
a compromise: procurators would command investigations of serious
political corruption and other high profile cases. In such cases, sometimes
procurators begin independent investigations, and sometimes they take
control after police begin cases. The open reason for having procurators
control cases that excite great public attention is the need for highly
trained procurators to deal with difficult economic, accounting, and legal
problems; the behind the screen reason is the fear that retired police officials, who have taken positions in private industry or entered politics, will
sabotage investigations.[53] Another reason procurators make use of their
power to direct investigations, given by a retired procurator, is that procurators do not want police to grow too powerful.[54] "Prosecutor executives
do so most forcefully in 'redball' cases which are most likely to enhance (or
diminish) public regard for the procuracy. Indeed, it is hardly coincidence
that such actions simultaneously serve to protect procuracy turf against
real or perceived police encroachments."[55] Indeed, it is in these high-profile cases, which procurators know stimulate great public interest, that
procurators most completely dominate police.[56]

Judge Oppler, who played a prominent role in revising various codes
and laws, published his reminiscences in 1976. Oppler recalls that changing the Criminal Procedure Code was the most difficult reform, because
of the numerous legal safeguards in the new constitution.[57] Reviewing
these safeguards, Oppler notes that the American-Japanese team of
reformers usually chose a middle-of-the-road approach, with American
lawyers showing restraint.[58] In connection with criminal trials, he writes,
"our 'experiment with the adversary system' again was not a radical one but
moved along the middle road. The revised Code shows traits distinctively
adversary as well as inquisitional. . . . The effect of all of this is that the
character of the criminal trial will never be the same again."[59] Kurt Steiner,

who worked with Oppler, recalls that Oppler "insisted on the required sensitivity to Japanese desires and viewpoints. . . . Given these restraints in objectives and procedures, Oppler could expect the reforms over which he presided to last—as, indeed, they did."[60] Readers probably complete Oppler's account with the impression that the hybrid code produced by his team adequately protects the rights of criminal suspects and defendants.

Chief Justice Ishida Kazuto (well remembered for likening Teijin trial procurators' evidence to an attempt by a monkey to scoop up the moon's watery reflection) presented a paper on the rights of Japanese criminal suspects and defendants at an international judicial conference in April 1970. The judge took the audience step-by-step through the process of arrest, detention, interrogation, prosecution, and trial; protective safeguards were the paper's dominant theme.[61]

Hugh Borton wrote that effective political reform, since it was linked to changes in people's mentality, would take a long time. He might well have been writing about the criminal justice system. Judge Oppler also made the point that reforms would not take hold overnight: "I believe these difficulties are unavoidable in the evolution from an inquisitorial to at least a partially accusatorial criminal process."[62] The revised Criminal Procedure Code, however, has now been in force for half a century, and several generations of police, procurators, and judges have implemented its provisions. Thus, it is not too early to evaluate SCAP's aim to instill "a fundamental change in the criminological attitude" of officials.[63]

Confession

As John Haley notes, "Confession, repentance, and absolution provide the underlying theme of the Japanese criminal process."[64] Since the Tokugawa era, authorities have considered a case without a confession incomplete. Furthermore, outstanding among official abuses spotlighted during the Teijin trial was the issue of forced self-confessions. Therefore, it is revealing to look at the impact of Occupation reforms on methods used by authorities in obtaining confessions.

According to Daniel Foote, an authority on the postwar criminal justice system, physical abuse of suspects is rare,[65] which is a major change from the pre-1945 situation.[66] However, postwar reforms have not changed "the inquisitorial nature of the system and the 'criminological attitude' regarding the central role of confessions."[67] Police are permitted to hold a suspect for forty-eight hours, by which time they must release him or her, or hand the suspect over to procurators. Procurators then are entitled to hold that suspect for twenty-four hours, after which they may request that a judge grant ten more days (later they may request ten additional days). As Foote notes, judges seldom deny these requests. During this period of up to twenty-three days, suspects are usually in holding cells of police stations (so-called substitute prisons), where authorities have easy access to them. Meetings between suspects and defense lawyers are severely limited (both in number and in duration) during this twenty-three-day period. Suspects are informed of their right to remain silent at least once, but no time limit applies to the length of interrogations. Relentlessly, interrogations continue until suspects begin to reply to questions. Given this situation, investigators have ample time to pry open suspects and obtain confessions.[68] Foote notes that an official handbook on investigative techniques continues to state that "obtaining confessions is . . . indispensable to criminal investigations."[69] Moreover, although regulations that permit the holding of suspects in order to prevent destruction of evidence or flight were probably not intended to give investigators more time to question suspects, "in practice, however, prosecutors routinely use detention time to firm up their case by obtaining detailed confessions from the suspect."[70] One Justice Ministry official, in a roundtable discussion, stated: "When all is said and done, preindictment detention in Japan is for the purpose of questioning the suspect, demanding a confession, and pursuing other crimes. If someone were to tell you otherwise, I'd say that's a lie."[71]

Foote argues persuasively that criminal justice officials expect investigation to produce a confession: police think that procurators will not indict without a confession; procurators appear to believe that judges want a confession; and judges, for the most part, rarely refuse to accept confessions as evidence.[72] "Moreover, many judges appear to regard the admission of guilt as an essential part of the psychological catharsis needed to put the defendant on the road to rehabilitation. Failure to confess may be seen as a sign that the defendant is beyond redemption."[73] If the public media's handling of criminal cases is considered a reflection of public attitudes about confessions, then one must conclude that confessions are expected.[74] In sum, Foote notes that procurators feel disgraced if an indictment does not produce a conviction, and judges expect a detailed confession. It is not surprising, therefore, that confessions play such a key role.[75] "Courts appear well aware of the various techniques utilized by investigators in obtaining confessions, yet in practice condone extended questioning and psychological pressure utilized by investigators. At least in these respects the Occupation's goal of 'a fundamental change in the criminological attitude' does not appear to have occurred."[76]

The sociologist Patricia Steinhoff, in a review essay on Japan's criminal justice system, points out that detectives usually get confessions "not because police flagrantly violated the law to coerce confession, but rather because the legal environment itself was so enabling. Because they had nearly complete control over the interrogation of isolated suspects for extended periods of time, detectives could cajole them and wear down their resistance. . . . The heavy emphasis on confession tended to distort the investigative process and lead detectives into systematically bending the rules."[77] Standard interrogation procedures and legal requirements for a conviction, according to Steinhoff, also distort investigations. For example, no transcript is kept of an interrogation. Thus, the record is not the suspect's statement but a detective's construction, which easily leads to misstatements of facts.[78] Detectives, who are required legally to demonstrate motives for crimes, sometimes concocted "plausible motives to fit the emerging confessions. . . . Once they had embarked on a particular strategy, it was pursued doggedly even if the suspect confessed to improbable facts that kept changing under pressure."[79] Moreover, it appears that, once a false confession was made, suspects were unlikely to disavow it, and lawyers, procurators, and judges were not motivated to question the confession's authenticity.[80]

David Johnson, who has researched procuratorial methods, explains that procurators usually accept police confessions after confirming details.[81] To arrive at the "truth," procurators "filter through the raw materials suspects provide, using the parts deemed most relevant to assemble the suspects' confession."[82] Usually, suspects do not read a confession before signing it but instead hear it read. It is difficult, says Johnson, for suspects to digest details in a long, quickly read document. These methods of arriving at the "truth," however, benefit procurators, because they produce "closely-knit and logically consistent accounts which judges may find difficult to resist."[83]

Former Judge Ishimatsu Takeo (Osaka Appeals Court) states that criminal trials are merely a public ceremony, because the important fact finding is done beforehand in secret. At the investigative stage of criminal cases, evidence favorable to the prosecution is compiled, and other material is discarded. Thus, judges never see inconsistent or contradictory evidence. Instead, they see the material that proves the investigators' case.[84] Moreover, states Judge Ishimatsu, "the core of the investigation consists of obtaining testimony from the suspects and witnesses that accords with the hunches of investigators, and there is a tendency to play down the importance of original evidence and physical evidence (including documents)."[85] This matter of "the over-expansion of the investigation and practice by courts of merely confirming the results of the investigation—practices that have been going on ever since before the war . . . have become even more pronounced since that time."[86] In conclusion, says Ishimatsu, "the lengthy and thorough questioning of suspects, especially those held in substitute confinement, tends to lead to egregious trampling of human rights."[87]

The distinguished legal scholar Hirano Ryūichi sees serious problems in criminal procedure. Unlike the situation in many European nations and the United States, courtrooms are merely places where procuratorial investigations are authenticated.[88] "Accordingly, the real substance of criminal procedure in Japan lies in the investigative process. Moreover, this investigative process is an inquisitorial process performed by the prosecutors and police. Therein lies the truly distinctive character of Japanese criminal procedure."[89] In fact, writes Hirano, much of the authority of the old system's preliminary judges has been informally shifted to procurators. As a result, criminal suspects, who are kept in police holding cells, are subjected to long periods of interrogation.[90] This practice arises, says Hirano, because "detailed, corroborated confessions are demanded. . . . Suspects and defendants are questioned not only with respect to the details of the crime itself, but also with respect to motives, background and other matters. The results of the questioning are then introduced into evidence in the form of a confession statement." This document, from the procurators' viewpoint, must be airtight, in case it is challenged in court. Thus, "it is not enough for the confession simply to be fully . . . certain; rather it must be more than fully . . . certain. In order to achieve that level, one or two sessions of questioning is not enough. The confession must be matched carefully with the testimony of witnesses and other evidence. In order to do so, it is necessary to place suspects at the disposal of the investigators—namely, in holding cells—or to permit suspects to be called into such holding cells easily."[91] Courts, which act on received documents, including a confession statement, usually do not aim to make factual conclusions but rely on investigation documents. Judges, according to Hirano, avoid distinguishing fact from fiction in a courtroom; instead, they review the trial dossier in private.[92] Thus, "the real investigation of evidence goes on in the judges' chambers."[93] Hirano concludes that "it would probably be better to simply discard the fiction that the trial is the place where evidence and factual conclusions are formed."[94]

Criminal justice system reformers express special dissatisfaction with the "substitute prison" (*daiyō kangoku*) and lawyers' lack of access to criminal suspects. For example, *Tōkyō shinbun* journalist Iimuro Katsuhiko writes: "Japan is the only industrial democracy whose penal code allows police to incarcerate a suspect for up to 23 days in a holding cell prior to indictment. The police can extend confinement an additional 23 days for each new charge." Human rights advocates, notes Iimuro, claim "that lengthy detention, around-the-clock surveillance and grueling interrogations are a carryover from Japan's prewar police state. Moreover, detainees are denied legal counsel during questioning." The Japan Federation of Bar Associations argues that "the isolation of a holding cell and police interrogation methods cause severe psychological stress. Such treatment constitutes a form of physical and mental torture."[95]

Attorney Igarashi Futaba, who investigated the "substitute prison" system for the Tokyo Bar Association, states that long periods of uninterrupted surveillance, extremely poor food, lack of sleep, lack of a bath, forced sitting in painful positions, and night and day interrogations can produce false confessions. Outside contacts, according to Igarashi, are limited severely (lawyers, for example, are often given only fifteen minutes per visit with clients).[96] Igarashi concludes that given "the overwhelming power of the examining police official . . . anyone can be made to confess."[97] Her contention that lawyers are denied adequate access to clients is supported by the Japan Civil Liberties Union.[98]

The "substitute prison" system mentioned by Igarashi, Hirano, and others is rooted in the Prison Law (Law No. 28, March 28, 1908). Article 1, paragraph 3, reads: "The police jail may be substituted for a prison; provided that a convicted person sentenced to penal servitude or imprisonment shall not be detained therein continually for one month or more."[99] The Meiji government, as it submitted the Prison Law Bill to the Diet, acknowledged that police jails were not the proper place to hold criminal suspects and promised to construct proper facilities. Thus, the government and the legislators saw the "substitute prison" system as a temporary solution to a lack of funds for prison construction.[100]

This review of the criminal justice system, which focuses on confession, indicates that, despite postwar legal reforms, the essence of the old system remains intact. The "substitute prison" system remains in place, and police and procurators, at the risk of ignoring other evidence, strive to obtain the all-important confession. Procurators, today as before, dominate the court system; attorneys, today as before, play a very limited role. Judges, today as before, usually preside over a ceremony in which they sanctify the procurators' documents. Indeed, as David Johnson neatly puts it: "The current system places so much power in the procuracy's hands that only a

colossal abrogation of prosecutor prerogatives will produce more significant change in the balance of advantage in Japanese criminal procedure."[101]
One wonders if Alfred Oppler's sanguine view of the reformed criminal
justice system would be modified if the judge were alive today!

Kensatsu fassho

Unfortunately for procurators, the passage of over six decades has not
removed the public image of procuratorial misconduct. Indeed, it is unusual to read about the Teijin Incident and not find the term "prosecution fascism" (*kensatsu fassho*).

The political critic Yayama Tarō begins an article on the Recruit
Scandal of 1988–1989 with "the lesson of the Teijin affair."[102] After a sketch
of the Teijin case, Yayama writes: This affair is "a perfect example of procuratorial fascism, a case cooked up by right-wingers and reformist bureaucrats. . . . Because the masses believed the reports in the media, the
procurators expected to [win]. . . . But when the not guilty verdict came
through, it undermined people's trust in the procurator's office. . . . I can see
many features in [procurators'] . . . handling of the [Recruit Scandal] . . . that
parallel the Teijin case. . . . In the Teijin Affair, the procurator's office
leaked bits and pieces of what is called 'confessions' until it had turned public opinion solidly against its opponents. . . . Much of what the procurator's
office is doing now smacks of such practices."[103]

Yayama Tarō's criticism is not unique. Author Nishimoto Shōmei wrote
an editorial in the *Asahi Newspaper* on December 5, 1993, saying that many
people must doubt that complete procuratorial control of political corruption cases is a good thing. Some other critics also feel that procurators
abuse their unchecked power, which they use in undemocratic ways. Not
unexpectedly, reformist procurators are sometimes compared with pre-
1945 "fascist" predecessors.[104]

Former justice minister Hatano Akira, in "Questioning the Great
Crime of Prosecution Fascism" (*Kensatsu fassho no taizai o tou*) (published
in February 1994), discusses the Lockheed scandal that surfaced in 1976
and eventually put former prime minister Tanaka Kakuei in the dock. After
reminding readers that "prosecution fascism" originated during the Teijin
trial, Hatano explains that out-of-control procurators created the incident
out of whole cloth. Unfortunately, says Hatano, procurators could not tell
the real thing from an illusion.[105] In fact, the Teijin matter was a simple
business deal, and the criminal case constructed by procurators was based

on an "incident that never existed" (*jiken sonomono ga sonzai shinai*).[106] Next Hatano quotes parts of Judge Fujii's verdict, saying that the action of the judges was courageous, in light of the times. One of the lessons this case teaches, opines Hatano, is that the justice minister has a duty to use Article 14 of the Public Procurators' Office Law (Law No. 61, April 16, 1947) as a brake to halt overzealous procurators.[107] "I believe," writes Hatano, "that this article grew out of a review of the Teijin Incident of 1934."[108] Judge Ishida Kazuto's comments on the Teijin case, writes Hatano, illustrate the similarities between the procuratorial mood at the time and today's aggressive action by procurators. Overzealous procurators today, concludes Hatano, should reflect on mistakes made during the Teijin investigation and trial.[109]

The *Daily Yomiuri* of March 11, 1998, published an article titled "Pushing Panic Button Will Not Solve Problems behind Scandals" in which the Teijin Incident is cited as the benchmark against which to measure financial-political scandals. "There were times during the period of militarism in the Showa era (1926–1989) when the prosecution arm of the judicial system ruled over Japan with Fascist-like authoritarianism. The most typical case was the 1934 'Teijin incident' [which] . . . was regarded as a militarist-rightist plot to overthrow [Saitō's] government." The court found the defendants innocent and criticized procurators for presenting a no-facts case. "The ruling became a famous one and the judges' conscience and courage were imprinted on history."[110]

In the postwar era it has not been uncommon for corruption case suspects to capitalize on the dark public image of Teijin trial procurators. For example, in the Lockheed scandal, which involved former prime minister Tanaka Kakuei, most defendants confessed (Tanaka did not) but later repudiated their confessions, claiming that procurators had fabricated them.[111] During the Tokyo Sagawa Express Company scandal, which was revealed in August 1992, the charge of "prosecution fascism" surfaced again.[112]

Echoes of the past are also heard in low-profile criminal cases. Normally, procurators will not risk prosecuting when they have doubts about gaining a conviction. If they do prosecute, however, and the case results in an acquittal, they are harshly condemned. "Indeed, even acquittals or partial acquittals in minor theft and assault cases generate media headlines and public fury about the procuracy's 'sloppy investigations' . . . 'reckless practices' . . . and 'fascist intentions.'"[113]

Justice officials, especially procurators, are aware of the stigma attached to the Teijin scandal investigation. For example, Procurator Mihori

Hiroshi, who published *Summarizing the Crime of Bribery* (*Wairozai han-ron*) in 1957, draws on the Teijin investigation as an example of how not to obtain self-confessions. Using a posttrial publication by defendant Mitsuchi Chūzō as a textbook, Mihori instructs less experienced procurators in proper methods: use extreme care in getting confessions, and do not make mistakes.[114]

The Teijin case casts a long shadow. Debate continues among justice officials and scholars over the origins and exact meaning of Article 14 in the Public Procurators' Office Law (see above). One view is that this article was placed in the law to control excessive independence on the part of procurators by permitting the justice minister to reach out via the procurator general to restrain overzealous procurators in particular cases.[115] Former justice minister Hatano claims there is a direct link between the sensational Teijin prosecution and the creation of Article 14. This ministerial power should be used with caution, he writes, but it is an important tool for restraining out-of-control procurators.[116] Itō Shigeki, who became procurator general in 1986 and the postwar era's most famous procurator,[117] disagreed with Hatano in print, claiming that it was a procurator general's duty to disobey a minister's order to interfere in a particular case.[118] It appears that Itō's conviction was untested when he died of cancer in 1988. Perhaps Itō's unusual public rebellion against the highly centralized procuratorial command structure resulted from his being the first person to become procurator general who was not a procurator before 1945. Despite Itō's disagreement, Hatano's viewpoint has solid support. For example, Matsumoto Ichirō, writing on "Prosecution Fascism" in 1981, points out that, as a result of the Teijin case, the postwar reform of the procuratorial corps included Article 14, giving the minister the power to prevent reoccurrences of "prosecution fascism."[119] Several decades before Hatano, Matsumoto, and Itō were writing about whether a minister could legally use Article 14, it was employed by Justice Minister Inukai Takeru in April 1954 to prevent the procurator general from obtaining an arrest warrant.[120]

Banchōkai

Like "prosecution fascism," the term "Banchōkai" was not fated to disappear from public discourse and fade into the realm of scholarship, at least not as long as the group's members were active politically. Although Baron Gō declared the informal dinner club dissolved (in mid-May 1934), the public, it appears, saw a continuing interaction among its members, who were well versed in political intrigue. In brief, Nagano Mamoru and Kawai Yoshinari, who held lower house seats, also held postwar cabinet posts. Shōriki Matsutarō, too, became a state minister. Nakajima Kumakichi (an honorary member of the Banchōkai) was president of the Japan Foreign Trade Association and together with Nagasaki Eizō was an important figure in the shadowy world where politics meets high finance. Kobayashi Ataru (incorrectly identified as a Banchōkai member) was the first president of the Japan Development Bank and a powerful figure in the world where business and government overlap.[121]

"Will the Banchōkai Be Resurrected? (*Banchōkai wa fukkatsu*)" was published by Miyake Seiki in *Kaizō* in December 1952. According to Miyake, Nagano and Godō Takuo were instrumental in bringing together a feuding Prime Minister Yoshida Shigeru and Hatoyama Ichirō.[122] It was Nagano's role in this important deal between powerful political figures that prompted Miyake's question.[123] "Some people are beginning to predict," writes Miyake, "that the old Banchōkai will be resurrected."[124] The author, after outlining the Teijin scandal and trial, concludes that without Baron Gō (who died in 1942) behind them the Banchōkai group would be less successful than earlier.[125] Miyake was mistaken, as the "New Banchōkai" engaged in successful behind-the-curtain political maneuvering throughout the 1950s and 1960s. In another sense, however, Miyake was correct, because a key player in the "New Banchōkai," Kobayashi Ataru, was not an original member of the group. Kobayashi was identified with the Banchōkai in the Teijin scandal and was a defendant at the trial, but Kawai Yoshinari disputes his membership.[126] Nevertheless, as a postwar superstar entrepreneur, Kobayashi headed a Tuesday Club whose members played key roles in finance and politics.[127] This group "is credited with having engineered the reappointment of Prime Minister Yoshida in 1952, the merger of the two conservative parties in 1955, the selection of Prime Minister Kishi Nobusuke in 1957, and of his successor Ikeda Hayato in 1960."[128] Given Kobayashi's involvement in the Teijin Incident, it is not surprising that the public labeled the Tuesday Club the "New Banchōkai." In fact, Nagano, Kawai, and other former Banchōkai members were but one among numerous groups supporting Kobayashi.[129]

The mistaken identification of Kobayashi as a member of the "abode of demons" (see Chapter 2 for Mutō Sanji's characterization of the Banchōkai) did not damage a spectacular career, but, according to Nakajima Kumakichi, this was an unusual outcome. In a postwar autobiography, Nakajima writes: "Even today, people who write about the

Banchōkai characterize it as an evil crowd (*yōun*) in its actions in the financial and political worlds. Irresponsible writers even add new names to the membership of the Banchōkai."[130] Being stamped with the Banchōkai label, claims Nakajima, could severely damage a career in the financial field.[131]

CHAPTER 8
Conclusion

TOKYO DISTRICT COURT PROCURATORS had the authority to suspend prosecution or to indict Teijin stock sale suspects. Without indictments, this business scandal would probably have faded from public view with the conclusion of the *Jiji shinpō* series. But Procurators Kuroda Etsurō and Biwada Gensuke zealously pursued this investigation, indicting important politicians, bureaucrats, and businessmen. What motivated Kuroda and Biwada? Already noted is their disgust with corrupt members of the elite who sought personal gain at the expense of community and national interests. Moreover, Kuroda and Biwada worked at the epicenter of the state's anticorruption campaign; the Tokyo bureau during the early Showa era indicted suspects in a number of high-profile corruption cases. Indeed, the bureau's success must have emboldened Kuroda and Biwada. Furthermore, as explained earlier, Kuroda, together with colleagues, was eager to settle a score with Finance Ministry bureaucrats.

Although these reasons are enough to explain Kuroda's and Biwada's motive, they are inadequate in explaining why two seasoned professionals managed to wade ever deeper into a "no facts" legal quagmire. A clue is provided by a look at the investigative culture in which these procurators operated. David Johnson has produced the best work in English on this procuratorial culture. Although Johnson focuses primarily on the postwar era, his conclusions are also applicable to the 1930s. Most procurators, he writes, want to secure justice (the reader should recall that Procurator Shiono Suehiko, head of the Tokyo bureau, stressed the pursuit of justice in the face of strong resistance). A cardinal objective of procurators, notes Johnson, is the discovery of truth; the most direct and perfect route to this goal is a suspect's confession.[1] A veteran procurator told Johnson: "Only God knows the truth. . . . But if we try hard we can come closer to the truth, even if we are never able to see it perfectly. . . . We have constructed a system of prosecution that makes finding the truth our first priority."[2] To clarify "truth," procurators prepare a dossier during the investigation, of which the section containing a suspect's confession is the crucial part.[3] "Prosecutors . . . do not record confessions verbatim. Instead, they prepare a summary statement which organizes and summarizes the suspect's testimony. These summaries often synthesize statements the suspect has given over several sessions (or even days) of testimony. . . . Prosecutors frequently filter through the raw materials suspects provide, using the parts deemed most relevant to assemble the suspect's confession."[4] When this process is complete, procurators have constructed the "truth." Thus, it is clear that procuratorial attitudes and goals in the prewar and postwar eras are remarkably similar.

Kuroda and Biwada, positive that the defendants were guilty, interrogated isolated suspects repeatedly as they compiled an official version of "truth." Readers will recall that when suspects' stories did not mesh, procurators reconstructed facts as required. Kuroda and Biwada, who had carried out earlier investigations in this manner, may even have felt that the stressed suspects were telling the truth as they confessed to various crimes. Nevertheless, this normal investigative procedure, which worked in some investigations, resulted in multiple errors and flawed confessions in the Teijin case. Ironically, Kuroda's and Biwada's relentless pursuit of "truth," which involved a manipulation of facts, resulted in a "no facts" court verdict. Thus, in a sense, the procurators were victims of the same flawed system that victimized the sixteen defendants.

In analyzing why the Tokyo bureau did so well in earlier corruption cases but so poorly in the Teijin case, one can conclude that Kuroda's team was careless, forgetting important points made by Shiono Suehiko, who ran the bureau until October 1930. In one pep talk to subordinates, Shiono stressed strong performance and pride of accomplishment as they carried on the important work of maintaining justice. Facing each case with a letter of resignation in hand, he said, procurators should do their duty. Interestingly, he added that procurators must understand social conditions and must possess common sense.[5] In his memoirs, Shiono points out that the Tokyo bureau picked corruption targets with care, playing off one major political party against the other. Shiono notes: "If we had not used the scalpel skillfully, our own heads would have been in danger."[6] Kuroda and Biwada either forgot or simply ignored these instructions about common sense and limiting investigative targets, because they attacked simultaneously elite members of the political, bureaucratic, and business worlds. A plaintive comment by procurator Hirata Susumu during the prosecution's summation, that the harsh courtroom criticism and abuse of procurators was almost unprecedented, indicates that procurators did not understand, until too late, the strength of the sixteen defendants' social and political networks. For example, Vice-Minister Kuroda Hideo, who was a member of the House of Peers and who was regarded as a candidate for finance minister, had extensive ties in the political, bureaucratic, and business worlds. Minister Mitsuchi Chūzō was a former bureaucrat and powerful politician who was scheduled to receive a very high imperial decoration. Several businessmen on trial were connected with Baron Gō, a leading figure in the financial world. Minister Nakajima Kumakichi had deep contacts in politics, business, and the bureaucracy. Nagasaki Eizō, president of the Asahi Oil Company, was married to the daughter of former prime minister Katsura Tarō. Ōkubo Teiji, head of the Finance Ministry Banking Bureau, was married to the sister of Chief Supreme Court Justice Ikeda Torajirō. Ōno Ryūta, chief of the Special Banking Section, Finance Ministry, was married to Hara Yoshimichi's daughter. Hara was not only a prominent attorney and bar association head, but also a former justice minister. Moreover, Hara was close to Hiranuma Kiichirō, who handpicked him for the justice post (Tanaka Cabinet).

This brief outline suggests that Kuroda and Biwada had taken on formidable opponents. Finance Ministry Aoki Kazuo states: "The suspects were powerful people who placed no limits on expenses; they used over fifty well-known lawyers." Because of the lawyers' skillful preparation for the trial, "they were able to shoot to pieces each item the procurators introduced in court. This would not have been an easy thing for ordinary suspects to do."[7] Finally, Kuroda disobeyed Chief Procurator Miyagi's order not to involve the Bank of Japan. Although none of its directors were prosecuted, two were listed as bribees and sucked into this corruption scandal: they appeared before the preliminary court. Again, one must question Kuroda's and Biwada's common sense.

"Revisionist bureaucrats" or "new bureaucrats" in the 1930s were united in an effort to change the Japanese economic, political, and social order. Although scholars have identified a number of revisionist bureaucrats, they have neglected justice officials. Procurator Kuroda Etsurō, however, appears a good fit for the "revisionist" title. Kuroda viewed businessmen, politicians, and most government officials as corrupt. If he were to become procurator general, he told suspects, he would root out corruption and reform society from top to bottom.[8]

It is not unusual for Japanese scholars to identify Hiranuma Kiichirō as the "evil" force behind the Teijin affair, by pointing out that his supporters dominated the Justice Ministry, especially the procuratorial corps. Unfortunately, some foreign scholars simply repeat this viewpoint. Gordon Berger, for example, writes that Hiranuma "directed from behind the scenes the prosecution by the Ministry of Justice, of the Banchōkai."[9] Missing in this perspective is the fact that Hiranuma was an old-line bureaucrat dedicated to the status quo and a vocal opponent of revisionist bureaucrats. Hiranuma "believed the reform programs of the so-called 'New Bureaucrats' were inspired by European fascist parties and were therefore simply another facet of foreign threats to the unique Japanese order."[10] As Richard Yasko points out, "Hiranuma was a conservative who sought to preserve essential Japanese social and political values. . . . After briefly participating in nascent political alliances . . . in the early thirties, the Hiranuma faction disavowed the fascist movement and broke with the radical right."[11] Hiranuma and other conservative bureaucrats, then, resisted not only excessive democratic impulses, but also totalitarianism. Hiranuma protected "the internally coherent qualities of the Japanese political system, [and] chief among these qualities was the fundamental principle that imperial rule was to be administered by a bureaucracy that combined legal expertise and moral rectitude."[12] In sum, "Hiranuma's ideological and political stance throughout the 1920's and thirties had been invariably conservative. Neither he nor his organizations . . . had ever advocated institutional reform or political reorganization."[13] Political journalist Baba Tsunego, writing in April 1939, pointed out that the Hiranuma Cabinet, established three months earlier, "stands for the maintenance of the *status quo.* . . . Immediately after he had taken office Hiranuma told newspaper reporters that he would respect the Diet, for Japan had a constitutional government, and therefore could not disregard the political parties. . . . [Moreover,] he declared he had no intention of reorganizing the nation."[14]

Thus, it is inconceivable that Hiranuma would have approved of Kuroda's radical reform objectives. Furthermore, as a legalist famous for moral rectitude and adherence to the law, Hiranuma would not have approved of Kuroda's interrogation methods. Nevertheless, one can assume that Hiranuma's small army of supporters were engaged continually in political intrigue with the purpose of toppling the cabinet, as were the supporters of other political hopefuls. This fact does not add up to a conspiracy by procurators to manufacture an incident designed to bring down the government. Once the Teijin investigation began, however,

Hiranuma and his supporters must have used this corruption case for political gain. As Richard Yasko neatly frames it, Hiranuma's and his supporters' efforts to undermine the cabinet "should not be considered an intrinsically evil political act. Such acts were quite common within the Japanese political context. . . . Since the nation lacked a legally established order for changing the reins of government, incessant political maneuvering was the means by which political power was shared and balanced."[15]

There are those who insist that some procurators were engaged in a conspiracy to destroy the Saitō Cabinet. Political journalist Aritake Shūji, for example, in a postwar interview, claims that Shiono Suehiko, head of the Penal Administration Bureau (former head of the Tokyo District Court procurators), knew about Kuroda's dealing in Meitō stock shares and blackmailed Kuroda into handling the Teijin case. This was a rumor that circulated at the time, says Aritake. More proof, states Aritake, is found in Metropolitan Police Board head Fujinuma Shōhei's *Watakushi no issho* (My life). Shiono, knowing about Kuroda's illegal stock transactions, wrote Fujinuma, forced Kuroda to open the Teijin case. This fact was well known by informed people; Kuroda even mentioned it to Okazaki, noted Fujinuma.[16] One should ask, however, if it was necessary to blackmail Kuroda. Indeed, is a conspiracy theory required to explain Kuroda's agressive handling of the Teijin investigation? The answer is no.

Procurator Kuroda's actions are better understood if they are evaluated in light of the superabundance of corruption cases that he and his colleagues handled during the late 1920s and early 1930s. Although Kuroda's early death deprives us of a trial record from which to deduce his feelings about corruption cases, pretrial comments illustrate a festering anger over his public humiliation during the Meiji Sugar Company investigation. These feelings bubbled to the surface during his interrogation of Nagano. Certainly, this part of Nagano's memoir rings with truth: Kuroda's obsession with corruption crimes is reflected in his interrogation of Takagi as well, when he again brought up the Meiji Sugar Company case.[17] Shimada also reported that Kuroda "bitterly abused politicians . . . and businessmen as being all corrupt."[18] Kuroda told Kawai as well that some parts of society were rotten and must be purged; Finance Ministry officials were included in the rotten part.[19] Kuroda's overzealous actions during the Teijin investigation, then, must be viewed against this background. Like Mutō Sanji, Kuroda needed no prompting from "evil forces" offstage; he was eager to pin to the wall with legal nails corrupt financial officials, businessmen, and politicians. Finally, it is important to recall that Chief Procurator Miyagi ordered Kuroda to keep Bank of Japan directors out of the Teijin scandal investigation, because their involvement would damage the nation's international image. Kuroda, however, in overzealous efforts to construct an airtight legal case against Takagi, brought in the names of Nagaike Chōji (the bank's Business Department director) and Shijō Takahide (another director) as bribees (¥5,000 to the former and ¥3,000 to the latter). Like Mutō, Kuroda marched to his own drumbeat.

This book illustrates continuities in the criminal justice system that are apparent whether one looks at the procedures for the handling of criminal suspects or the dominant role of procurators. As in the prewar era, police and procurators rely heavily on confession and use isolation and intensive interrogation to obtain the documentation demanded by courts. Patricia Steinhoff writes of the "substitute prisons" of the pre-1945 era: "Suspects were totally at the mercy of their police interrogators 24 hours a day, with no access to defense lawyers and no supervision of interrogations by officials outside the protective police hierarchy."[20] This situation applies today as well. Despite the Occupation reforms, "the Japanese criminal justice system . . . is still operating under essentially the same criminal law, criminal procedure, and penal code as it did prior to 1945."[21] The role of procurators, too, reflects transwar continuity. After the Occupation, revisions in the Criminal Procedure Code restored most procuratorial power. Thus, procurators continue to dominate criminal investigations; police may resent this dominant role, but they normally comply. This dominance, notes David Johnson, is based on custom and law.[22] Although postwar reforms reenforced the tradition of judicial independence, judges seldom use this increased power to challenge procuratorial behavior. "Whether during investigation, at trial or concerning the charge decision," writes Johnson, "Japanese procurators appear to get what they want from judges with notably few exceptions."[23]

   Transwar continuity can be perceived in public perception of judges as well. As noted in Chapter 1, judges were considered the most trustworthy of all state officials. John Haley is of the opinion that, "in the view of the public, the Japanese judiciary has remained one of the most trusted institutions of postwar Japanese governance."[24] Haley bases this evaluation on public opinion polls, which "consistently find significantly higher levels of public trust in courts than in any other major . . . institution."[25] It appears, then, that citizens feel that courts are managed by objective judges who provide equitable justice. It was the Teijin scandal trial together with other trials in which judges displayed professional independence that produced this public view.

Finally, one must conclude that, even during the stressful war years, judges cherished the bench's independence, and the public impression of an independent judiciary remained alive. Teijin trial judges reenforced this perception that courts dispensed equitable justice. Indeed, the important verdict by Teijin case judges, issued during the crisis-filled decade of the 1930s, should be ranked in importance near the famous Ōtsu case judgment, the benchmark for judicial independence from the executive.

Notes

Abbreviations

AS   Aritake Shūji, *Shōwa Ōkurashō gaishi*

JWC   *Japan Weekly Chronicle*

NM   Nonaka Moritaka, *Teijin o sabaku*

OT   Ōshima Tarō, *Teijin jiken: Shōkanshū o mamotta ishoku no hanketsu*

Introduction

1. Andō Yoshio, *Shōwa keizai shi e no shōgen* 2:8.
2. Murobushi Tetsurō, *Jitsuroku Nihon oshoku shi*, 224.
3. Yayama Tarō, "The Recruit Scandal," 93.
4. Senshū daigaku Imamura hōritsu kenkyū shitsu, ed., *Teijin jiken*, 4.
5. Hasegawa Masayasu, *Shōwa kenpō shi*, 78; Itō Takashi, *Shōwa shi o saguru*, 143.
6. Imamura Rikisaburō, *Teijin jiken benron*, 10.
7. Richard Mitchell, *Thought Control in Prewar Japan*, 188–189.
8. Stanley Payne, *A History of Fascism, 1914–1945*, 336.
9. Ben-Ami Shillony, *Politics and Culture in Wartime Japan*, 177.
10. Elise Tipton, *Japanese Police State*, 142.

Chapter 1: Criminal Justice System

1. Mitchell, *Janus-Faced Justice*, 1.
2. Dan Henderson, *Conciliation and Japanese Law*, 1:44–45, 50, 54, 56–57.
3. Ibid., 59, 61.
4. Ibid., 67.
5. Henderson, "Law and Political Modernization in Japan," 410 n. 44.
6. Tsuji Tatsuya, "Politics in the Eighteenth Century," 446–447.

7. Ibid., 448.
8. Michiko Aoki and Margaret Dardess, comps. and eds., *As the Japanese See It*, 263–274, contains a translation of six Judge Ōoka tales.
9. Irwin Scheiner, "Benevolent Lords and Honorable Peasants," 44.
10. Ibid., 47.
11. Ibid., 46.
12. Ibid.
13. Anne Walthall, *Social Protest and Popular Culture in Eighteenth-Century Japan*, 91.
14. Walthall, "Narratives of Peasant Uprisings in Japan," 576–577; Walthall, "Japanese *Gimin*," 1076, 1083–1084; also see Aoki and Dardess, *As the Japanese See It*, 275–282.
15. Conrad Totman, *Early Modern Japan*, 515–518; Richard Rubinger, *Private Academies of Tokugawa Japan*, 188–189; Tetsuo Najita, "Ōshio Heihachirō," 174.
16. Ibid., 178.
17. Michael Lewis, *Rioters and Citizens*, 252.
18. Quoted in James White, *Ikki*, 47.
19. Herman Ooms, *Tokugawa Village Practice*, 348.
20. Mitchell, *Janus-Faced Justice*, 4–5.
21. Hiramatsu Yoshirō, "Summary of Tokugawa Criminal Justice," 121.
22. Ibid., 121–122.
23. Mitchell, *Janus-Faced Justice*, 10–13.
24. Ishii Ryōsuke, ed., *Japanese Legislation in the Meiji Era*, 275, 277–278, 286–287.
25. Ibid., 286.
26. Ibid., 288; Henderson, *Conciliation and Japanese Law*, 2:189.
27. Mitchell, *Janus-Faced Justice*, 12–13.
28. Ibid., 13.
29. Hugh Borton, *Japan's Modern Century*, 582.
30. John Haley, *Authority without Power*, 80.
31. Tanaka Hideo, ed., *The Japanese Legal System*, 626–627; Ishii, *Japanese Legislation*, 488–489.
32. Tanaka, 627.
33. Ishii, *Japanese Legislation*, 489 (italics in original).
34. Mitchell, *Thought Control in Prewar Japan*, 35.
35. See Mitchell, *Censorship in Imperial Japan*, and Mitchell, *Janus-Faced Justice*.
36. J. Ramseyer and Frances Rosenbluth, *The Politics of Oligarchy*, 87. Ramseyer and Rosenbluth distort my view on pre-1945 judicial independence. These scholars state that "John Haley (1991:80) leans toward complete independence

in the pre-World War II years. . . . So does Mitchell (1992)" (p. 184 n. 1). I do no such thing! I do say about court decisions I cover in *Janus-Faced Justice* that judges often did not go along with what procurators wanted: they sometimes dropped charges, reduced sentences, and freed leftist political criminal suspects. I point out, however, that judges' decisions were influenced by the trend of the times, especially in trials involving rightists. For example, I write on page 151: "There was an erosion of judicial independence during the period between 1933 and 1945, especially in connection with trials involving rightists who claimed to kill in defense of the *kokutai*."

37. Ishii, *Japanese Legislation*, 291–292.
38. "Kanketsu ni atatte (zadankai)," 589.
39. Ishii, *Japanese Legislation*, 291–292.
40. Mitchell, *Thought Control in Prewar Japan*, 35–36.
41. Mitchell, *Political Bribery in Japan*, 37.
42. B. J. George, "The Impact of the Past upon the Rights of the Accused in Japan," 63.
43. Mitchell, *Janus-Faced Justice*, 71.
44. Tanaka, *Japanese Legal System*, 550–551.
45. Mitchell, *Janus-Faced Justice*, 159.
46. Abe Haruo, "Criminal Justice in Japan," 558.
47. Tanaka, *Japanese Legal System*, 637 (italics in original).
48. Robert Epp, "The Challenge from Tradition," 20–21.
49. Ibid., 26.
50. Ibid., 25–26; Ishida Takeshi, "The Introduction of Western Political Concepts into Japan," 12–13.
51. Quoted in Mukai Ken and Toshitani Nobuyoshi, "The Progress and Problems of Compiling the Civil Code in the Early Meiji Era," 38 n. 23.
52. Ishii, *Japanese Legislation*, 398.
53. Ukai Nobushige, "The Individual and the Rule of Law under the New Japanese Constitution," 733; Henderson, "Law and Political Modernization in Japan," 421.
54. George Uyehara, *The Political Development of Japan, 1867–1909*, 183–184.
55. Mitchell, *Janus-Faced Justice*, 30–34, 58–61.
56. Ibid., 70–73, 79–80.
57. Morinaga Eizaburō, *Nihon bengoshi retsuden*, 210.
58. Mitchell, *Political Bribery in Japan*, 22–25, 28–37.
59. Ibid., 50–55; Mitchell, *Thought Control in Prewar Japan*, 81, 86; Shiono Suehiko kaikoroku kankōkai, *Shiono Suehiko kaikoroku*, 242, 248–249, 439.
60. Mitchell, *Janus-Faced Justice*, 50–55; Shiono, *Shiono Suehiko kaikoroku*, 242, 248–249, 439.

61. Norman Hastings, "The Seiyūkai and Party Government in Japan, 1924–1932," 129–130.
62. Chō Yukio, "Exposing the Incompetence of the Bourgeoisie," 494.
63. Hastings, "Seiyūkai," 130.
64. Shiono, *Shiono Suehiko kaikoroku*, 248–249; Mitchell, *Janus-Faced Justice*, 50–54.
65. Shiono, 248.
66. Ōshima Tarō, "Kunshō—tetsudō gigoku jiken: Seitō seiji ni okeru oshoku no rotei," 311.
67. Basil H. Chamberlain, *Things Japanese*, 281; Miyakawa Masuji, *Life of Japan*, 120–122; Tanabe Kohji, "The Process of Litigation," 74, 76.
68. Ibid., 76.
69. Ibid.
70. Hattori Takaaki, "The Legal Profession in Japan," 130.
71. Tanabe, "Litigation," 74.
72. Yazawa, "The Legal Structure of Corporate Enterprise," 557.
73. Ibid., 558.
74. Haley, *The Spirit of Japanese Law*, 101.
75. *JWC*, May 12, 1932, 602.
76. Hattori, "The Legal Profession in Japan," 122.
77. Hattori, "The Role of the Supreme Court of Japan," 74.
78. Tanaka, *The Japanese Legal System*, 485.

Chapter 2: Background of the Scandal

1. Byron Marshall, *Capitalism and Nationalism in Prewar Japan*, 94, 97–101.
2. Ibid., 101.
3. Quoted in ibid., 103.
4. Quoted in ibid.
5. Ibid., 104.
6. Maruyama Masao, *Thought and Behaviour in Modern Japanese Politics*, 45.
7. Marshall, *Capitalism and Nationalism*, 108.
8. Chalmers Johnson, *MITI and the Japanese Miracle*, 111.
9. Nakamura Takafusa, "Depression, Recovery, and War, 1920–1945," 451.
10. Andō, *Shōwa keizai shi e no shōgen*, 1:35; John Roberts, *Mitsui*, 242.
11. Quoted in Andō, *Shōwa keizai shi*, 1:35.
12. Roberts, *Mitsui*, 203.
13. Nakamura Takafusa, "Depression, Recovery, and War," 455–456; Kaneda Hiromitsu, "Agricultural Stagnation in the 1920's," 44, 50.

14. Kaneda, 46.
15. Chō, "Exposing the Incompetence," 493–494.
16. Tamaki Norio, *Japanese Banking*, 146, 148–149; also see Morikawa Hidemasa, *Zaibatsu*, 176.
17. Chō, "Exposing the Incompetence," 494–497; Nakamura Takafusa, "Depression, Recovery, and War," 457.
18. Matsuo Takayoshi, "Teijin Incident"; Arthur Tiedemann, "Big Business and Politics in Prewar Japan," 294; Stock shares issued by the Teijin Company totaled 420,000. *JWC*, July 4, 1935, 17.
19. *JWC*, January 3, 1935, 14.
20. Chō, "From the Shōwa Economic Crisis to Military Economy," 575, 579; Rōyama Sōichi, "Money and the Japanese," 179.
21. Quoted in Dick Nanto and Shinji Takagi, "Korekiyo Takahashi and Japan's Recovery from the Great Depression," 370.
22. William Lockwood, *The Economic Development of Japan*, 209.
23. Ibid., 200.
24. *JWC*, January 22, 1931, 74.
25. William Fletcher, *The Japanese Business Community and National Trade Policy, 1920–1942*, 204.
26. *JWC*, January 22, 1931, 74.
27. Ibid., 74–75.
28. Takahashi Kamekichi, *Kabushiki-kaisha bōkoku ron*, i–ii.
29. Ibid., 4.
30. Ibid., 4–5.
31. Ibid., 4.
32. Teranishi Jūrō, "Loan Syndication in War-Time Japan and the Origins of the Main Bank System," 55, 58.
33. *JWC*, January 22, 1931, 68.
34. Harry Wildes, *Japan in Crisis*, 69.
35. *JWC*, September 15, 1932, 360; ibid., April 19, 1934, 525.
36. *The New Encyclopedia Britannica*, 967; *Academic American Encyclopedia*, 97; *Encyclopaedia of the Social Sciences*, 588; James Scherer, *Japan's Advance*, 122.
37. Zaikai no shinbunsha, ed., *Mugen ka genjitsu ka, Teijin jiken no shinsō*, 177–181; Yano Tsuneta and Shirasaki Kyōichi, *Nippon*, 268, 271 note.
38. Scherer, *Japan's Advance*, 121–124; Mitsubishi Economic Research Bureau, *Japanese Trade and Industry*, 280; Yano and Shirasaki, *Nippon*, 271 note; Kenkoku kinen jigyo kyōkai, *Japan in Advance*, 122.
39. Mitsubishi Economic Research Bureau, *Japanese Trade and Industry*, 272.
40. Ibid., 274.

41. Kawai Yoshinari, *Teijin jiken*, 26–27; *JWC*, May 31, 1934, 729; William Fletcher, *The Japanese Business Community and National Trade Policy*, 4; Y. Takenobu, *The Japan Year Book, 1928*, 71 (appendix A); Alan Campbell and David Noble, eds., *Japan: An Illustrated Encyclopedia*, 1:801. There is confusion over the Banchōkai membership. Matsuo Takayoshi claims that Kobayashi Ataru was a member (see Matsuo, "Teijin Incident"). Kawai, a founding member, disagrees. Kawai writes: "Most people mentioned by the *Jiji shinpō* or others talking about the Teijin Incident were people who had nothing to do with the Banchōkai. For example, Kobayashi Ataru and Nagasaki Eizō had absolutely no connection. I think that Mr. Gō did not even know them." Kawai, 27.

42. Fletcher, *Japanese Business Community*, 4; Takenobu, *Japan Year Book*, 71; Campbell and Noble, *Japan*, 801.

43. Kawai, *Teijin jiken*, 28.

44. Chitoshi Yanaga, *Big Business in Japanese Politics*, 57.

45. Fletcher, 4, *Japanese Business Community*, 120–121; Tiedemann, "Big Business and Politics in Prewar Japan," 294.

46. Ibid.

47. Nakajima Kumakichi, *Seikai zaikai gojūnen*, 219.

48. Tiedmann, "Big Business," 294; Ichihara Ryōhei, "Seitō rengō undō no hasan (sono ni)," 168.

49. AS, 521; Kawai, *Teijin jiken*, 27.

50. OT, 58.

51. Yanaga, *Big Business*, 59: Nakamura Hideichirō, "The Activities of the Japan Economic Federation," 413.

52. Ichihara, "Seitō rengō undō," 168.

53. Ibid.

54. Ichihara Ryōhei, "Ichi Nihon riberarisuto no shakaiteki 'sebone' (III)," 75; Ichihara, "Seitō rengō undō," 167–168.

55. *JWC*, January 3, 1935, 14.

56. Tiedemann, "Big Business," 294–295.

57. Chō, "Exposing the Incompetence," 496.

58. Johnson, *MITI and the Japanese Miracle*, 90.

59. OT, 53.

60. Ibid., 54; *JWC*, August 12, 1937, 321; Shiono Suehiko kaikoroku kankōkai, *Shiono Suehiko kaikoroku*, 259; Ōshima Tarō, "Kunshō," 310, 316; George Akita, "The Other Ito," 352–353.

61. OT, 54.

62. Ibid.; *JWC*, January 3, 1935, 14.

63. *JWC*, January 3, 1935, 14; OT, 55–56; Andō, *Shōwa keizai shi e no shōgen*, 2:26.

64. Andō, 26–27; OT, 55–56; *JWC*, January 3, 1935, 14.

65. *JWC*, January 3, 1935, 15; OT, 56–57.

66. Miyake Seiki, "Banchōkai wa fukkatsu suru ka," 94–95.

67. Ibid., 94.

68. Wildes, *Japan in Crisis*, 174–175.

69. OT, 55.

70. Chalmers Johnson, "Tanaka Kakuei, Structural Corruption, and the Advent of Machine Politics in Japan," 25.

71. Hans Baerwald, "Fund-Raising in Japan," 1.

72. Befu Harumi, "Gift-Giving in a Modernizing Japan," 445, 450.

73. OT, 57–59; Kawai, *Teijin jiken*, 21–22; John Vandenbrink, "State and Industrial Society in Modern Japan," 147; Tokenobu, *Japan Year Book*, 68 (appendix A).

74. Ichihara, "Ichi Nihon riberarisuto," 68–69; OT, 58; Kawai, "Teijin mondai no shinkyō ittan," 365; Suzuki Yoshio denki kankōkai, *Suzuki Yoshio*, 404.

75. Ishiwata Sōtarō denki hensankai, *Ishiwata Sōtarō*, 163.

76. Some sources use January 16. For example, Ōuchi Tsutomu, *Nihon no rekishi*, 370.

77. Quoted in Ichihara, "Ichi Nihon riberarisuto," 69; also quoted in Ōuchi, *Nihon no rekishi*, 371.

78. Quoted in Ichihara, 70.

79. Another source begins this fifty-six-issue series on January 17. Kawai, *Teijin jiken*, 21.

80. Quoted in Ichihara, "Seitō rengō undō," 175; also quoted in Ichihara, "Ichi Nihon riberarisuto," 70–71.

81. Ibid., 74.

82. Quoted in ibid., 75.

83. Quoted in ibid., 81.

84. Vandenbrink, "State and Industrial Society," 140.

85. *JWC*, March 15, 1934, 335.

86. Sanseidō henshūjo, ed., *Konsaisu jinmei jiten*, 1107.

87. *JWC*, March 15, 1934, 334.

88. Vandenbrink, "State and Industrial Society," 136–138; Takenobu, *Japan Year Book*, 68 (appendix A).

89. *JWC*, March 15, 1934, 352; ibid., April 12, 1934, 490.

90. Vandenbrink, "State and Industrial Society," 145.

91. Ibid., 146, 146 n. 16.

92. Ibid., 148–149.
93. *JWC*, March 15, 1934, 334.
94. Vandenbrink, "State and Industrial Society," 147.
95. "Mutō Sanji"; Fletcher, *Japanese Business Community*, 39.
96. Quoted in Chō, "Exposing the Incompetence," 494.
97. Fletcher, *Japanese Business Community*, 39.
98. *JWC*, June 11, 1931, 644.
99. Ibid.
100. Ibid., April 12, 1934, 490.
101. Kawai, *Teijin jiken*, 29.
102. Sources that discuss Mutō's death contain a lot of misinformation. For example OT, 58, and Ōuchi, *Nihon no rekishi*, 374, list the death on March 9. The latter source states as well that he was killed by a "young man."
103. *JWC*, March 15, 1934, 352.
104. Ibid.
105. *JWC*, March 15, 1934, 334.
106. *JWC*, March 22, 1934, 388.
107. Ibid.
108. Kawai, *Teijin jiken*, 51.
109. *JWC*, April 12, 1934, 490.
110. Ibid.
111. Johnson, *MITI and the Japanese Miracle*, 122.

Chapter 3: Saitō Cabinet

1. Sandra Wilson, "Bureaucrats and Villagers in Japan," 125; Shinobu Seizaburō, "From Party Politics to Military Dictatorship," 672–675.
2. Gordon Berger, "Politics and Mobilization in Japan, 1931–1945," 101–102, 107.
3. Hiranuma and Suzuki had outstanding careers in the Justice Ministry, rising to the post of minister one after another (Hiranuma, September 1923–January 1924; Suzuki, January to June 1924). Suzuki, whom Hiranuma treated like a brother, was viewed by outsiders as Hiranuma's loyal follower, but from the mid-1920s, while their political views remained similar, their approach to achieving the premiership diverged. Hiranuma chose the Privy Council route, letting numerous followers act as his agents; Suzuki plunged into open politics. It appears that their long, deep relationship was strained in 1931–1932, as some political leaders called for a unified political party cabinet that would cooperate more fully with the military. The gulf between the two comrades widened, one can surmise, after Saitō

was chosen as premier, because even Hiranuma opposed the appointment of Suzuki. Given the way the gossip mill functioned, Suzuki must have heard about Hiranuma's objection. Kawahara Hiroshi, " 'Chian ijihō' suishin-shatachi—'Chian ijihō no seiji katei,' " 6–7, 10; Suzuki Kisaburō sensei denki hensankai, *Suzuki Kisaburō*, 382–383; Norman Hastings, "The Seiyūkai and Party Government in Japan, 1924–1932," 298–299; Berger, *Parties Out of Power in Japan*, 52.

4. Berger, "Politics and Mobilization," 101–102, 107–108; Berger, *Parties Out of Power*, 48–49; James Crowley, *Japan's Quest for Autonomy*, 178–179.
5. Stephen Large, *Emperors of the Rising Sun*, 52.
6. Sharon Minichiello, *Retreat from Reform*, 87–88.
7. Berger, *Parties Out of Power*, 52–53.
8. *JWC*, August 25, 1932, 231.
9. Minichiello, *Retreat from Reform*, 90–91.
10. Berger, *Parties Out of Power*, 93, 99, 100.
11. Tiedemann, "Big Business and Politics in Prewar Japan," 293–296.
12. Ichihara, "Seitō rengō undō," 161, 168–170.
13. Kawai, *Teijin jiken*, 29.
14. *JWC*, October 27, 1932, 553; ibid., May 21, 1931, 557; ibid., June 4, 1931, 609; Hattori Takaaki, "The Legal Profession in Japan," 120; John Haley, *The Spirit of Japanese Law*, 100.
15. *JWC*, June 11, 1931, 639; ibid., June 25, 1931, 694; Matsuzaka Hiromasa den kankōkai, *Matsuzaka Hiromasa den*, 66.
16. Ohara Naoshi kaikoroku hensankai, *Ohara Naoshi kaikoroku*, 221; Matsuzaka, 67.
17. *JWC*, December 1, 1932, 755.
18. Robert Spaulding, *Imperial Japan's Higher Civil Service Examinations*, 173.
19. *JWC*, December 1, 1932, 755.
20. Spaulding, *Imperial Japan*, 173.
21. *JWC*, November 2, 1933, 551; ibid., December 7, 1933, 697; ibid., February 15, 1934, 220; ibid., July 12, 1934, 63.
22. Nihon, Kōan chōsachō, ed., *Senzen ni okeru uyoku dantai no jōkyō*, 581–583, 585–586.
23. *JWC*, April 27, 1933, 584.
24. Mitchell, *Thought Control in Prewar Japan*, 36–37; Mitchell, *Political Bribery in Japan*, 24–25.
25. Mitchell, *Political Bribery*, 57–61.
26. *JWC*, March 24, 1932, 399; ibid., April 21, 1932, 531; AS, 484.
27. AS, 484–486.
28. Ibid., 486–487.

29. Zaikai no shinbunsha, ed., *Mugen ka genjitsu ka*, 41.
30. AS, 492–493.
31. Ibid., 487–488; *JWC*, August 25, 1932, 247.
32. *JWC*, August 25, 1932, 247.
33. Ibid.
34. Ibid., 231.
35. Ibid.
36. Ishiwata Sōtarō denki hensankai, *Ishiwata Sōtarō*, 149, 153–154.
37. *JWC*, September 8, 1932, 311.
38. Ishiwata Sōtarō denki hensankai, *Ishiwata Sōtarō*, 154–155.
39. *JWC*, January 26, 1933, 130; Andō, *Shōwa keizai shi e no shōgen*, 2:23.
40. *JWC*, January 26, 1933, 130.
41. Ibid., February 9, 1933, 188.
42. Ibid., 190.
43. Ibid., September 1, 1932, 295; ibid., September 15, 1932, 358; ibid., February 9, 1933, 207; Kyōto daigaku bungakubu kokushi kenkyū shitsu, ed., *Nihon kindai shi jiten*, 186.
44. *JWC*, November 10, 1932, 620.
45. AS, 480–481.
46. *JWC*, January 25, 1934, 91.
47. For the trials, see David Sneider, "Action and Oratory," 1–66.
48. *JWC*, February 1, 1934, 141.
49. Ibid., 151.
50. Chalmers Johnson, *MITI and the Japanese Miracle*, 103–104, 108.
51. Ibid., 108.
52. Ibid., 109–110, 119.
53. Jerome Cohen, *Japan's Economy in War and Reconstruction*, 25–26; Mitsubishi Economic Research Bureau, *Japanese Trade and Industry*, 204–205.
54. *JWC*, February 8, 1934, 169–170.
55. Ibid., 188.
56. Ibid., 174.
57. "Ashikaga Takauji," in Alan Campbell and David Noble, eds., *Japan*, 1:66–67.
58. Reinhard Zöllner, "The Sun Also Rises," 518–519.
59. *JWC*, February 8, 1934, 187; ibid., February 15, 1934, 202; Eguchi Keiichi, *Shōwa no rekishi*, 255.
60. Quoted in *JWC*, February 15, 1934, 208.
61. Eguchi, *Shōwa*, 255.
62. *JWC*, February 15, 1934, 204, 206.
63. Ibid., January 15, 1934, 208.

64. Nakajima, *Seikai zaikai gojūnen*, 203, 209–210.
65. *JWC*, February 15, 1934, 203.
66. Ibid.
67. Ibid.
68. Ibid.
69. Ibid., July 21, 1932, 77; ibid., December 7, 1933, 702–703; ibid., December 21, 1933, 769.
70. Ibid., February 8, 1934, 173; ibid., February 15, 1934, 203.
71. Ibid., 207.
72. Ibid., February 22, 1934, 234, 239.
73. Ibid., 240.
74. *JWC*, February 22, 1934, 234–235.
75. Ibid., 239; for information about the Decoration Bureau Scandal, see Mitchell, *Political Bribery in Japan*, 53.
76. *JWC*, February 22, 1934, 239–240.
77. Ibid., 240; ibid., March 1, 1934, 277–278.
78. Ibid., 278–279.
79. Ibid., 308–309.
80. Ibid., 279, 308–310.
81. Ibid., March 15, 1934, 342–343.
82. Hatoyama Ichirō, *Watakushi no jijoden*, 298.
83. Tiedemann, "Big Business," 295; *JWC*, February 22, 1934, 238.
84. Ichihara, "Ichi Nihon riberarisuto," 73.
85. For information about Hiranuma's support network, see Itō Takashi, *Shōwa shoki seiji shi kenkyū*; Richard Yasko, "Hiranuma Kiichirō and Conservative Politics in Prewar Japan"; Takeuchi Kakuji den kankōkai, *Takeuchi Kakuji den*.
86. Ichihara, "Ichi Nihon riberarisuto," 72, 74.
87. *JWC*, March 15, 1934, 348.
88. Ibid., April 19, 1934, 513.
89. Ibid., April 5, 1934, 445.
90. R. L. Sims, *A Political History of Modern Japan*, 216–217; Ōuchi, *Nihon no rekishi*, 367. Also see Susan Weiner, "Bureaucracy and Politics in the 1930s."
91. Ishiwata Sōtarō denki hensankai, *Ishiwata Sōtarō*, 163.
92. AS, 523; OT, 59.
93. AS, 520–522.
94. Wildes, *Japan in Crisis*, 197–198.
95. Ibid., 199.
96. Quoted in Kawai, *Teijin jiken*, 42–43.
97. *JWC*, January 3, 1935, 15; OT, 59.

98.   AS, 525; Iwamura Michiyo den kankōkai, *Iwamura Michiyo den*, 81.

99.   Quoted in AS, 525.

100. Ibid.

101. OT, 59; *JWC*, January 3, 1935, 15. Baron Gō dissolved the Banchōkai in mid-May 1934. *JWC*, May 24, 1934, 701.

102. Aoki Kazuo, *Seizan zuisō*, 298–301.

103. *JWC*, May 31, 1934, 729.

104. Ibid.

105. Andō, *Shōwa keizai shi*, 2:23; AS, 526.

106. For details about police-procurator rivalry and conflict, see Mitchell, *Thought Control in Prewar Japan*, and Mitchell, *Janus-Faced Justice*.

107. AS, 526.

108. Ibid., 598.

109. AS, 592, 594–595.

110. Suzuki Yoshio denki kankōkai, *Suzuki Yoshio*, 406–407, 410.

111. Kawai, *Teijin jiken*, 285.

112. Robert Spaulding, "The Bureaucracy as a Political Force, 1920–1945," 62.

113. OT, 60–61.

114. *JWC*, February 7, 1935, 161.

115. Nakajima, *Seikai zaikai gojūnen*, 220–221.

116. Ibid., 221.

117. *JWC*, June 28, 1934, 876.

118. Ibid., July 5, 1934, 22.

119. AS, 537–538; OT, 61.

120. Imamura Rikisaburō, *Teijin jiken benron*, 9.

121. OT, 60.

122. NM, 67–69; also see Kawai, *Teijin jiken*, 110–111. Judge Ishida Kazuto considered the involvement of Takahashi's son as "the direct cause" of the cabinet's collapse. Quoted in ibid., 111.

123. Berger, *Parties Out of Power*, 81.

124. Ibid., 80–85.

125. Ibid., 99–100.

126. Ibid., 100.

127. Tiedemann, "Big Business," 293–294.

128. Ibid., 295–296.

129. Ōuchi, *Nihon no rekishi*, 367–370.

130. Ibid., 370.

131. Ibid., 371.

132. Ibid., 373.

133. Ibid.

134. Eguchi, *Shōwa no rekishi*, 255.
135. Ichihara, "Seitō rengō undō," 161, 170.
136. Ibid., 170.
137. Ibid., 178.
138. Ibid.
139. Nakamura Kikuo, *Shōwa seiji shi*, 118, 124 note.
140. Ōshima Kiyoshi, *Takahashi Korekiyo*, 178.
141. Andō, *Shōwa keizai shi*, 2:23.
142. Ibid.; AS, 527.
143. Imamura Rikisaburō, *Teijin jiken benron*, 202.
144. Quoted in NM, 167.
145. Nakajima, *Seikai zaikai gojūnen*, 209.
146. Ibid., 221.
147. Christopher Szpilman, "The Politics of Cultural Conservatism," 152.
148. Ibid., 159.
149. Imamura Rikisaburō, *Teijin jiken benron*, 10.
150. *JWC*, January 3, 1935, 15.

Chapter 4: Preparation for the Trial

1. AS, 535, 578.
2. Kawai, *Teijin jiken*, 313, 316.
3. AS, 563, 565, 567, 569, 571, 573.
4. Imamura Takeo, *Takahashi Korekiyo*, 203.
5. Mitsuchi Chūzō, *Shōnan hōjōki*, 15.
6. AS, 584–586.
7. *JWC*, July 12, 1934, 46.
8. Ibid., July 26, 1934, 127.
9. Ibid., August 2, 1934, 159.
10. Ibid., August 9, 1934, 214.
11. Ibid., August 30, 1934, 310.
12. Ibid.
13. Ibid., September 6, 1934, 323.
14. AS, 573.
15. *JWC*, September 20, 1934, 401; NM, 138, 153.
16. *JWC*, July 12, 1934, 51.
17. Weiner, "Bureaucracy and Politics," 121.
18. Berger, *Parties Out of Power*, 101; Janet Hunter, comp., *Concise Dictionary of Modern Japanese History*, 283.
19. AS, 582.

20. Ohara Naoshi kaikoroku hensankai, *Ohara Naoshi kaikoroku*, 250.

21. Mitchell, *Political Bribery in Japan*, 31–33.

22. Takai Kenzō, *Shihō keisatsu ron*, 1–2,10,13–16, 80–8l; Mitchell, *Thought Control in Prewar Japan*, 187.

23. Mitchell, *Janus-Faced Justice*, 149.

24. *JWC*, July 12, 1934, 51.

25. Harold Quigley, *Japanese Government and Politics*, 283.

26. *JWC*, July 26, 1934, 127.

27. Ibid., September 20, 1934, 401.

28. Mitchell, *Thought Control in Prewar Janan*, 99.

29. Suzuki Yoshio denki kankōkai, *Suzuki Yoshio*, 412.

30. Kawai, *Teijin jiken*, 186.

31. Quigley, *Japanese Government*, 283 n. 18.

32. Yamabe Kentarō, ed., *Gendai shi shiryō*, xiii–ix.

33. Reprinted from the *Yoshin* in Zaikai no shinbunsha, *Mugen ka genjitsu ka*, 6, 34.

34. William Sebald, trans., *The Criminal Code of Japan*, 216–217.

35. Ibid., 218.

36. Ibid., 219.

37. Wagatsuma Sakae, ed., *Shin hōritsugaku jiten*, 980.

38. *JWC*, July 25,1935, 121.

39. Sebald, *Criminal Code*, 142.

40. Ibid., 147.

41. Ibid., 124.

42. Ibid., 125.

43. Ibid., 142; Wagatsuma Sakae, ed., *Kyū hōrei shū*, 449.

44. Wagatsuma, *Kyū hōrei shū*, 504; *JWC*, October 31, 1935, 541.

45. Mitchell, *Political Bribery in Japan*, 99–100, 142–143.

46. Senshū daigaku Imamura hōritsu kenkyū shitsu, ed., *Teijin jiken*. This is volume 1 in a planned series. The list of defense lawyers is at the end of the volume. Failure to list Nagawa Kanichi as one of Vice-Minister Kuroda's lawyers suggests that this list should be used with care.

47. Ibid. The chart shows only five defendants covered by Imamura; he added Nakajima later.

48. Aoki Kazuo, *Seizan zuisō*, 300.

49. AS, 587; NM, 219.

50. Byron Marshall, *Academic Freedom and the Japanese Imperial University, 1868–1939*, 42–43.

51. Nagano Kunisuke, ed., *Hōsō hyakunen shi*, 903.

52. Senshū daigaku, *Teijin jiken*, unnumbered appendix.

53. Nagano, *Hōsō hyakunen shi*, 947–948.
54. Ibid., 869–871.
55. Senshū daigaku, *Teijin jiken*, 22 n. 7.
56. *JWC*, December 6, 1934, 771–772.
57. Ibid., 772.
58. Ibid., January 10, 1935, 31.
59. Ibid.
60. Ibid., January 3, 1935, 14–15.
61. Ibid., November 15, 1934, 670–671.
62. Ibid., January 3, 1935, 14–15.
63. Ibid., January 17, 1935, 76.
64. Ibid., January 24, 1935, 107.
65. Ibid., January 31, 1935, 125.
66. Ibid., 126.
67. Ibid.
68. Ibid.; Iwamura Michiyo den kankōkai, *Iwamura Michiyo den*, 88.
69. NM, 33.
70. Quoted in ibid.
71. *JWC*, February 7, 1935, 161.
72. Quoted in ibid.
73. Ibid.
74. Ibid.
75. Quoted in ibid., January 31, 1935, 134.
76. Ibid.
77. Ibid., February 7, 1935, 161.
78. Quoted in ibid.
79. Ibid.
80. Ibid., 164.
81. Ibid., January 31, 1935, 118–119; for more information on the treatment of regular and political criminals, see Mitchell, *Janus-Faced Justice*.
82. *JWC*, February 7, 1935, 167.
83. Ibid., January 3, 1935, 21; ibid., March 7, 1935, 315.
84. Ibid., February 21, 1935, 226.
85. Mitchell, *Janus-Faced Justice*, 135.
86. *JWC*, January 31, 1935, 126.
87. Zaikai no shinbunsha, *Mugen ka genjitsu ka*, 2.
88. Quoted in ibid.
89. Ibid.
90. Ibid., 9–12.
91. Ibid., 13.

92. Ibid., 43.
93. Ibid., 43–45.
94. Ibid., 45.
95. Ibid., 45–47.
96. Ibid., 47.
97. Ibid., 48.
98. Ibid.
99. Ibid., 48–49.
100. For information on jail and prison conditions, see Mitchell, *Janus-Faced Justice.*
101. OT, 67.
102. *JWC*, March 28, 1935, 406.
103. Ibid.
104. Ibid., July 4, 1935, 34.
105. OT, 57.
106. Mitchell, *Political Bribery in Japan*, 52.
107. AS, 531.
108. *JWC*, June 29, 1933, 893.
109. Ibid., January 30, 1936, 138; ibid., February 27, 1936, 272.
110. Ibid., May 21, 1936, 645.
111. Quoted in ibid.
112. Ibid., July 5, 1934, 9; ibid., July 12, 1934, 65; ibid., September 19, 1935, 375; ibid., November 7, 1935, 590; ibid., November 21, 1935, 646.
113. Ibid., July 16, 1936, 86; ibid., February 18, 1937, 208; ibid., April 22, 1937, 490.
114. Mitchell, *Political Bribery in Japan*, 64.

Chapter 5: Trial

1. NM, 3–4; AS, 544–546, 551, 533; *JWC*, January 3, 1935, 14. Also see "The Law" in Chapter 4.
2. AS, 455–456, 563, 565, 567.
3. Ibid., 569, 571, 573.
4. NM, 5–8.
5. Ibid., 8.
6. Ibid., 9; *JWC*, June 27, 1935, 837.
7. NM, 9–10; *JWC*, June 27, 1935, 837.
8. *JWC*, July 4, 1935, 16–17; ibid., July 11, 1935, 48; ibid., July 18, 1935, 80.
9. Quoted in ibid., July 4, 1935, 16.
10. Ibid., July 11, 1935, 48.

11. Quoted in ibid.
12. Ibid., 49.
13. Quoted in ibid., July 18, 1935, 80.
14. Ibid.
15. Ibid., July 11, 1935, 48.
16. Ibid., July 25, 1935, 121.
17. Quoted in ibid.
18. Ibid. July 4, 1935, 17.
19. Ibid., July 11, 1935, 48.
20. Ibid., July 25, 1935, 121.
21. Quoted in ibid., August 8, 1935, 190.
22. NM, 24–25.
23. Ibid., 26.
24. Quoted in ibid., 25.
25. Ibid., 26, 29.
26. *JWC*, August 8, 1935, 189.
27. Quoted in ibid.
28. Ibid.
29. Quoted in ibid.
30. NM, 49, 51.
31. Mitsuchi Chūzō, *Yūshū tsurezure gusa*, 1–5, 11.
32. Ibid., 11.
33. Ibid., 18–364.
34. *JWC*, August 29, 1935, 277.
35. Quoted in ibid., September 5, 1935, 310.
36. Quoted in ibid.
37. Quoted in ibid.
38. Ibid.
39. Quoted in ibid., September 12, 1935, 342.
40. Ibid., October 3, 1935, 429; Shiono Suehiko kaikoroku kankōkai, *Shiono Suehiko kaikoroku*, 259.
41. Quoted in *JWC*, September 26, 1935, 398.
42. Ibid.
43. Quoted in ibid., October 3, 1935, 429.
44. Ibid.
45. Ibid., October 10, 1935, 455.
46. Ibid.
47. Ibid., October 24, 1935, 510.
48. Quoted in ibid., October 31, 1935, 541.
49. Ibid.

50. Ibid.; ibid., January 30, 1936, 138.
51. Ibid., February 13, 1936, 196; ibid., February 27, 1936, 265.
52. Quoted in ibid., February 13, 1936, 196.
53. Ibid.
54. Ibid., February 27, 1936, 272.
55. For details on the February 26, 1936, army coup, see Shillony, *Revolt in Japan*.
56. Quoted in Kawai, *Teijin jiken*, 109.
57. *JWC*, May 21, 1936, 645.
58. Ibid., June 11, 1936, 747.
59. Quoted in ibid.
60. Quoted in ibid., July 16, 1936, 91.
61. Imamura Rikisaburō, *Teijin jiken benron*, 41.
62. NM, 126–131.
63. Ibid., 131.
64. Ibid., October 22, 1936, 535.
65. Ibid.
66. Ibid., October 29, 1936, 573.
67. NM, 31–32.
68. Ibid., 33.
69. Ibid., 38–39.
70. Quoted in ibid., 33–35.
71. Ibid., 35–37.
72. Quoted in ibid., 39–40, 43–44.
73. Ibid., 57.
74. Quoted in *JWC*, November 5, 1936, 602.
75. Ibid.
76. Quoted in NM, 70.
77. Ibid., 71.
78. AS, 606–607.
79. Quoted in ibid., 609.
80. Ibid., 609–610.
81. Ibid., 610.
82. Ibid., 612.
83. Quoted in ibid., November 5, 1936, 602.
84. NM, 92–104.
85. *JWC*, December 10, 1936, 754,
86. Quoted in NM, 211.
87. Ibid., 211–212.
88. Ibid., 212.

89. Ibid., 213.
90. Quoted in ibid., 213.
91. Ibid., 214–215.
92. Quoted in ibid., 205–206.
93. Ibid., 206–209.
94. Ibid., 208.
95. Ibid., 209.
96. *JWC*, December 24, 1936, 827.
97. Quoted in ibid.
98. Quoted in NM, 136.
99. Quoted in ibid., 138.
100. Quoted in ibid., 139.
101. Quoted in ibid., 140–141.
102. Ibid., 143–144.
103. Quoted in ibid., 144.
104. Quoted in ibid., 146.
105. Ibid., 147.
106. Quoted in ibid., 167.
107. Ibid., 168.
108. Quoted in ibid., 169.
109. Ibid., 169–170.
110. Mitsuchi, *Teijin jiken to watashi no shinkyō (kōhantei ni okeru Mitsuchi Chūzō shi chinjutsu sokki)*.
111. *JWC*, February 11, 1937, 174; NM, 253–261.
112. Ibid., February 25, 1937, 243; Mitchell, *Political Bribery in Japan*, 243.
113. *JWC*, February 25, 1937, 243.
114. Ibid., March 4, 1937, 259.
115. Ibid., 251.
116. Ibid., March 18, 1937, 337.
117. Ibid., April 22, 1937, 494; ibid., April 29, 1937, 530; NM, 255.
118. NM, 75–76.
119. Quoted in ibid., 76.
120. Ibid., 77–78, 80–81.
121. Ibid., 36, 83–84.
122. Ibid., 132–133.
123. Quoted in ibid., 133.
124. Ibid., 134–135.
125. *JWC*, May 22, 1937, 656.
126. Ibid.
127. Imamura Rikisaburō, *Teijin jiken benron*, 39.

128. *JWC*, June 17, 1937, 750.
129. Quoted in ibid.
130. Imamura Rikisaburō, *Teijin jiken benron*, 41.
131. *JWC*, June 17, 1937, 750.
132. Quoted in ibid., 751.
133. Ibid.
134. Ibid.
135. Ibid., 751–752.
136. Suzuki Yoshio, "Gōmon," 469, 473.
137. Ibid., 477.
138. *JWC*, June 3, 1937, 695.
139. Gujō Korekazu, ed., *Teijin jiken*, 57–69.
140. Ibid., 58–68.
141. Ibid., 1–56.
142. *JWC*, June 17, 1937, 738–739.
143. Mikiso Hane, *Modern Japan*, 275–277.
144. Wada Hidekichi, "Watakushi no mita Teijin jiken," 322–323.
145. Ibid., 324–328.
146. Ibid., 329.
147. Ibid.
148. Ibid., 330.
149. Ibid., 333.
150. Ibid., 335.
151. Kawai Yoshinari, "Teijin mondai no shinkyō ittan," 364–365.
152. Ibid., 365.
153. Ibid., 366–367.
154. Ibid., 367.
155. *JWC*, August 12, 1937, 231; Kawai,"Teijin mondai," 373.
156. Quoted in *JWC*, August 12, 1937, 231.
157. Ibid., 230.
158. Ibid., 231.
159. Quoted in ibid., 230.
160. Ibid., August 19, 1937, 270.
161. Ibid.
162. Imamura Rikisaburō, *Teijin jiken benron*, 10–11.
163. Ibid., 12–19.
164. Ibid., 19.
165. Ibid., 19, 39.
166. Ibid., 78, 81.
167. Ibid., 168–232.

168. Ibid., 168.
169. Ibid., 232–233.
170. Ibid., 236.
171. Ibid., 262, 265, 268, 281–283, 286, 288.
172. NM, 216, 227–231.
173. Ibid., 232–233, 235.
174. Quoted in ibid., 237.
175. Ibid., 245–246.
176. Quoted in ibid., 247.
177. Ibid., 247.
178. Quoted in ibid., 249.
179. Ibid., 251.
180. AS, 614–620.
181. Suzuki Yoshio denki kankōkai, *Suzuki Yoshio*, 394, 398–399, 402–406; Suzuki Yoshio, *Teijin jiken benron*, 1.
182. Gujō, *Teijin jiken*, 96–97.
183. Ibid., 97.
184. Ibid., 97–99.
185. Ibid., 99.
186. Ibid.
187. Ibid., 101.
188. Ibid., 106.
189. Inui Masahiko, *Teijin jiken benron*, 1.
190. Ibid., 2, 49–52, 60.
191. Ibid., 77–110.
192. Ibid., 111.
193. Ibid.
194. Ibid., 112.
195. *JWC*, October 14, 1937, 510.
196. AS, 536–538.
197. *JWC*, December 23, 1937, 835; NM, 461–462.
198. *JWC*, December 23, 1937, 835.
199. Ibid.
200. Quoted in Morinaga Eizaburō, *Shidan saiban*, 267.
201. AS, 622.
202. Ibid.
203. *JWC*, December 23, 1937, 835.
204. Quoted in AS, 621.
205. *JWC*, December 23, 1937, 818.
206. Ibid., 836.

207. Ibid.; ibid., December 30, 1937, 873.
208. Matsuzaka Hiromasa den kankōkai, *Matsuzaka Hiromasa den*, 156–158.
209. *JWC*, December 30, 1937, 873.
210. Shiono Suehiko kaikoroku kankōkai, *Shiono Suehiko kaikoroku*, 278–280.
211. Ohara Naoshi kaikoroku hensankai, *Ohara Naoshi kaikoroku*, 256.
212. Ibid., 257.
213. Quoted in Nomura Masao, *Hōsō fūunroku*, 2:71.
214. Quoted in Kawai, *Teijin jiken*, 108–111.
215. *JWC*, December 30, 1937, 852.
216. Ibid., 853.
217. Morinaga, *Shidan saiban*, 262.
218. Ibid., 263–266.
219. For information on torture of criminal suspects, see "torture" in the index of Mitchell, *Janus-Faced Justice.*
220. Morinaga, *Shidan saiban*, 267.

Chapter 6: Aftermath

1. Imamura Rikisaburō, *Teijin jiken benron*, 9–10, 117–120, 132–133.
2. Morishita Sumio, "Imamura Rikisaburō," 135.
3. NM, 11–12.
4. Ibid., iii–iv.
5. Ibid., vii–viii.
6. Mitsuchi Chūzō, "Teijin jiken o kaeri mite," 159.
7. Ibid., 160.
8. Ibid., 162–163.
9. Ibid., 163–164.
10. Ibid., 166, 168–169.
11. Ibid., 170.
12. Ibid.
13. Ibid., 172.
14. Mitchell, *Censorship in Imperial Japan*, 163.
15. Mitsuchi, "Teijin jiken o kaeri mite," 169–170.
16. Hozumi Shigetō, "Saiban to shinjitsu no hakken," 126.
17. Quoted in "The Teikoku Rayon Scandal," 708.
18. *JWC*, January 6, 1938, 27.
19. Ibid., December 30, 1937, 873; ibid., February 3, 1938, 134.
20. Ibid.
21. Ibid., 142.
22. Ibid., February 10, 1938, 170.

23. Ibid., February 3, 1938, 142.
24. Shiono Suehiko kaikoroku kankōkai, *Shiono Suehiko kaikoroku*, 278–279.
25. *JWC*, February 10, 1938, 172.
26. Ibid., February 17, 1938, 201.
27. Ibid., February 24, 1938, 272–273.
28. Ibid., 273.
29. Ibid., 238.
30. Ibid., March 10, 1938, 304–305.
31. Ibid., June 17, 1937, 752; ibid., December 23, 1937, 836.
32. Ibid.
33. Ibid., March 10, 1938, 312.
34. Mitchell, *Janus-Faced Justice*, 108–110.
35. Ibid., 111.
36. *JWC*, February 3, 1938, 149; ibid., May 5, 1938, 555.
37. Ōuchi, *Nihon no rekishi*, 373.
38. Mitchell, *Thought Control in Prewar Japan*, 142.
39. Hattori Takaaki, "The Legal Profession in Japan," 125.
40. Quoted in ibid., note 50.
41. *JWC*, August 8, 1935, 189; Ibid., February 7, 1935, 161.
42. Ibid., December 23, 1937, 836.
43. Wolfgang Bauer, *China and the Search for Happiness*, 213.
44. S. N. Eisenstadt, *Japanese Civilization*, 341.
45. Andō, *Shōwa keizai shi e no shōgen*, 2:23.
46. Mitchell, *Political Bribery in Japan*, 54.
47. *JWC*, February 25, 1937, 237.
48. Quoted in ibid.
49. Ibid.
50. Ibid.
51. Ibid., August 12, 1937, 224.
52. For a brief review of the system of government awards, see Takane Masaaki, *The Political Elite in Japan*, 34–35. Beginning at the top, decorations were ranked Supreme Order of the Chrysanthemum (men only), Order of the Rising Sun (men only), Order of the Precious Crown (for women), Order of the Sacred Treasure (for both). These awards were ranked from first to eighth class. Military men received the Order of the Golden Kites. Mitsuchi's award was very high. See Hashimoto Nobuyuki, "Decorations," 81.
53. Sanseidō henshūjo, *Konsaisu jinmei jiten*, 420, 801, 1073; Janet Hunter, *Concise Dictionary of Modern Japanese History*, 291–293, 304; *JWC*, December 30, 1937, 873; Chitoshi Yanaga, *Big Business in Japanese Politics*, 57, 217; Shinobu Seizaburō, *Sengo Nihon seiji shi*, 587; "Kobayashi Ataru."

54. AS, 630–631; *JWC*, May 31, 1934, 729; ibid., December 23, 1934, 836; ibid., December 30, 1937, 873; ibid., February 17, 1938, 220. For information on the North China Development Joint-Stock Company, see Ramon Myers, "Creating a Modern Enclave Economy," 163–164.

55. Nomura Masao, *Hōsō fūunroku*, 2:72, 283, 293; Hiroshi Itoh and Lawrence Beer, eds., *The Constitutional Case Law of Japan*, 252; Kyōto daigaku bungakubu kokushi kenkyū shitsu, *Nihon kindai shi jiten*, 87, 609; Hunter, *Concise Dictionary*, 288; John Maki, *Court and Constitution in Japan*, 430.

56. *JWC*, January 8, 1931, 25.

57. Mitchell, *Janus-Faced Justice*, discusses this topic in detail.

58. Iwagiri Noboru, ed., *Motoji Shinkuma den*, 120–121.

59. Quoted in ibid., 121–122.

60. Ibid., 122–123.

61. Ibid., 123.

62. Kawakami Kan, *Iwayuru jinken jūrin mondai ni tsuite*, 122, 127.

63. Ibid., 116, 130–131.

64. Quoted in ibid., 116.

65. Ibid., ii, 133–135, 139–140, 143–144.

66. "Kanketsu ni atatte (zadankai)," 579–580.

67. Ibid., 580–581.

68. Ibid., 580.

69. *JWC*, March 21, 1935, 371.

70. Ibid., April 4, 1935, 436.

71. Nihon, Shihōshō, *Shihō enkakushi*, 484.

72. Quoted in *JWC*, May 30, 1935, 692.

73. Quoted in *JWC*, June 18, 1936, 783.

74. Quoted in *JWC*, March 26, 1936, 382.

75. Ibid., July 30, 1936, 142.

76. Ibid., July 9, 1936, 65.

77. Ibid., 45.

78. Ibid., August 20, 1936, 238.

79. Ibid., July 9, 1936, 39–40.

80. Ibid., March 11, 1937, 293; ibid., April 1, 1937, 396.

81. Ibid., March 17, 1938, 332; Nihon, *Shihō enkakushi*, 526–527.

82. *JWC*, January 19, 1939, 76.

83. Ibid., 56–57.

84. Haley, *Spirit of Japanese Law*, 227 n. 26.

85. *JWC*, February 22, 1940, 218.

86. Ōuchi, *Nihon no rekishi*, 373.

87. Hatano Akira, "Kensatsu fassho no taizai o tou," 76.

88. Murobushi, *Jitsuroku Nihon oshoku shi*, 234.
89. *JWC*, August 12, 1937, 224.
90. Haley, *Spirit of Japanese Law*, 62.
91. Ibid., 62–63.
92. *JWC*, October 29, 1938, 447.
93. Ibid., February 9, 1939, 160.
94. Ibid., June 8, 1939, 702.
95. Berger, "Politics and Mobilization," 111.
96. Matsuo, "Teijin Incident."
97. Haley, *Spirit of Japanese Law*, 62–63.

Chapter 7: Postwar

1. For details about treatment of regular and political criminal suspects, see Mitchell, *Janus-Faced Justice*.
2. Carol Gluck, "Entangling Illusions," 179–180; Also see Marlene Mayo, "American Wartime Planning for Occupied Japan."
3. Mayo, 6–7, 16–18.
4. Ibid., 18.
5. Quoted in ibid., 20.
6. Ibid., 37.
7. Borton, *Japan's Modern Century*, 567–568.
8. Mayo, "American Wartime Planning," 45–47.
9. Borton, *Japan's Modern Century*, 462; Christopher Aldous, *The Police in Occupation Japan*, 47–48.
10. Charles Kades, "The American Role in Revising Japan's Imperial Constitution," 219.
11. David Danelski, "The Constitutional and Legislative Phases of the Creation of the Japanese Supreme Court," 35.
12. John Maki, "The Japanese Constitutional Style," 9.
13. Hata Ikuhiko, "Japan under the Occupation," 367–368.
14. Masumi Junnosuke, *Postwar Politics in Japan, 1945–1955*, 53–54.
15. Ibid., 55.
16. Justin Williams, *Japan's Political Revolution under MacArthur*, contains useful profiles of officials who drafted the constitution, 52–54.
17. Ibid., 52.
18. Ibid.
19. Kades, "American Role," 227.
20. Ibid., 227.
21. Danelski, "Constitutional and Legislative Phases," 62.

22. Ibid., 41.
23. For interesting comments on the drafting of human rights provisions, see Koseki Shōichi, *The Birth of Japan's Postwar Constitution*, 86–89.
24. Wildes, *Japan in Crisis*, 144–154.
25. Masumi, *Postwar Politics*, 55.
26. Quoted in ibid., 55–56.
27. Maki, "Japanese Constitutional Style," 9.
28. Ibid., 12.
29. Borton, *Japan's Modern Century*, 575–576.
30. Ibid., 576.
31. Ibid., 582–583.
32. Ibid., 582.
33. Williams, *Japan's Political Revolution*, 64–65.
34. Alfred Oppler, *Legal Reform in Occupied Japan*, 129.
35. Ibid., 137–139, 143, 147.
36. Ibid., 143.
37. Ibid.
38. Ibid., 136.
39. Richard Appleton, "Reforms in Japanese Criminal Procedure under Allied Occupation," 416.
40. Wagatsuma Sakae, ed., *Shin hōritsugaku jiten*, 465–466.
41. Harry Wildes, "The Japanese Police," 393.
42. Wildes, *Japan in Crisis*, 145.
43. Walter Ames, "Police System"; Hane, *Modern Japan*, 352.
44. Hane, *Modern Japan*, 352.
45. Oppler, *Legal Reform*, 104; Thomas Blakemore, "Post-War Developments in Japanese Law," 642.
46. Takayanagi Kenzō, "A Century of Innovation," 23; Nagashima Atsushi, "The Accused and Society," 302; Ushiomi Toshitaka, "The Prosecution at the Crossroads," 84–85.
47. Oppler, *Legal Reform*, 138.
48. Appleton, "Reforms," 408.
49. Ames, "Police System," 198; Hane, *Modern Japan*, 357; John Dower, *Empire and Aftermath*, 346–348.
50. Dower, 347–348.
51. Ames, "Police System," 198.
52. David T. Johnson, "The Japanese Way of Justice," 144.
53. Ibid., 147.
54. Ibid., 169.
55. Ibid.

56. Ibid., 167.
57. Oppler, *Legal Reform*, 136.
58. Ibid., 138, 142, 148.
59. Ibid., 142.
60. Ibid., xi.
61. Ishida Kazuto, "The Rights of the Suspect and of the Accused in Criminal Procedure in Japan."
62. Oppler, *Legal Reform*, 140.
63. Quoted in Daniel Foote, "Confessions and the Right to Silence in Japan," 426–427.
64. John Haley, "Sheathing the Sword of Justice in Japan," 269.
65. Foote, "Confessions," 427.
66. Mitchell, *Janus-Faced Justice*.
67. Foote, "Confessions," 428.
68. Ibid., 430–437.
69. Quoted in ibid., 437.
70. Ibid., 431.
71. Quoted in ibid.
72. Ibid., 461 n. 223, 462.
73. Ibid., 465–466.
74. Ibid., 466–467, 469.
75. Ibid., 471–472.
76. Ibid., 469–470.
77. Patricia Steinhoff, "Pursuing the Japanese Police," 844.
78. Ibid., 845.
79. Ibid., 845–846.
80. Ibid., 846. For more information on this subject, see Miyazawa Setsuo, *Policing in Japan*.
81. David Johnson, "Japanese Way of Justice," 341.
82. Ibid., 340.
83. Ibid.
84. Ishimatsu Takeo, "Are Criminal Defendants in Japan Truly Receiving Trials by Judges?" 141, 150–151.
85. Ibid., 151.
86. Ibid., 152.
87. Ibid.
88. Hirano Ryūichi, "Diagnosis of the Current Code of Criminal Procedure," 129–131.
89. Ibid., 131.
90. Ibid., 131–133.

91. Ibid., 136–137.
92. Ibid., 138–140.
93. Ibid., 141.
94. Ibid., 142.
95. Iimuro Katsuhiko, "Rainbow Reflections," 1–2.
96. Igarashi Futaba, "Forced to Confess," 195–211. For additional information on the "substitute prison," see Japan Federation of Bar Associations, *The Documents Concerning the Daiyo-Kangoku (Japan Substitute Prison System)*.
97. Igarashi, 213.
98. Kazuo Itoh, "On Publication of the 'Citizens' Human Rights Reports," 55–60. Also see Frank Bennett, "Pretrial Detention in Japan," 68.
99. Nihon, Prison Law, 1.
100. Japan Federation of Bar Associations, *Documents*, 2.
101. David Johnson, "Japanese Way of Justice," 237.
102. Yayama, "The Recruit Scandal," 93.
103. Ibid., 95–96.
104. David Johnson, "Japanese Way of Justice," 171.
105. Hatano Akira, "Kensatsu fassho no taizai o tou," 75–76.
106. Ibid., 76.
107. Ibid., 75–76.
108. Ibid., 76.
109. Ibid.
110. "Pushing Panic Button Will Not Solve Problems Behind Scandals."
111. Mitchell, *Political Bribery in Japan*, 121–122.
112. Peter Herzog, *Japan's Pseudo-Democracy*, 269; also see Mitchell, *Political Bribery in Japan*, 127, 139.
113. David Johnson, "Japanese Way of Justice," 285.
114. Mihori Hiroshi, *Wairozai hanron*, 219.
115. Hattori Takaaki, "The Legal Profession in Japan," 135.
116. Hatano, "Kensatsu fassho," 75–76.
117. David Johnson, "Japanese Way of Justice," 159.
118. Hatano, "Kensatsu fassho," 77.
119. Matsumoto Ichirō, "Kensatsu fassho," 313.
120. Mitchell, *Political Bribery In Japan*, 111–112; Hattori, "Legal Profession," 135 n. 101.
121. Shinobu, *Sengo Nihon seiji shi*, 587; Mitchell, *Political Bribery in Japan*. 87.
122. Miyake Seiki, "Banchōkai wa fukkatsu suru ka," 95. Also see Yanaga, *Big Business in Japanese Politics*, 57.
123. Miyake, 93, 95.
124. Ibid., 93.
125. Ibid., 95.

126. Since Kawai was a founding member of the group, his comment about Kobayashi is probably correct.

127. John Roberts, *Mitsui*, 442.

128. Ibid. Although Roberts presents some interesting material on "teahouse politics," readers must tread with care. For example, he states that Kobayashi Ataru "spent some years in prison because of his implication in that [Teijin] affair." Perhaps Roberts was thinking about the time in jail as police and procurators pushed for a confession, but that time does not add up to "some years."

129. Suzuki Matsuo, *Zaikai oyabun-kobun*, 189.

130. Nakajima, *Seikai zaikai gojūnen*, 219.

131. Ibid.

Chapter 8: Conclusion

1. David Johnson, "Japanese Way," 259, 267, 335.

2. Quoted in ibid., 330.

3. Ibid., 340.

4. Ibid., 339–340.

5. Shiono Suehiko kaikoroku kankōkai, *Shiono Suehiko kaikoroku*, 439.

6. Ibid., 248.

7. Aoki, *Seizan zuisō*, 313.

8. Suzuki Yoshio denki kankōkai, *Suzuki Yoshio*, 404–405.

9. Gorden Berger, "Hiranuma Kiichirō."

10. Richard Yasko, "Hiranuma Kiichirō and Conservative Politics in Pre-War Japan," 25.

11. Ibid., 3–4.

12. Ibid., 4–5.

13. Ibid., 130.

14. *JWC*, April 16, 1939, 419.

15. Yasko, "Hiranuma Kiichirō," 77.

16. Andō, *Shōwa keizai shi e no shōgen*, 2:23.

17. *JWC*, August 8, 1935, 189.

18. Ibid., September 26, 1935, 398.

19. Kawai, *Teijin jiken*, 57.

20. Patricia Steinhoff, "Review Section," 492.

21. Ibid., 495.

22. David Johnson, "Japanese Way," 144, 148–149, 152.

23. Ibid., 182.

24. Haley, *Spirit of Japanese Law*, 108.

25. Ibid., 230 n. 47.

Bibliography

Abe Haruo. "Criminal Justice in Japan: Its Historical Background and Modern Problems." *American Bar Association Journal* 47 (June 1961): 555–559.

Academic American Encyclopedia 16:97. Danbury, Conn.: Grolier, 1998.

Akita, George. "The Other Ito: A Political Failure." In Alber M. Craig and Donald H. Shively, eds., *Personality in Japanese History*. Berkeley: University of California Press, 1970.

Ames, Walter. "Police System." In Itasaka Gen, ed., *Encyclopedia of Japan*, 6:198. Tokyo: Kōdansha, 1983.

Aldous, Christopher. *The Police in Occupation Japan: Control, Corruption, and Resistance to Reform*. London: Routledge, 1997.

Andō Yoshio. *Shōwa keizai shi e no shōgen* (Testimony about Showa economic history). Vols. 1 and 2. Tokyo: Mainichi shinbunsha, 1965.

Aoki Kazuo. *Seizan zuisō* (My reflections). Tokyo: Nihon keizai Shinbunsha, 1959.

Aoki, Michiko Y., and Margaret B. Dardess, comps. and eds. *As the Japanese See It: Past and Present*. Honolulu: University of Hawai'i Press, 1981.

Appleton, Richard B. "Reforms in Japanese Criminal Procedure under Allied Occupation." *Washington Law Review and State Bar Journal* 24 (November 1949): 401–430.

Aritake Shūji. *Shōwa Ōkurashō gaishi* (An unofficial history of the Finance Ministry). Vol. 1. Tokyo: Shōwa Ōkurashō gaishi kankōkai, 1967.

"Ashikaga Takauji." In Alan Campbell and David S. Noble, eds., *Japan: An Illustrated Encyclopedia*, 1:66–67. Tokyo: Kōdansha, 1993.

Baerwald, Hans H. "Fund Raising in Japan: A Sasakawa Saga." *JPRI Occasional Paper*, no. 3 (May 1995).

Bauer, Wolfgang. *China and the Search for Happiness: Recurring Themes in Four Thousand Years of Chinese Cultural History*. New York: Seabury Press, 1976.

Befu Harumi. "Gift-Giving in a Modernizing Japan." *Monumenta Nipponica* 23 (Winter 1968): 63–83.

Bennet, Frank. "Pretrial Detention in Japan: Overview and Introductory Note." *Law in Japan: An Annual* 23 (1990): 67–71.

Berger, Gordon. "Hiranuma Kiichirō (1867–1952.)" In Itasaka Gen, ed., *Encyclopedia of Japan*, 3:144. Tokyo: Kōdansha, 1983.

———. *Parties Out of Power in Japan, 1931–1941*. Princeton, N.J.: Princeton University Press, 1977.

———. "Politics and Mobilization in Japan, 1931–1945." In Peter Duus, ed., *The Cambridge History of Japan*, volume 6: *The Twentieth Century*. Cambridge, Great Britain: Cambridge University Press, 1988.

Blakemore, Thomas L. "Post-War Developments in Japanese Law." *Wisconsin Law Review* (1947): 632–653.

Borton, Hugh. *Japan's Modern Century*. New York: Ronald Press, 1970.

Campbell, Alan, and David S. Noble, eds. *Japan: An Illustrated Encyclopedia*, vol. 1. Tokyo: Kōdansha, 1993.

Chamberlain, Basil H. *Things Japanese: Being Notes on Various Subjects Connected with Japan for the Use of Travellers and Others*. London: John Murray, 1905.

Chō Yukio. "Exposing the Incompetence of the Bourgeoisie: The Financial Panic of 1927." *Japan Interpreter* 8 (Winter 1974): 492–501.

———. "From the Shōwa Economic Crisis to Military Economy: With Special Reference to the Inoue and Takahashi Financial Policies." *The Developing Economies* 5 (December 1967): 568–596.

Cohen, Jerome B. *Japan's Economy in War and Reconstruction*. Minneapolis, Minn.: University of Minnesota Press, 1949.

Crowley, James B. *Japan's Quest for Autonomy: National Security and Foreign Policy, 1930–1938*. Princeton, N.J.: Princeton University Press, 1966.

Danelski, David, J. "The Constitutional and Legislative Phases of the Creation of the Japanese Supreme Court." In L. H. Redford, ed., *The Occupation of Japan: Impact of Legal Reform*. Norfolk, Va.: MacArthur Memorial, 1978 [?].

Dower, John W. *Empire and Aftermath: Yoshida Shigeru and the Japanese Experience, 1878–1954*. Cambridge, Mass.: Harvard University Press, 1979.

Eguchi Keiichi. *Shōwa no rekishi* (A History of Showa). Vol. 4. Tokyo: Shōgakukan, 1982.

Eisenstadt, S. N. *Japanese Civilization: A Comparative View*. Chicago, Ill.: University of Chicago Press, 1995.

Encyclopaedia of the Social Sciences 2:18, 588. New York: MacMillan Co., 1934.

Epp, Robert. "The Challenge from Tradition: Attempts to Compile a Civil Code in Japan, 1866–78." *Monumenta Nipponica* 22 (Spring and Summer 1967): 15–48.

Fletcher, William M. *The Japanese Business Community and National Trade Policy, 1920–1942*. Chapel Hill, N.C.: University of North Carolina Press, 1989.

Foote, Daniel H. "Confessions and the Right to Silence in Japan." *Georgia Journal of International and Comparative Law* 21 (1991): 415–488.

George, B. J. "The Impact of the Past upon the Rights of the Accused in Japan." *Civil Law and Military Journal* 5 (July–December 1969): 57–76.

Gluck, Carol. "Entangling Illusions: Japanese and American Views of the Occupation." In Warren I. Cohen, ed., *New Frontiers in American-East Asian Relations: Essays Presented to Dorothy Borg*. New York: Columbia University Press, 1983.

Gujō Korekazu, ed. *Teijin jiken: Ōkurashō kankei benron danpen* (Teijin Incident: A portion of the summation in connection with the Finance Ministry). Tokyo: Gujō Korekazu, 1938.

Haley, John O. *Authority without Power: Law and the Japanese Paradox*. London: Oxford University Press, 1991.

———. "Sheathing the Sword of Justice in Japan: An Essay on Law without Sanctions." *Journal of Japanese Studies* 8 (Summer 1982): 265–281.

———. *The Spirit of Japanese Law*. Athens, Ga.: University of Georgia Press, 1998.

Hane, Mikiso. *Modern Japan: A Historical Survey*. Boulder, Colo.: Westview Press, 1992.

Hasegawa Masayasu. *Shōwa kenpō shi* (A history of the constitution during Showa). Tokyo: Iwanami shoten, 1975.

Hashimoto Nobuyuki. "Decorations." In Itasaka Gen, ed., *Encyclopedia of Japan*, 2:81. Tokyo: Kōdansha, 1983.

Hastings, Norman S. "The Seiyūkai and Party Government in Japan, 1924–1932." Ph.D. dissertation, University of Kansas, 1977.

Hata Ikuhiko. "Japan under the Occupation." *Japan Interpreter* 10 (Winter 1976): 361–380.

Hatano Akira. "Kensatsu fassho no taizai o tou" (Questioning the great crime of prosecution fascism). *Hōseki* (February 1994): 61–79.

Hatoyama Ichirō. *Watakushi no jijoden* (My autobiography). Tokyo: Kaizōsha, 1951.

Hattori Takaaki. "The Legal Profession in Japan: Its Historical Development and Present State." In Arthur von Mehren, ed., *Law in Japan: The Legal Order in a Changing Society*. Cambridge, Mass.: Harvard University Press, 1963.

———. "The Role of the Supreme Court of Japan in the Field of Judicial Administration." *Washington Law Review* 60 (1985): 69–86.

Henderson, Dan Fenno. *Conciliation and Japanese Law: Tokugawa and Modern*. Vols. 1 and 2. Seattle: University of Washington Press, 1965.

———. "Law and Political Modernization Japan." In Robert E. Ward, ed., *Political Development in Modern Japan*. Princeton, N.J.: Princeton University Press, 1968.

Herzog, Peter J. *Japan's Pseudo-Democracy*. New York: New York University Press, 1993.

Hiramatsu Yoshirō. "Summary of Tokugawa Criminal Justice." *Law in Japan: An Annual* 22 (1989): 105–128.

Hirano Ryūichi. Diagnosis of the Current Code of Criminal Procedure." *Law in Japan: An Annual* 22 (1989): 129–142.

Hozumi Shigetō. "Saiban to shinjitsu no hakken: Teijin jiken kōhantei ni okeru benron" (The trial and discovering the truth: Summation at the Teijin public trial). *Chūō kōron* 53 (February 1938): 126–158.

Hunter, Janet E., comp. *Concise Dictionary of Modern Japanese History*. Berkeley: University of California Press, 1984.

Ichihara Ryōhei. "Ichi Nihon riberarisuto no shakaiteki 'sebone' (III): Mutō Sanji no '*Jiji shinpō*' jidai to 'Teijin jiken' " (The social backbone of a Japanese liberalist (III): Mutō Sanji's *Jiji shinpō* era and the Teijin Incident). *Keizai ronshū* 3 (January 1954): 51–81.

———. "Seitō rengō undō no hasan (sono ni): Teijin jiken o shōten to shite" (Bankruptcy of the political parties coalition movement (part 2): Focus on the Teijin Incident). *Keizai ronsō* 73 (February 1955): 161–182.

Igarashi Futaba. "Forced to Confess." In Gavan McCormack and Yoshio Sugimoto, eds., *Democracy in Contemporary Japan*. Armonk, N.Y.: M. E. Sharpe, 1986.

Iimuro Katsuhiko. "Rainbow Reflections." *New York Nichibei*, December 15, 1988.

Imamura Rikisaburō. *Hōtei gojūnen* (Fifty years at court). Tokyo: Senshū daigaku, 1948.

———. *Teijin jiken benron* (Teijin Incident summation). Tokyo: Kanaishi Kazuo, 1938.

Imamura Takeo. *Takahasi Korekiyo* (Takahashi Korekiyo). Tokyo: Jijitsushinsha, 1985.

Inui Masahiko. *Teijin jiken benron* (Teijin Incident summation). Tokyo: Kanaishi Kazuo, 1937.

Ishida Kazuto. "The Rights of the Suspect and of the Accused in Criminal Procedure in Japan." In *Record of the Fourth Asian Judicial Conference, Canberra, April 1970*. Canberra: Australian Government Publication Service, 1971.

Ishida Takeshi. "The Introduction of Western Political Concepts into Japan." *Nissan Occasional Paper Series*, no 2. Oxford: Nissan Institute of Japanese Studies, 1986.

Ishii Ryōsuke, ed. *Japanese Legislation in the Meiji Era*. Tokyo: Pan-Pacific Press, 1958.

Ishimatsu Takeo. "Are Criminal Defendants in Japan Truly Receiving Trials by Judges?" *Law in Japan: An Annual* 22 (1989): 143–153.

Ishiwata Sōtarō denki hensankai. *Ishiwata Sōtarō*. Tokyo: Ishiwata Sōtarō denki hensankai, 1954.

Itō Takashi. "Conflict and Coalitions in Japan, 1930: Political Groups [and] the London Naval Disarmament Conference." In Sven Groennings et al., eds., *The Study of Coalition Behavior: Theoretical Perspectives and Cases from Four Continents*. New York: Holt, Rinehart and Winston, 1970.

———. *Shōwa shi o saguru* (Searching for the history of Showa). Vol. 1. Tokyo: Mitsumura tosho shuppan kabushiki-kaisha, 1984.

———. *Shōwa shoki seiji shi kenkyū* (Research in the political history of early Showa). Tokyo: Tōkyō daigaku shuppankai, 1969.

Itoh, Hiroshi, and Lawrence Ward Beer, eds. *The Constitutional Case Law of Japan: Selected Supreme Court Decisions, 1961–70*. Seattle: University of Washington Press, 1978.

Itoh, Kazuo. "On Publication of the 'Citizens' Human Rights Reports.' " *Law in Japan: An Annual* 20 (1987): 29–73.

Iwagiri Noboru, ed. *Motoji Shinkuma den* (Biography of Motoji Shinkuma). Tokyo: Chūō shuppansha, 1955.

Iwamura Michiyo den kankōkai. *Iwamura Michiyo den* (Biography of Iwamura Michiyo). Tokyo: Iwamura Michiyo kankōkai, 1971.

Japan Federation of Bar Associations. *The Documents Concerning the Daiyo-Kangoku (Japan Substitute Prison System)*. Tokyo: Japan Federation of Bar Associations, 1989.

Japan Weekly Chronicle. 1931–1940.

Johnson, Chalmers. *Conspiracy at Matsukawa*. Berkeley: University of California Press, 1972.

———. *MITI and the Japanese Miracle: The Growth of Industrial Policy, 1925–1975*. Stanford, Calif.: Stanford University Press, 1982.

———. "Tanaka Kakuei, Structural Corruption, and the Advent of Machine Politics in Japan." *Journal of Japanese Studies* 12 (Winter 1986): 1–28.

Johnson, David T. "The Japanese Way of Justice: Prosecuting Crime in Japan." Ph.D. dissertation, University of California at Berkeley, 1996.

Kades, Charles L. "The American Role in Revising Japan's Imperial Constitution." *Political Science Quarterly* 104 (Summer 1989): 215–247.

Kaneda Hiromitsu. "Agricultural Stagnation in the 1920's: A Macroeconomic Perspective." *Hitotsubashi Journal of Economics* 29 (June 1988): 44–57.

"Kanketsu ni atatte (zadankai)" (Toward a conclusion, a roundtable talk). In Wagatsuma Sakae, ed., *Nihon seiji saiban shiroku, Shōwakō* (A history of political trials in Japan, latter Showa). Tokyo: Daiichi hōki shuppan kabushiki-kaisha, 1970.

Kawahara Hiroshi. " 'Chian ijihō' no suishinshatachi—'Chian ijihō no seiji katei' " (Promoters of the Peace Preservation Law—the political process of the Peace Preservation Law). *Shakai kagaku tōkyū* 38 (August 1968): 1–25.

Kawai Yoshinari. *Teijin jiken: Sanjūnen-me no shōgen* (Teijin Incident: Testimony on the thirtieth anniversary). Tokyo: Kōdansha, 1970.

———. "Teijin mondai no shinkyō ittan" (My partial opinion on the Teijin problem). *Chūō kōron* 52 (September 1937): 364–373.

Kawakami Kan. Iwayuru jinken jūrin mondai ni tsuite (About so-called infringement of human rights). In Shihōshō chōsaka (Justice Ministry, research section), *Shihō kenkyū (hōkokusho)* (Justice research, report), 24, no. 14 (February 1938).

Kenkoku kinen jigyo kyōkai, *Japan in Advance*. Tokyo: Kenkoku kinen jigyō kyōkai, 1936.

Kitazawa, Naokichi. *The Government of Japan*. Princeton, N.J.: Princeton University Press, 1929.

"Kobayashi Ataru." In Alan Campbell and David S. Noble, ed., *Japan: An Illustrated Encyclopedia*, 1:801.

Koseki Shōichi. *The Birth of Japan's Postwar Constitution*. Boulder, Colo.: Westview, 1997.

Kyōto daigaku bungakubu kokushi kenkyū shitsu, ed. *Nihon kindai shi jiten* (Dictionary of modern Japanese history). Tokyo: Tōyō keizai shinpōsha, 1958.

Large, Stephen S. *Emperors of the Rising Sun: Three Biographies*. Tokyo: Kōdansha International, 1997.

Lewis, Michael. *Rioters and Citizens: Mass Protest in Imperial Japan*. Berkeley: University of California Press, 1990.

Lockwood, William W. *The Economic Development of Japan: Growth and Structural Change, 1868–1938*. Princeton, N.J.: Princeton University Press, 1954.

Maki, John M. *Court and Constitution in Japan: Selected Supreme Court Decisions, 1948–60*. Seattle: University of Washington Press, 1964.

———. "The Japanese Constitutional Style." In Dan Fenno Henderson, ed., *The Constitution of Japan: Its First Twenty Years, 1947–67*. Seattle: University of Washington Press, 1968.

Marshall, Byron K. *Academic Freedom and the Japanese Imperial University, 1868–1939*. Berkeley: University of California Press, 1992.

———. *Capitalism and Nationalism in Prewar Japan: The Ideology of the Business Elite, 1868–1941*. Stanford, Calif.: Stanford University Press, 1967.

Maruyama Masao. *Thought and Behaviour in Modern Japanese Politics.* London: Oxford University Press, 1963.

Masumi Junnosuke. *Postwar Politics in Japan, 1945–1955.* Berkeley: University of California Press, 1985.

Matsumoto Ichirō. "Kensatsu fassho" (Prosecution fascism). *Hōgaku seminā zōkan,* August 1981, 313.

Matsuo Takayoshi. "Teijin Incident." In Itasaka Gen, ed., *Encyclopedia of Japan,* 7:375. Tokyo: Kōdansha, 1983.

Matsuzaka Hiromasa den kankōkai. *Matsuzaka Hiromasa den* (Biography of Matsuzaka Hiromasa). Osaka: Dai Nihon insatsu kabushiki-kaisha, 1969.

Mayo, Marlene J. "American Wartime Planning for Occupied Japan." In Robert Wolfe, ed., *Americans as Proconsuls: United States Military Government in Germany and Japan, 1944–1952.* Carbondale and Edwardsville, Ill.: Southern Illinois University Press, 1984.

Meyers, Howard. "Revisions of the Criminal Code of Japan during the Occupation." *Washington Law Review and State Bar Journal* 25 (1950): 104–134.

Mihori Hiroshi. *Wairozai hanron* (Summarizing the crime of bribery). Tokyo: Musashi shobō, 1957.

Minichiello, Sharon. *Retreat from Reform: Patterns of Political Behavior in Interwar Japan.* Honolulu: University of Hawai'i Press, 1984.

Mitchell, Richard H. *Censorship in Imperial Japan.* Princeton, N.J.: Princeton University Press, 1983.

———. *Janus-Faced Justice: Political Criminals in Imperial Japan.* Honolulu: University of Hawai'i Press, 1992.

———. *Political Bribery in Japan.* Honolulu: University of Hawai'i, 1996.

———. *Thought Control in Prewar Japan.* Ithaca, N.Y.: Cornell University Press, 1976.

Mitsubishi Economic Research Bureau. *Japanese Trade and Industry: Present and Future.* London: Macmillan and Co., 1936.

Mitsuchi Chūzō. *Shōnan hōjōki* (Thoughts in my Shōnan study). Tokyo: Yamamoto Sansei, 1936.

———. "Teijin jiken o kaeri mite" (A Review of the Teijin Incident). *Chūō kōron* 53 (February 1938): 159–172.

———. *Teijin jiken to watashi no shinkyō (kōhantei ni okeru Mitsuchi Chūzō shi chinjutsu sokki)* The Teijin Incident and my mental state (a shorthand record of Mitsuchi Chūzō's statement at the public trial). Tokyo: Ogasawara Yoshitarō, 1937.

———. *Yūshū tsurezure gusa* (Essays done during prison idleness). Tokyo: Chikura Yutaka, 1935.

Miyakawa Masuji. *Life of Japan*. New York: Neale Publishing Co., 1910.

Miyake Seiki. "Banchōkai wa fukkatsu suru ka" (Will the Banchōkai be resurrected?). *Kaizō* 33 (December 1952): 93–96.

Miyazawa Setsuo. *Policing in Japan: A Study on Making Crime*. Albany, N.Y.: State University of New York Press, 1992.

Morikawa Hidemasa. *Zaibatsu: The Rise and Fall of Family Enterprise Groups in Japan*. Tokyo: University of Tokyo Press, 1992.

Morinaga Eizaburō. *Nihon bengoshi retsuden* (Biographical series on Japanese lawyers). Tokyo: Shakai shisō sha, 1984.

———. *Shidan saiban* (A study of historic trials). Vol. 1. Tokyo: Nippon hyōronsha, 1966.

Morishita Sumio. "Imamura Rikisaburō." In Ushiomi Toshitaka, ed. *Nihon no bengoshi* (Japanese lawyers). Tokyo: Nippon hyōronsha, 1972.

Mukai Ken and Toshitani Nobuyoshi. "The Progress and Problems of Compiling the Civil Code in the Early Meiji Era." *Law in Japan: An Annual* 1 (1967): 25–59.

Murobushi Tetsurō. *Jitsuroku Nihon oshoku shi* (A history of Japanese corruption: An authentic account). Tokyo: Chikuma bunko, 1988.

"Mutō Sanji." In Itasaka Gen, ed., *Encyclopedia of Japan*, 5:288. Tokyo: Kōdansha, 1983.

Myers, Ramon H. "Creating a Modern Enclave Economy: Economic Integration of Japan, Manchuria, and North China, 1932–1945." In Peter Duus et al., eds., *The Japanese Wartime Empire, 1931–1945*. Princeton, N.J.: Princeton University Press, 1996.

Nagano Kunisuke, ed. *Hōsō hyakunen shi* (A centennial judicial history). Tokyo: Hōsō kōronsha, 1969.

Nagashima Atsushi. "The Accused and Society: The Administration of Criminal Justice in Japan." In Arthur T. von Mehren, ed., *Law in Japan: The Legal Order in a Changing Society*. Cambridge, Mass.: Harvard University Press, 1963.

Najita, Tetsuo. "Ōshio Heihachirō (1793–1837)." In Albert M. Craig and Donald H. Shively, eds., *Personality in Japanese History*. Berkeley: University of California Press, 1970.

Nakajima Kumakichi. *Seikai zaikai gojūnen* (Fifty years in the world of politics and finance). Tokyo: Dai Nihon bengokai kōdansha, 1951.

Nakamura Hideichirō. "The Activities of the Japan Economic Federation." In Dorothy Borg and Shumpei Okamoto, eds., *Pearl Harbor as History: Japanese-American Relations, 1931–1941*. New York: Columbia University Press, 1973.

Nakamura Kikuo. *Shōwa seiji shi* (A political history of Showa). Tokyo: Keiō tsūshin, 1958.

Nakamura Takafusa. "Depression, Recovery, and War, 1920–1945." In Peter Duus, ed., *The Cambridge History of Japan*, volume 6: *The Twentieth Century*. Cambridge, Great Britain: Cambridge University Press, 1988.

Nanto, Dick K., and Shinji Takagi. "Korekiyo Takahashi and Japan's Recovery from the Great Depression." *American Economic Association Papers and Proceedings* 75 (May 1985): 369–374.

Naramoto Tatsuya. *Nihon no rekishi* (A history of Japan). Vol. 17. Tokyo: Chūō kōronsha, 1966.

The New Encyclopedia Britannica. Vol. 9. Chicago, Ill.: Encyclopedia Britannica, 1998.

Nihon. Kōan chōsachō (Public security investigation agency), ed. *Senzen ni okeru uyoku dantai no jōkyō* (Condition of rightist groups before the war). Vol. 1. Tokyo: Kōan chosachō, 1964.

———. Prison Law (Law No. 28, March 28, 1908). *EHS Law Bulletin Series*.

———. Shihōshō (Justice Ministry). *Shihō enkakushi* (Historical record of the Justice [Ministry]). Tokyo: Hōsōkai, 1939.

Nomura Masao, ed. *Hōsō fūunroku: Anohito konohito hōmonki* (Record of affairs in judicial circles: Interviews of various people). Vol. 2. Tokyo: Asahi shinbunsha, 1966.

Nonaka Moritaka. *Teijin o sabaku* (Judgment on Teijin). Tokyo: Heibonsha, 1938.

Ohara Naoshi kaikoroku hensankai. *Ohara Naoshi kaikoroku* (The memoir of Ohara Naoshi). Tokyo: Ohara Naoshi kaikoroku hensankai, 1966.

Ooms, Herman. *Tokugawa Village Practice: Class, Status, Power, Law*. Berkeley: University of California Press, 1996.

Oppler, Alfred C. "Courts and Law in Transition." *Contemporary Japan* 21, nos. 1–2 (1952): 19–55.

———. *Legal Reform in Occupied Japan: A Participant Looks Back*. Princeton, N.J.: Princeton University Press, 1976.

Ōshima Tarō. "Kunshō—tetsudō gigoku jiken: Seitō seiji ni okeru oshoku no rotei" (Decorations—railway scandal incidents: Exposing corruption in political party politics). In Wagatsuma Sakae, ed., *Nihon seiji saiban shiroku, Shōwazen* (A history of political trials, early Showa). Tokyo: Daiichi hōki shuppan kabushiki-kaisha, 1970.

———. "Teijin jiken: Shōkanshū o mamotta ishoku no hanketsu" (Teijin Incident: A unique judgment protected commercial practices). In Wagatsuma Sakae, ed., *Nihon seiji saiban shiroku, Shōwakō* (A history of political trials, later Showa). Tokyo: Daiichi hōki shuppan kabushiki-kaisha, 1970.

Ōshima Kiyoshi. *Takahashi Korekiyo*. Tokyo: Chūō kōronsha, 1969.

Ōuchi Tsutomu. *Nihon no rekishi* (A history of Japan). Vol. 24. Tokyo: Chūō kōronsha, 1967.

Passin, Herbert. *The Legacy of the Occupation—Japan*. New York: Columbia University, Occasional Papers of the East Asian Institute, 1968.

Payne, Stanley G. *A History of Fascism, 1914–1945*. Madison: University of Wisconsin, 1995.

"Pushing Panic Button Will Not Solve Problems behind Scandals." *Daily Yomiuri*, March 11, 1998 (Lexis-Nexis).

Quigley, Harold S. *Japanese Government and Politics: An Introductory Study*. New York: Century, 1932.

Ramseyer, J. Mark, and Frances M. Rosenbluth. *The Politics of Oligarchy: Institutional Choice in Imperial Japan*. Cambridge, Great Britain: Cambridge University Press, 1995.

Roberts, John G. *Mitsui: Three Centuries of Japanese Business*. New York: Weatherhill, 1973.

Rōyama Shōichi. "Money and the Japanese." In Carol Gluck and Stephen R. Graubard, eds., *Shōwa: The Japan of Hirohito*. New York: W. W. Norton, 1992.

Rubinger, Richard. *Private Academies of Tokugawa Japan*. Princeton, N.J.: Princeton University Press, 1982.

Sanseidō henshūjo, ed. *Konsaisu jinmei jiten* (A concise biographical dictionary). Tokyo: Sanseidō kabushiki-kaisha, 1976.

Scheiner, Irwin. "Benevolent Lords and Honorable Peasants: Rebellion and Peasant Consciousness in Tokugawa Japan." In Tetsuo Najita and Irwin Scheiner, eds., *Japanese Thought in the Tokugawa Period*. Chicago, Ill.: University of Chicago Press, 1978.

Scherer, James A. B. *Japan's Advance*. Tokyo: Hokuseidō Press, 1934.

Sebald, William J., trans. *The Criminal Code of Japan*. Kobe: Japan Chronicle Press, 1936.

Senshū daigaku Imamura hōritsu kenkyū shitsu (Senshū University Imamura Legal Research Center), ed. *Teijin jiken*. Vol. 1. Tokyo: Senshū daigaku Imamura hōritsu kenkyū shitsu, 1993.

Shillony, Ben-Ami. *Politics and Culture in Wartime Japan*. Oxford: Clarendon Press, 1981.

———. *Revolt in Japan: The Young Officers and the February 26, 1936, Incident*. Princeton, N.J.: Princeton University Press, 1973.

Shinobu Seizaburō. "From Party Politics to Military Dictatorship." *The Developing Economies* 4 (December 1967): 666–684.

————. *Sengo Nihon seiji shi, 1945–1952* (Postwar Japanese political history, 1945–1952). Vol. 2. Tokyo: Keisō shobō, 1968.

Shiono Suehiko kaikoroku kankōkai. *Shiono Suehiko kaikoroku* (The memoir of Shiono Suehiko). Tokyo: Shiono Suehiko kaikoroku kankōkai, 1958.

Sims, R. L. *A Political History of Modern Japan.* New Delhi: Vikas, 1991.

Sneider, David A. "Action and Oratory: The Trials of the May 15 Incident of 1932." *Law in Japan: An Annual* 23 (1990): 1–66.

Spaulding, Robert M. "The Bureaucracy as a Political Force, 1920–1945." In James W. Morley, ed., *Dilemmas of Growth in Prewar Japan.* Princeton, N.J.: Princeton University Press, 1971.

————. *Imperial Japan's Higher Civil Service Examinations.* Princeton, N.J.: Princeton University Press, 1967.

Steinhoff, Patricia G. "Pursuing the Japanese Police." *Law and Society Review* 27, no. 4 (1993): 827–850.

————. "Review Section." *Journal of Japanese Studies* 19 (Summer 1993): 488–495.

Suzuki Kisaburō sensei denki hensankai. *Suzuki Kisaburō.* Tokyo: Suzuki Kisaburō sensei denki hensankai, 1945.

Suzuki Matsuo. *Zaikai oyabun-kobun* (Leaders and followers in the financial world). Tokyo: Jitsugyō no Nihonsha, 1955.

Suzuki Yoshio. "Gōmon" (Torture). *Chūō kōron* 52 (June 1937): 469–477.

Suzuki Yoshio denki kankōkai. *Suzuki Yoshio.* Tokyo: Suzuki Yoshio denki kankōkai, 1964.

————. *Teijin jiken benron* (Teijin Incident summation). Tokyo: Takaya Ichijirō, 1938.

Szpilman, Christopher W. "The Politics of Cultural Conservatism: The National Foundation Society in the Struggle against Foreign Ideas in Prewar Japan, 1918–1936." Ph.D. dissertation, Yale University, 1993.

Takahashi Kamekichi. *Kabushiki-kaisha bōkoku ron* (Joint-stock companies, ruination of the nation). Tokyo: Banrikaku shobō, 1930.

Takai Kenzō. *Shihō keisatsu ron* (On justice police). Tokyo: Ganshōdō, 1924.

Takane Masaaki. *The Political Elite in Japan: Continuity and Change in Modernization.* Berkeley: University of California Press, 1981.

Takayanagi Kenzō. "A Century of Innovation: The Development of Japanese Law, 1868–1961." In Arthur T. von Mehren, ed., *Law in Japan: The Legal Order in a Changing Society.* Cambridge, Mass.: Harvard University Press, 1963.

Takenobu, Y., ed. *The Japan Year Book, 1928.* Tokyo: Japan Year Book Office, 1928.

Takeuchi Kakuji den kankōkai. *Takeuchi Kakuji den* (A Biography of Takeuchi Kakuji). Tokyo: Sakai shobō, 1960.

Tamaki Norio. *Japanese Banking: A History 1859–1959.* Cambridge, Great Britain: Cambridge University Press, 1995.

Tanabe Kohji. "The Process of Litigation: An Experiment with the Adversary System." In Arthur T. von Mehren, ed., *Law in Japan: The Legal Order in a Changing Society*. Cambridge, Mass.: Harvard University Press, 1963.

Tanaka Hideo, ed. *The Japanese Legal System: Introductory Cases and Materials*. Tokyo: University of Tokyo Press, 1976.

"The Teikoku Rayon Scandal." *Contemporary Japan* 6 (March 1938): 708–710.

Teranishi Jūrō. "Loan Syndication in War-Time Japan and the Origins of the Main Bank System." In Masahiko Aoki and Hugh Patrick, eds., *The Japanese Main Bank System: Its Relevance for Developing and Transforming Economies*. New York: Oxford University Press, 1994.

Tiedemann, Arthur E. "Big Business and Politics in Prewar Japan." In James W. Morley, ed., *Dilemmas of Growth in Prewar Japan*. Princeton, N.J.: Princeton University Press, 1971.

Tipton, Elise K. *The Japanese Police State: The Tokkō in Interwar Japan*. Sydney, Australia: Allen and Unwin, 1990.

Totman, Conrad. *Early Modern Japan*. Berkeley: University of California Press, 1993.

Tsuji Tatsuya. "Politics in the Eighteenth Century." In John Whitney Hall, ed., *The Cambridge History of Japan*, volume 4: *Early Modern Japan*. Cambridge, Great Britain: Cambridge University Press, 1991.

Ukai Nobushige. "The Individual and the Rule of Law under the New Japanese Constitution." *Northwestern University Law Review* 51 (1957): 733–744

Ushiomi Toshitaka. "The Prosecution at the Crossroads." *Annals of the Institute of Social Science* 9 (1968): 84–85.

Uyehara, George E. *The Political Development of Japan, 1867–1909*. New York: E. P. Dutton, 1910.

Vandenbrink, John D. "State and Industrial Society in Modern Japan: The Liberal Critique, 1916–1926." Ph.D. dissertation, University of Chicago, 1985.

Wada Hidekichi. "Watakushi no mita Teijin jiken" (My view of the Teijin Incident). *Chūō kōron* 52 (August 1937): 322–335.

Wagatsuma Sakae, ed. *Kyū hōrei shū* (A collection of old laws and regulations). Tokyo: Yūhikaku, 1968.

———. *Shin hōritsugaku jiten* (A new jurisprudence dictionary). Tokyo: Yūhikaku, 1967.

Walthall, Anne. "Japanese *Gimin*: Peasant Martyrs in Popular Memory." *American Historical Review* 91 (December 1986): 1076–1102.

———. "Narratives of Peasant Uprisings in Japan." *Journal of Asian Studies* 42 (May 1983): 571–587.

———. *Social Protest and Popular Culture in Eighteenth-Century Japan*. Tucson: University of Arizona Press, 1986.

Weiner, Susan B. "Bureaucracy and Politics in the 1930s: The Career of Gotō Fumio." Ph.D. dissertation, Harvard University, 1984.

White, James W. *Ikki: Social Conflict and Political Protest in Early Modern Japan.* Ithaca, N.Y.: Cornell University Press, 1995.

Wildes, Harry E. *Japan in Crisis.* New York: Macmillan, 1934.

———. "The Japanese Police." *Journal of Criminal Law, Criminology and Police Science* 19 (November 1928): 390–398.

———. *Social Currents in Japan: With Special Reference to the Press.* Chicago, Ill.: University of Chicago Press, 1927.

Williams, Justin, Sr. *Japan's Political Revolution under MacArthur: A Participant's Account.* Athens: University of Georgia Press, 1979.

Wilson, Sandra. "Bureaucrats and Villagers in Japan: *Shimin* and the Crisis of the Early 1930s." *Social Science Japan Journal* 1 (April 1998): 121–140.

Yamabe Kentarō, ed. *Gendai shi shiryō* (Materials on contemporary history). Vol. 16. Tokyo: Misuzu shobō, 1965.

Yanaga, Chitoshi. *Big Business in Japanese Politics.* New Haven, Conn.: Yale University Press, 1968.

Yano Tsuneta and Shirasaki Kyōichi. *Nippon: A Charted Survey of Japan.* Tokyo: Kokuseisha, 1936.

Yasko, Richard. "Hiranuma Kiichirō and Conservative Politics in Pre-war Japan." Ph.D. dissertation, University of Chicago, 1973.

Yayama Tarō. "The Recruit Scandal: Learning from the Causes of Corruption." *Journal of Japanese Studies* 16 (Winter 1990): 93–114.

Yazawa Makoto. "The Legal Structure for Corporate Enterprise: Shareholder-Management Relations under Japanese Law." In Arthur T. von Mehren, ed., *Law in Japan: The Legal Order in a Changing Society.* Cambridge, Mass.: Harvard University Press, 1963.

Zaikai no shinbunsha, ed. *Mugen ka genjitsu ka, Teijin jiken no shinsō* (Dream? reality? truth about the Teijin Incident). Tokyo: Zaikai no shinbunsha, 1935.

Zöllner, Reinhard. "The Sun Also Rises: Go-Daigo in Revolt." *Monumenta Nipponica* 53 (Winter 1998): 517–527.

Index

About the Author

Richard H. Mitchell is the author of six books on Japanese history, among them *Thought Control in Prewar Japan* (1976), *Censorship in Imperial Japan* (1983), *Janus-Faced Justice: Political Criminals in Imperial Japan* (1992), and *Political Bribery in Japan* (1996). He is Curators' Professor of Japanese history at the University of Missouri–St. Louis.